Trading Information

Trading Information

Nicholas Jones

POLITICO'S

First published in Great Britain 2006 by
Politico's Publishing Ltd, an imprint of
Methuen Publishing Ltd
11–12 Buckingham Gate
London
SW1E 6LB

10 9 8 7 6 5 4 3 2 1

A CIP catalogue record for this book is available from the British Library.

ISBN-10: 1-84275-090-9
ISBN-13: 978-1-84275-090-2

Typeset by SX Composing DTP, Rayleigh, Essex
Printed and bound in Great Britain by The Cromwell Press Ltd, Trowbridge, Wiltshire

Contents

Introduction

In the twenty years in which I have been writing about the way politicians and public figures seek to exploit the news media, I have overlooked the extent to which the man or woman in the street has often become as adept as the professionals at finding ways to influence the headlines. Political spin doctors, public relations consultants, lobbyists, advertising agents and a host of other potential manipulators of the media have benefited from the expansion in press and broadcasting and now the internet. What I had not realised was the degree to which ordinary members of the public have kept pace with these advances in communication techniques and are sometimes quite capable of working out for themselves how to have an impact on what is being reported or broadcast. Such have been the long-term effects of the way in which we have all been bombarded by news, advertising and entertainment that some researchers are suggesting that an inner under-standing of what interests and excites the media is now being reflected in our genes and indeed has become a component of the 21st-century genome. For example, activists of all shades of opinion have shown repeatedly how they can outsmart the government of the day and seize the headlines with audacious action; aggrieved workers are much more likely than before to become whistleblowers or to leak confidential information, perhaps to embarrass their employers or to expose abuses.

However misguided it might seem to the authorities or the management, the driving force behind the leaking of sensitive or secret data is sometimes a desire to serve the common good. My aim in this book is to examine the power which resides with those whom I call the information traders, be they professional manipulators or the whistleblowers who put their jobs on the line. What made them realise that information is like a currency which can be traded to their advantage, to support a cause or perhaps expose an injustice? How did they acquire an acute understanding of the inner mechanics of the media? Why is it that journalists are sometimes eager to trade precious editorial space and airtime in return for what may be suspect material? Any casual reader, viewer or listener cannot help but get confused by the vast array of 'leaks' on offer. Perhaps a secret document has been exposed; confidential data might have leaked out unexpectedly; private correspondence has suddenly reached the public domain; or a correspondent has obtained an exclusive insight into a controversial step being planned by government or big business. Unfortunately journalists are not always prepared to come clean: is this leak the work of a genuine whistleblower or has the reporter accepted a plant from a publicist or spin doctor who is only too happy to see the information dressed up as an exclusive story in return for a favourable slant?

Powerful groups which seek to control the flow of information either from a position of authority or through their commercial strength have had to come to terms with the fact that they must do business in a crowded marketplace which contains many other players who might be equally knowledgeable about how to capitalise on the competitive forces which have been unleashed by the new environment of rolling news and entertainment, twenty-four hours a day, seven days a week. When this media-savvy generation see an opportunity to influence the reporting of events, there can be input from unexpected quarters and the well-placed leak is usually a sure-fire way to attract attention. Only occasionally do we get the chance to identify and appreciate the hidden influence of the vast array of characters who give tip-offs or supply secret documents, be they genuine whistleblowers or political spin doctors. Rare indeed is the reporter who will ignore the journalists' code and wilfully reveal the identity of a source. But have we the journalists become corrupted and too dependent on these trade-offs? Indeed, have the information traders got the upper hand? I realise most journalists who benefit from the trade in confidential information will probably be irritated by my book. What is the point, they will ask, in trying to make life more difficult for those who have become regular and reliable sources of data which would otherwise be withheld from public scrutiny? I accept that my endeavour to understand and expose the culture of leaking might be seen as a step too far.

Nonetheless no journalist can ignore the fact that the calculated way in which information is being fed to the media on an unattributable and off-the-record basis has hastened a decline in editorial standards. I have no wish to profit personally from my inquiries or be thought to have taken financial advantage of other journalists, and all my proceeds from *Trading Information* are being donated to the Journalists' Charity (www.journalistscharity. org.uk), of which I was chairman during 2005–6 when I was researching and writing this book.

Chapter 1

Before going any further into my exploration of the many surreptitious ways in which information can be traded with the news media, I owe readers of this book a frank account of what some might consider has been my own highly dubious conduct in the past. In seeking to investigate the motives and experiences of those who have leaked secret or confidential material, I have to admit that I do write with a degree of experience or, to use criminal parlance, perhaps I should say I have 'form'. I too have behaved in a manner which others will consider was underhand or perhaps even disreputable. I am not so naive as to think that my own conduct during thirty years' employment as a BBC industrial and political correspondent was regarded as having been beyond reproach. In fact I knew all along that some of my editors and producers did occasionally have their concerns about the reliability of my reporting and the methods I used when gathering information. Indeed, on one celebrated occasion I was told in no uncertain terms that the BBC's management feared that I had become 'excitable and untrustworthy'. Despite having been reprimanded so forthrightly, I secretly rather liked being portrayed in such emotive terms, as well might other reporters sharing a predilection for sailing close to the wind.

Nonetheless, even when having made allowances for the well-known deviousness and volatility of journalists, I accept there are lines which should not be crossed. We do owe a debt of loyalty to whoever it is that publishes or broadcasts our stories; the confidence and trust of the colleagues with whom we work, and on whom we depend, should be respected; their future employment must not be put in jeopardy by foolhardy exploits or by our own pursuit of personal publicity. In offering a *mea culpa* for action which at the time caused intense embarrassment and annoyance not only to the editorial hierarchy of the BBC but also to the then Prime Minister, I do acknowledge in hindsight that my activities placed others at risk. Rather than having the guts to put my own head on the block, I did take cover and allow BBC managers to mount a robust defence of the corporation's staff which, in the words of that famous phrase, was 'economical with the truth', at least as far as I was concerned. Although I am writing about an incident which happened well over a decade ago, fresh in my mind are the calamitous events which engulfed the BBC early in 2004 after the conclusion of the inquiry by Lord Hutton into the death of the celebrated weapons inspector Dr David Kelly.

The row provoked by my action was nothing like the no-holds-barred confrontation which led to Kelly's exposure after a BBC reporter, Andrew Gilligan, had accused the Downing Street director of communications, Alastair Campbell, of having 'sexed up' the British government's dossier on Iraq's weapons of mass destruction. However, while it was in a different league, the set-to that I precipitated did put the BBC at odds with the government of the day and prompted questions about the ethics of those BBC journalists and technicians who had the misfortune to find they were under suspicion as a result of my duplicity. What struck me so forcibly while conducting research for this book, and in reflecting on my own misdemeanours on that occasion, was the realisation that for a brief period my behaviour mirrored that of those who, for whatever reason, have similarly thrown caution to the wind and have often as a result faced a far greater threat to their own futures because of the way they have abused privileged access, broken confidences and handed over confidential material to journalists.

In my own case I recall that my responses followed a pattern which I have subsequently found was common among those who have leaked information: I too had felt frustrated by authority, in my case the management of the BBC; like many other leakers, I could not resist seizing an opportunity to publicise information which I considered was being suppressed; and once my story was out in the newspapers and all over the airwaves, I felt a sense of empowerment through having had the satisfaction of knowing that I had succeeded in causing quite a stir yet had escaped unscathed. My claim to the briefest of mentions in the roll call of infamous leaks was that I was the secret instigator of stories about what became known in the tabloid press as 'Bastardgate'. I had eavesdropped on what the two participants had regarded as a private conversation; I had taken a shorthand note of what I had overheard; and then I had given a verbatim quote of what had been said to another journalist. While an exchange of information between two reporters might not on the face of it seem all that unusual, this was no run-of-the-mill quotation. In disclosing what I had seen and heard, I knew full well that once the story was out it would give newspaper headline writers a field day because of the beleaguered position of the then Prime Minister, John Major.

Major had faced months of turmoil within the Conservative Party because of mounting criticism over the terms of British membership of the European Union. The conversation which I spied on took place in July 1993 in the immediate aftermath of his defeat in the House of Commons at the hands of rebel Tory MPs opposed to the Maastricht Treaty. Rather unwisely, on completing a series of television interviews, the Prime Minister chose to speak privately, with a considerable degree of frankness, about the activities of the former Tory ministers who he believed had been stirring up dissent. As he relaxed and continued to chat away to Michael Brunson, the political editor of ITN, the focus of their conversation turned to the possibility that Major might be forced to demand the resignation of the three members of his Cabinet who were known to be Eurosceptics. Apparently the prospect of having to contend with another trio of ex-ministers causing trouble on the back benches so alarmed the Prime Minister that he turned to Brunson and posed this highly revealing question in what were clearly pretty sensational terms: 'Would you like three more of the bastards out there?' I knew instantly on hearing Major describe three of his Cabinet colleagues as 'bastards' that his remark was political dynamite.

What gave me a pivotal position in the unfolding drama of 'Bastardgate' was that Major and Brunson had no idea their conversation had been overheard, nor did they know that anyone had recorded their remarks, let alone taken a full shorthand note of what they had said. In the event the way in which the story emerged was truly bizarre given the fierce competition which exists for exclusive political stories. Furthermore the whole episode does raise some fundamental questions about the rules of news gathering. Why, in his own report that evening for *News at Ten*, did Brunson fail to reveal Major's deep unease about the possibility of a Cabinet split involving his Eurosceptic ministers? And, if it was really the case that this insight into the parlous state of the Prime Minister's relationship with his colleagues was known about by political correspondents within the BBC, why did the corporation give up the opportunity to break the story?

Given all these circumstances, what was it that finally prompted a BBC correspondent to defy his own management and leak the contents of that private conversation to a Sunday newspaper? Some political observers will undoubtedly dismiss the sequence of events which followed as nothing more than a typical example of the incestuous and irrelevant goings-on within the Westminster village.

That might have been the case but for the fact that, as Major confirmed in his memoirs, the circumstances he faced were dire. His government had been on 'the brink of collapse' over the Maastricht defeat. He felt the subsequent media frenzy over 'Bastardgate' served only to fuel the resentment of the Eurosceptics and had 'reduced the chances of a much-needed reconciliation across the Conservative Party'. In revealing for the first time my unseemly role in what Major deemed 'an unhappy episode', I need to explain why, late that Friday afternoon in July 1993, I found myself feverishly writing down the contents of a private conversation. Because of my long-standing curiosity about the way public figures seek to exploit the news media, I have always been on the look-out for unusual insights into the way politicians react when interviewed. Of particular interest are glaring inconsistencies between what politicians say publicly, either on air or to the newspapers, and their true feelings. Once a broadcast has been completed, even the most controlled performer can sometimes be racked by self-doubt and desperate for feedback: 'What was it like? How did I do? Did I get that point across? Was I convincing?' It is at this moment, when their defences are down, that politicians are especially vulnerable.

In the course of a few anxious moments they might inadvertently let slip a nugget of information, perhaps give a hint as to precisely what was really bothering them or reveal what hitherto had been a hidden agenda. On most days BBC journalists conduct a wide range of live and pre-recorded political interviews and because I had a fast shorthand note I was frequently assigned the task of listening across to what was being said in case something news-worthy emerged. Gathering the latest reaction from prominent politicians cannot be left to chance and their comments, either in actuality or in reported speech, formed an essential part of the daily coverage of political news. A small monitor on each desk in the Westminster newsroom allows journalists to watch or listen to a vast range of television and radio output. By selecting the relevant channel, it is possible to monitor the output of each studio as well as a wide variety of incoming feeds from other locations, both at home or abroad. On the day in question, I had to keep an ear on what

Major was saying because I needed to select one of his responses for a radio report that I was preparing for broadcast that evening.

The events that week in the House of Commons had been sensational: one of the divisions on the Bill to ratify the Maastricht treaty had resulted in a tied vote of 317–317 and the government lost a second division by eight votes. Next day, Friday 23 July, after winning a confidence vote by the comfortable margin of thirty-nine votes, Major decided to reinforce his victory by giving a series of television interviews in his office in Downing Street. Whenever he was questioned at length I always tried either to monitor his appearances or replay the tapes at a later stage because over the years he had often surprised me by his acute understanding of the tricks of the trade. Unlike his predecessor, Margaret Thatcher, who was so suspicious of journalists and broadcasters that she always remained on her guard in their company and rarely indulged them with small talk, Major liked to fraternise with reporters, camera crews and technicians. A string of interviews of the kind which took place after Major won his vote of confidence is, in some respects, a semi-public event. Often those in attendance include a political reporter from the Press Association news agency, whose job it is to take a verbatim note of any newsworthy responses so that they can be supplied to newspapers and other news outlets under an embargo.

I had always worked on the assumption that from the moment the Prime Minister took his seat ready for the first interview he would have realised there was a fair chance that any of his utterances might have been heard by other people in the room or be picked up by one of the microphones. The interviews conducted late that Friday afternoon in Downing Street followed the usual pattern: Major remained seated and once each question-and-answer session was completed, another interviewer slipped into the seat in front of him. Although the televising inside Downing Street was being done by a single BBC crew on a pooled basis and the pictures were being fed from an outside broadcast vehicle parked nearby in Horse Guards Parade, it was up to each broadcasting organisation to record a copy of its own interview ready for transmission. Strict rules applied to the use of any footage. BBC television and radio programmes were under an obligation to broadcast only those answers which Major had given to the BBC's political editor, Robin Oakley; all other responses, however newsworthy they might have been, were the property of the relevant broadcasting outlet.

After I had selected one of the answers which the Prime Minister gave to Oakley, so that I could use it in one of my subsequent radio reports, I stopped watching the monitor and did not see the final interview conducted by Michael Brunson for ITN. However, other BBC journalists in the Millbank newsroom were still monitoring the continuous feed of the proceedings and they shouted across to alert me to the fact that Major had carried on talking after the last formal interview and he had suddenly become quite revealing about the problems he faced. The monitors on each desk have a replay facility and the key section was replayed for me and several other correspondents who had missed the exchange. I could see that although the main television lights had been dimmed, Major and Brunson remained seated in the interview position; their conversation was clearly audible. I was struck immediately by the frank, engaging manner which the Prime Minister had adopted. He said that if he had done all the 'clever, decisive things' which people had wanted him to, he would have 'split the Conservative Party into smithereens' and journalists would have said he had acted like 'a ham-fisted leader' and 'broken up' the party.

Although Major had provided me with intriguing insights on previous occasions, I had never heard him being anything like so forthcoming about the constraints he faced. I detected an almost conspiratorial air about the proceedings as Brunson played the occasion for all it was worth and followed up Major's remark about continuing 'bitterness' within the party over the government's European policy with a question of his own. Why had the Prime Minister not asked for the resignation of the three Eurosceptics in his Cabinet? Brunson, evidently conscious of the fact that there were other people in the vicinity, quickly added the rider that 'perhaps we had better not mention open names in this room'. Major needed no further prompting and seemed in no doubt as to whom Brunson had in mind: 'We all know which three that is.' He then proceeded, in a relaxed and easy manner, to outline the dilemma he faced. 'You are Prime Minister. You have got a majority of eighteen. You have got a party still harking back to a golden age that never was, but is now invented. And you have three right-wing members of the Cabinet actually resigned. What happens in the Parliamentary party?' At this point, much to my relief, Brunson interrupted Major.

I had been concentrating hard on my shorthand note, determined to write down the Prime Minister's every word, and I made just a quick summary of Brunson's suggestion that although he thought the outgoing ministers would probably 'create a lot of fuss' they could easily be replaced. Major acknowledged that he could bring other senior Tory MPs into the Cabinet:

That is right, but where do you think most of this poison has come from? It is coming from the dispossessed and the never possessed. You and I can think of ex-ministers who are going around causing all sorts of trouble. Would you like three more of the bastards out there?

Given the political climate in which he was having to operate, these remarks were sensational: here was a Prime Minister blaming ex-ministers for having spread 'poison' and accusing three of his Cabinet colleagues of being 'bastards'. Inevitably there was quite a hullabaloo in the Millbank newsroom as word spread among the correspondents and producers about the potential implications of what Major had been saying; there was an immediate debate as to whether the BBC should or could report what had been overheard.

I was the only correspondent to have taken a shorthand note of what had been said and after about half an hour's discussion my line manager, Bob Eggington, told me personally that I must not use something which the BBC had recorded by accident. Whatever Major might have said, it was part of a private conversation and was the exclusive property of ITN. As the *Six O'Clock News* was off the air by then, some of the correspondents went downstairs to have a Friday night drink in Rodin's, a café-bar in the basement of the Millbank building, which had become a popular rendezvous for broadcasters and newspaper journalists working in Westminster. Judging by the buzz in the BBC's newsroom I sensed that Major's gaffe about the three 'bastards' was bound to be the main talking point. Instead of joining my colleagues I set to work transcribing my shorthand note in order to add it to a daily diary which I kept about the insights which I obtained during the course of my work. I had already collected several other examples which supported one of the themes I was researching, that a chat with a politician, either during a warm-up to an interview or afterwards, often provided a better news line than the broadcast itself. Once I had printed off the two sheets of A4 paper which contained my notes I left for home.

I was anxious to watch *News at Ten* in order to see what use Brunson made of his exclusive insight into the Prime Minister's thinking. I had already observed how Major frequently adopted a friendly and engaging manner when talking to journalists. I had been flattered at having been on the receiving end of the same treatment but I considered it was a calculated act which he hoped would secure him sympathetic coverage. Having gone out of his way to take ITN's political editor into his confidence and to impress him with his indiscretions, I felt sure Major would be hoping for a pay-back and that, all things being equal, there was every likelihood that Brunson would be supportive in assessing the Prime Minister's position. In the event, as I suspected, *News at Ten* portrayed Major as being in a buoyant mood and made no mention of his fears about the potentially disruptive behaviour of his three Eurosceptic Cabinet colleagues. I thought Brunson could easily have alluded to this, as in the past he had regularly been quite tough on Major. After all, the Prime Minister had revealed the depths of his despair while delivering at the same time what could be interpreted as a warning shot across the bows of potential dissidents.

I concluded that the whole episode demonstrated a cunning streak in the Prime Minister and that he was not averse to going on a charm offensive with journalists if he thought that by doing so he could manipulate the media. Next morning, to my surprise, I was called at home by Paul Routledge, a political correspondent for the *Observer*, who asked for my help. Several journalists had told him that I was the only correspondent at Millbank who had taken a detailed note of what the Prime Minister had said and as he understood the BBC had a pirate video of the conversation, he wondered whether I had a copy of the tape and whether I could confirm that the Major had accused three Cabinet members of being 'bastards' and had blamed ex-ministers for 'spreading poison'. When I began playing for time, trying to think how to respond, Routledge started summarising earlier sections of the conversation which I had not heard. To my surprise he also disclosed that *Newsnight*'s presenter Jeremy Paxman had wanted to do the BBC's interview with the Prime Minister, rather than Robin Oakley, but that this request had been rejected. I sensed that Routledge was desperate to get first-hand verification of the 'bastards' quote.

For a loyal BBC employee there was only option: I should have told Routledge that I could not possibly discuss with him what had taken place in the Millbank newsroom; I certainly should not have leaked to him the contents of the conversation. It was at this point that I began to feel frustrated by what had happened: I was sure Major's mateyness had been deliberate, that he hoped Brunson would take pity on him – which, as it transpired, seemed to have been the case; I felt annoyed by the instruction I had been given that the BBC could make no mention of a highly revealing insight into the Prime Minister's thinking; and I was rather disconcerted to discover that newspaper journalists already had as much information as I possessed both about the scope of the conversation and about other circumstances relating to the interview. I had no intention of disobeying the instruction I had been given about not broadcasting what I had heard, nor did I have any wish to jeopardise the BBC's position, but I did have a strong sense of loyalty towards journalists with whom I had worked over many years. Throughout the late 1970s and early 1980s I had been one of the BBC's labour and industrial correspondents, while Routledge had been the labour editor of the *Times*; we had both covered the epic struggles of the era, such as the 1978–9 'winter of discontent' and the 1984–5 miners' strike.

Although employed by competing news outlets, reporters assigned to fast-moving stories such as industrial disputes often relied on each other when it came to obtaining or checking basic facts and quotes. While we would willingly trade information in this way, we would not discuss the top line to our individual stories or reveal a possible exclusive. As a radio reporter I had to spend hours outside union and management meetings waiting for the protagonists to arrive or depart. Often I would have the only recording of what had been said. I would happily play the tape so that newspaper reporters could get the quotes they needed; in return they would pass on background information which I might have missed. That Saturday morning, knowing that Routledge faced a deadline for next day's *Observer*, I felt I could not deny having heard Major refer to the 'bastards', so I read to him my shorthand note of the relevant quotes. Once I had put the telephone down I realised the risk I had taken but, judging by the information which Routledge had already obtained, I thought it was inevitable that the Sunday newspapers would publish the story anyway and that sooner or later the BBC would end up following suit.

Nonetheless I thought I had better alert Bob Eggington to the fact that I had been approached by the *Observer*, which was already aware of the main points from the conversation, and that Routledge was suggesting that the BBC possessed a pirate tape of what had been said. Eggington remained adamant that the BBC should not broadcast the story but he acknowledged that that might change depending on what the newspapers published. Later that afternoon I had another call from the *Observer*, this time from paper's political editor, Simon Hoggart, who told me the story was their front page splash but that they were anxious to check with me yet again that I had heard Major say the word 'bastards'. Hoggart needed to satisfy himself about the authenticity of that one remark and the fact that I was able to quote not from memory but from a shorthand note was the reassurance he needed. He left me with the clear impression that the paper had obtained information from a variety of sources and probably had a fuller account of what had happened than covered by my short extract, vital though that was to the punchline of the story. Next morning, despite having been tempted to rush out first thing to the nearest newsagent, I waited for the Sunday papers to be delivered.

My sense of foreboding was confirmed on seeing the *Observer*'s front page. The top story was under the joint by-line of Routledge and Hoggart: 'Major hits at Cabinet "bastards"'. It described how 'John Major's rage and frustration with right-wing Tories boiled over' in an outburst of 'anger and contempt' that was bound to 'keep open the party's wounds after the Maastricht furore'. By the time I got to the fourth and fifth paragraphs my heart sank. Routledge had reported in great detail what had happened inside the Millbank newsroom. He described how BBC staff monitoring the interview had been surprised to see an embittered Prime Minister under-mine his own 'nice guy' image. As a result they had made their own video recording of the conversation and then produced 'a bootleg transcription of the tape'. I knew instantly that Routledge's reference to the tape having been transcribed was tantamount to naming me as the source because the BBC's management already knew I was the only correspondent to have taken a shorthand note. Having lit the blue touch paper, Routledge predicted that the leak was 'certain to cause another row' between Downing Street and the BBC but then added the rider that the 'BBC cannot be blamed for the leak'.

That morning the telephone hardly stopped ringing. Eggington was the first to call demanding a full account of all that had transpired. He warned me that a full-scale investigation was underway because the Conservative Party chairman, Sir Norman Fowler, had been interviewed on *Sky News* that morning. He blamed the BBC for leaking the contents of the Prime Minister's private conversation and called on the corporation to 'put its house in order'. After Eggington reminded me that I was the only BBC correspondent to have taken a note, I assured him that although I had spoken to Routledge that Saturday morning, I was responding to his call and I had not tipped off the *Observer* nor had I spoken to any other newspaper about the story. Eggington replied rather ominously that he had further enquiries to make and told me to report to his office next day. As I discovered a decade later during my subsequent researches, most leakers would have recognised the dichotomy in the thoughts which were buzzing around my head that Sunday morning. On the one hand I could not stop thinking about the likely reaction of the BBC's management. I knew that if Fowler had sent his complaint direct to the corporation's director general, John Birt, there would be an in-depth inquiry and there was unlikely to be any doubt as to who was to blame.

Conversely I realised that it was my close interest in Major's behaviour which had prompted me to take a shorthand note in the first place and that without it the *Observer* would probably have been unable to stand its exclusive up. I had, in effect, helped to instigate a political row which seemed set to remain headline news for some days. Although the BBC had not benefited from my endeavours, I did take some satisfaction from the fact that the story had not been suppressed. For his part Routledge had done all he could to propel the story up the news agenda because he displayed no hesitation in identifying the three 'bastards' whom he thought Major had in mind: the Home Secretary, Michael Howard, the Secretary of State for Social Security, Peter Lilley, and the chief secretary to the Treasury, Michael Portillo. I was surprised by the inclusion of Howard in the *Observer*'s list because in my original note I had written that the third 'bastard' was probably the Secretary of State for Wales, John Redwood. Major's outburst provided the lead story for four of next day's newspapers; another four had it as the inside lead on page two. Most of the headlines predicted that what the *Sun* had dubbed 'Bastardgate' would spark off a new bout of party infighting over Europe.

'Major's gaffe renews Tory civil war' was the banner headline in the *Daily Telegraph* and this was mirrored on the front page of the *Times*: 'Major gaffe endangers Tory truce'. The front-page headline which stopped me in my tracks was in the *Daily Express*: 'Find the mole, Tories tell BBC'. The Conservative high command was said to be 'incensed' by what appeared to have been a 'dirty tricks campaign' to leak Major's private conversation.

Michael Brunson had weighed in too, accusing 'snoopers' at the BBC's studios in Millbank of listening in to what was clearly an off-screen chat between himself and the Prime Minister. BBC officials were quoted by the *Daily Express* as having insisted that they knew nothing about the alleged transcript but had promised that 'any guilty staff would be disciplined' by the corporation. Nonetheless, on reading through the daily papers, I could not help but feel rather pleased with myself: the quotes which I had taken down and given to Routledge had been widely reprinted and came almost entirely from that section of the conversation which I had monitored.

Although most of the newspapers were convinced that Major's off-the-cuff remarks would provide deadly ammunition for his enemies in the party, the Conservatives' deputy chairman, Gerry Malone, suggested on *Today* there was nothing wrong with the Prime Minister using strong language: 'If he always uses po-faced language about things then he's seen not to be in touch with real people . . . He's a strong individual, who has strong views and occasionally expresses them robustly.' I had wondered over the weekend whether these disclosures about Major's exasperation could be used to his advantage and Malone's light-hearted response was reflected that Monday afternoon in an editorial in the London *Evening Standard* which said the revelation that the Prime Minister 'sometimes feels annoyance' would have done him no harm with the public. Equally comforting was the *Standard*'s denunciation of Fowler for having failed to take 'the sting out of this row with a little philosophical humour'. Fowler's demand that the BBC should investigate and explain how the leak took place was 'both pointless and peevish'. While I was rather grasping at straws, I did feel a little easier about my position when I was interviewed by Bob Eggington later that afternoon.

He confirmed what I had suspected, that newspaper reporters first heard about Major's use of the word 'bastards' that Friday evening when a number of BBC correspondents and producers had gone for a drink to the café-bar in Millbank. Brunson, who was in the vicinity at the time, was apparently stopped by at least two BBC journalists who complimented him on having pulled off such a newsy encounter with the Prime Minister. Because there had been so much gossiping about what had taken place, the Downing Street press office was convinced that Rodin's was the source of the story.

Apparently a dozen BBC journalists and technicians had been questioned and Eggington told me his inquiries had confirmed that I was the only employee to have transcribed Major's conversation; the one video tape recorded by staff in the newsroom had already been handed in and destroyed, as had the master copy recorded in the control room. There was nothing for it, he said, but to wait for the director general's verdict on Fowler's complaint. That evening, rather to my surprise, I was assigned to the task of pulling together the latest political reaction to Major's indiscretion for inclusion in a report for the six o'clock bulletin on Radio 4.

My opening line was that ministers and senior party officials had rallied round the Prime Minister seeking to 'minimise the impact' of his reported criticism of the three Cabinet ministers. I rather relished the irony of the situation: I had ended up reporting a story which I had leaked yet no one listening knew of the part I had played. Within a few hours the story had taken another dramatic turn because it emerged that the *Daily Mirror* had obtained a video tape containing the entire off-air conversation. John

Williams, the paper's political editor, told me he had just watched the tape and the full transcript would be published next day. 'When you see it in full, it's not at all bad for Major . . . He comes across as being quite human.'

Almost simultaneously the Press Association published a statement from the BBC announcing that a two-day inquiry had not produced 'any evidence that a BBC employee was responsible for the leak'. It said that under the pooling arrangement which operated that Friday afternoon, the interviews could have been 'monitored and recorded either in vision or in sound' not only by the BBC, ITN and Sky News but also by a wide range of other British and overseas broadcasting outlets which had the ability to plug into the BBC's feed.

The signal had also been fed to the government itself via the Central Office of Information, where it was standard practice for civil servants to transcribe interviews given by the Prime Minister. As there were so many 'possible sources for the leak', there was 'no reason to think from our inquiries so far' that the information came from the BBC. Engineers had taken a broadcast-quality recording but this was 'neither copied nor played to any outsider'. The statement was in the name of the deputy director general, Bob Phillis, who had written to Fowler to assure him that inquiries were continuing. If any further evidence came to light to suggest that BBC staff were responsible, the party chairman would be informed, but as far as Phillis could establish, 'there is no truth' in the allegation that a BBC employee was to blame. I was taken aback by the forthright nature of the denial. Eggington had given me advance warning that the statement would be issued and he told me with wry amusement that I was probably the 'luckiest' person in the BBC because purely by chance Phillis had investigated the complaint in the absence of John Birt, who was on holiday that week. I was left with the clear impression that if Birt had dealt with the matter I would have been disciplined and might well have been sacked.

By taking a shorthand note and then volunteering the fact that I had spoken to Paul Routledge, I had virtually incriminated myself and could hardly have expected to escape without at least a reprimand. Since his appointment as director general the previous year, Birt had strengthened the BBC's complaints procedure and tightened up the internal systems for enforcing editorial standards. I knew from my own personal experience that he gave the highest priority to complaints from politicians and had already gained a reputation for being somewhat overzealous in his attempt to control the corporation's staff. Phillis, like the director general, had also held several senior positions within the broadcasting industry but before joining the BBC he had been chief executive of ITN, which by all accounts seemed able to maintain an easier-going relationship with the government of the day. I could only assume that Phillis must have realised that Major's attack on the Cabinet 'bastards' had obviously become hot gossip that Friday evening and that once news of this spread among journalists, and once other broadcasting organisations inspected their tapes, they too would have discovered they had a full recording of Major's off-the-cuff outburst.

When Phillis authorised the BBC's denial, which was issued shortly after 7 p.m., he would almost certainly not have known that another copy of the tape had surfaced and had already been given to the press. It was only after the publication of the first editions of the *Daily Mirror* at around 10 p.m. that the transcript of the entire conversation became available. Billed as the 'Scoop of the Year' it promised readers the 'Bastards' tape in full and it filled the first six pages of the paper. Bill Akass, a *Mirror* reporter, described how an informant named Latimer handed him the tape outside a west London tube station and demanded in return that a full, unedited version should be published because Major came across as 'a normal human being'. My impression all along had been that Major seized his opportunity that Friday afternoon and purposely made his conversation as enticing as possible in the hope of winning Michael Brunson's sympathy.

The tape showed the Prime Minister leaning back in his chair, unclipping a small microphone from beneath his tie, and then saying in a jocular tone, 'What I don't understand, Michael, is why such a complete wimp like me keeps winning everything.' At this point Brunson smiled broadly. Major, 'still smirking', turned to his press secretary, Gus O'Donnell, and remarked: 'I suppose Gus will tell me off for saying that, won't you, Gus?' Brunson interrupted him at this point: 'No, no, no . . . it's a fair point. The trouble is that people are not perceiving you as winning . . . Because rotten SOBs like me, I suppose, don't get the message.' As Brunson laughed at his own flippant aside, Major responded, 'No, no, no. I wasn't going to say that – well, partly that, yes, partly because S-H-one-Ts like you, yes, that's perfectly right.' At this point they both laughed. The *Mirror*'s lengthy transcript showed that I had monitored only a fraction of the conversation. I told Routledge that the feed had been cut after Major referred to the danger of there being 'three more of the bastards out there', but in fact a second camera had continued to roll and recorded several more questions and answers. In a comment column alongside the transcript, John Williams said the tape showed 'above all, an honest man, an honest politician'; there was 'no shifty excuse-making, no dodging or weaving'. If the Prime Minister's chief public relations officer had any sense, the video should be put out as a 'party political broadcast'.

Although the *Daily Mirror* had been highly complimentary, the *Sun* was not going to be outdone and in a rival exclusive it claimed that the 'storm over Premier John Major's swearing' had exploded again. After gaining access to other untransmitted BBC tapes, the *Sun*'s political correspondent, Simon Walters, discovered that the Prime Minister had used the 'F-word' after taking part in a televised phone-in during the 1992 general election. During an off-air chat with Jonathan Dimbleby, the presenter of *Election Call*, Major joked about there being 'a high fuck-up factor' among Tory voters. Within a matter of days it had become open season for exposing stories about the Prime Minister's indiscretions, but, despite having helped to instigate what was fast becoming a media feeding frenzy, I still felt a slight degree of trepidation when attending the 11 a.m. briefing in Downing Street. Until that moment I had managed to avoid face-to-face contact with the rest of the political correspondents at Westminster. Colleagues in the BBC whom I suspected of gossiping that Friday evening had been keeping their heads well below the parapet, no doubt fearing they might come under suspicion, and I thought the best tactic at the lobby briefing would be to sit on one side and keep my head down.

When Brunson arrived he was still in a state of high dudgeon about the insufferable behaviour of whoever it was in the BBC who had divulged details of Major's gaffe within an hour of his interview. ITN's political editor was in full flood: 'Every work position at BBC Millbank has a video recorder. There's no control there, they don't respect anything, they just record what they like . . . I know precisely where ITN's tape is. It's safe and sound and hasn't left our building.' At this point the various BBC journalists looked down rather sheepishly at their notebooks. My eye caught Brunson's but I did not detect the slightest sign that he held me responsible for causing so much mischief. When O'Donnell opened the proceedings he seemed relaxed and determined to make light of reporters' questions about the Prime Minister admission that he was a wimp. 'He hasn't expressed any thoughts about this . . . even hostile newspapers say this whole business has done the Prime Minister a power of good.' When asked whether he had advised Major to stop swearing, O'Donnell bridled: 'I am tempted to say "eff off" . . . I have never spoken to him about bad language.' As we were leaving the briefing,

Chris Moncrieff, the Press Association's political editor, told me that he had rarely seen O'Donnell looking so chipper.

Downing Street's success in turning the 'Bastardgate' tape to the Prime Minister's advantage had taken Moncrieff by surprise. 'Once the *Daily Mirror* came out with the full quotes, I started writing the story along the lines that these latest revelations would plunge the government into chaos but as soon as I got in touch with No.10 it was clear they didn't mind at all.' Moncrieff was told by the deputy press secretary, Jonathan Haslam, that it was 'bunkum and balderdash' to suggest the leak was going to damage Major. Although both the BBC and ITN had taken steps to prevent any misuse of their recordings, other news outlets had no such scruples. Clips of Major's indiscretions were broadcast on GMTV with the word 'bastards' bleeped out. Readers of the *Daily Mirror* were invited to hear the fourteen-minute tape in its entirely by calling a special number at a cost of 36 pence per minute and the *Sun,* anxious not to be upstaged, opened a phone line replaying its 'F-word' tape. Both newspapers were ordered immediately by the Independent Committee for the Supervision of Standards of Telephone Information Services to withdraw their 0891 numbers because replaying the interviews was deemed to be an 'unreasonable invasion of privacy' and infringed the code of practice for premium rate phone lines.

The *Sun* refused to back down and the *Daily Mirror* retaliated next day by offering readers a free cassette of its 'Bastardgate' recording. In the face of what was fast becoming a summer circulation war between the two newspapers, it was the telephone watchdog which ended up executing a smart about-turn. Amid much embarrassment, the committee reversed its previous ruling and said it had concluded there had been no 'unreasonable invasion of privacy' because although Major's conversations were private, there were a number of people present on both occasions and the two unguarded asides were 'not characterised by a high degree of intimacy'. While the tabloids were having fun at the Prime Minister's expense, the revelations about his habit of gossiping with journalists was seen as a dangerous weakness by his political opponents and some senior strategists in the Tory hierarchy. They recalled how once Margaret Thatcher had finished an interview, her minders always intervened and ushered her away so as to prevent broadcasters or journalists trapping her in casual conversation. Complaints by politicians about journalists eavesdropping their conversations and then leaking titbits to the newspapers were nothing new.

During his premiership, Harold Wilson protested on more than one occasion about the way the satirical magazine *Private Eye* managed to reprint the contents of private conversations which he had conducted while inside BBC premises. After one celebrated confrontation during a pre-recorded interview in 1989, the Labour leader, Neil Kinnock, found he was pilloried in the press for swearing. Annoyed at being asked an unexpected question about the economy, Kinnock let rip at the *World at One* presenter, James Naughtie: 'For Christ's sake, they are the government. They have cocked it up . . . The Chancellor has buggered it up totally . . . I'm not going to be bloody kebabbed talking about what the alternatives are.' Although the exchange was not broadcast, it was leaked to the newspapers and caused Kinnock great embarrassment. After his election as leader in 1992, John Smith found that he was always accompanied by a Labour press officer whose job it was to head off intrusive or unexpected questions. At a reception given by the shadow Cabinet in the week of the 'Bastardgate' row, Smith told me that Labour's media team were 'very good' at fielding awkward interruptions and he wondered why Major's team were not sufficiently streetwise to understand what was going on.

Privately I was rather amused to hear Smith's praise for his streetwise media handlers because I knew they were not averse themselves either to a spot of eavesdropping or leaking. Earlier that month Labour's director of communications, David Hill, had been forced to apologise to the BBC on behalf of at least one Labour press officer who had been seen inside the Millbank studios secretly watching a bad-tempered pre-recorded interview on a monitor and had then been caught tipping off newspapers about the bust-up he had witnessed. Hill thought it was a mistake on the part of Gus O'Donnell to have allowed Michael Brunson to have such an uninhibited discussion with the Prime Minister, especially when the room being used in No.10 had in effect been turned into a television set. He was also surprised how slow the Tories had been to exploit 'Bastardgate' and swing it to Major's advantage:

> Once they had seen the *Observer* that Sunday morning, the Tories' media team should have checked immediately to see what was on the tape and they would have discovered pretty quickly it was much more favourable to the Prime Minister than the press suggested. Instead Sir Norman Fowler made a complete botch-up of it and wasted forty-eight hours by being so critical of the BBC.

On the other side of Westminster, at Conservative Central Office, where staff were still recovering from the most divisive week of Major's premiership, the overriding concern had been to gauge the likely impact on party morale. Unlike Hill, who had found ways to exploit 'Bastardgate', the Conservatives' director of communications, Tim Collins, had been kept firmly on the defensive. It was only after the first couple of days, when it was clear that most telephone calls were in support of the Prime Minister, that Collins felt able to change to tack:

> Most callers told us how delighted they were to have discovered that Major had such considerable inner strength and was no shrinking violet. When people see him in the raw they realise he is extremely effective. If he was actually the grey man he is supposed to be, he wouldn't have become the youngest Prime Minister this century nor would he have won an general election when a lot of the press said he would crack up.

I knew I had been rather sneaky asking Collins to discuss his tactics when it was obvious his party chairman was still annoyed about getting the brush-off from the BBC over his protest about the leaking of Major's gaffe. ITN's chief executive, David Gordon, had also been told that the BBC could not be blamed for the leak.

Despite on the one hand feeling an utter fraud for allowing these denials to have been issued, the more I learned about the unexpected dividend there had been for the Prime Minister in terms of his personal popularity, the easier I felt about the way Bob Phillis has been so forthright in rebutting these complaints. All my own high and mighty self-justification for leaking newsworthy insights which I thought should not be suppressed had effectively disappeared in a puff of smoke. Here was the Prime Minister basking in a blitz of cheeky-chappy headlines; 'Bastardgate' had evolved into a powerful fillip to the Prime Minister's flagging fortunes. Although the heat had been taken off the BBC, I knew, just like any other leaker who had managed to avoid detection, that it would be unwise on my part to tempt providence and draw attention to what happened in the Millbank studios that Friday afternoon. In his letter to Fowler, Phillis had left open the possibility that the BBC would take action if any evidence emerged that an employee had leaked the contents of Major's conversation.

Several newspapers continued to pursue the story and a week later the *Sunday Times* reported that the 'mole hunt' was still underway because Downing Street officials remained convinced that a BBC employee had eavesdropped on Major's off-air remarks and then supplied the details to the

Observer. Brunson kept up the pressure by writing an article for the *Guardian* in which he deplored the way the usual rules of privacy and his own personal copyright had been violated so blatantly when it must have been obvious to whoever was the leaker that the conversation was being conducted on lobby terms. Therefore he regretted having been 'thrust into the limelight' in a way he would not have chosen. A chance to interview the Prime Minister was a rare event in itself but opportunities to talk for a few moments while 'microphones are being unclipped from jackets or ties, while lights are being doused, and, in an ideal world, when cameras are being switched off, are like gold dust'. Brunson then reinforced the view I had always held, that occasionally broadcasters could find themselves in a privileged position and obtain insights which were not available to newspaper journalists. He acknowledged that the intimacy generated during post-interview small talk might provide information which would allow a broadcaster to 'steal a march on those colleagues from the written press'.

On this occasion ITN's political editor had not availed himself of the insights he had obtained and he was forthright in rejecting the taunts of those political correspondents who considered that the Prime Minister's attack on the 'bastards' was pretty sensational and should have been reported first and exclusively on *News at Ten.* Brunson said that although the text of their exchanges had been 'printed in full around the world' it would remain for him a private conversation; both he and ITN intended to be robust in their determination to ensure this principle was not compromised in any way. Nevertheless he believed that operating procedures during pooled interviews would have to be tightened if off-the-cuff remarks were going to become public property. 'Even five years ago, a "leak" of almost anything was regarded as a serious matter. Now everyone is at it.' Almost two months elapsed before the leaker and the recipient had a chance to discuss their handiwork. We met up at the TUC conference in mid-September 1993 and although Paul Routledge made no direct mention of the 'mole hunt' which had taken place within the BBC, I could tell that he realised that for a time at least, it must have been touch and go whether I was exposed and reprimanded by the management.

He was effusive in his thanks for the help I had given him that Saturday morning and indicated with a couple of fingers that to start with he only had a smidgen of information about what Major had said. Without my shorthand note of the Prime Minister's remarks about the danger of there being 'three more of the bastards out there', the *Observer* would not have been prepared to run the story. By being able to flesh out so authoritatively the tip-off he had received, Routledge had effectively saved his reputation as a political journalist. When he wrote the story he was already under notice to leave, having been sacked by the paper, but on the strength of his 'bastards' splash he was hired by the *Independent on Sunday*. The fact that Routledge's exclusive had not been sufficient to persuade the *Observer* to keep him on their staff was, in Brunson's view, a 'delicious irony' because it was the 'best scoop the paper had published for years'. In his autobiography, *A Ringside Seat*, Brunson said he realised immediately he read the *Observer*'s report that someone in the BBC had given Routledge 'a great deal of information' not only about the off-air conversation but also about lighting and sound quality. Neither he nor the Prime Minister knew that every word they had spoken was being secretly recorded but 'technology, and some questionable behaviour by the BBC, had betrayed us'.

He still could not understand why technicians in the BBC's outside broadcast vehicle continued recording after he had completed his *News at Ten* interview. He had said 'thank you' to the crew and both he and Major had removed the small clip-on microphones from their ties, which was a clear signal to the Prime Minister that anything he said was on lobby terms and would be treated as off the record. It was not until later that evening at Millbank, after being complimented by BBC journalists for obtaining 'great stuff' in his interview, that he sensed something was wrong and told Gus O'Donnell that he feared Major's use of the word 'bastards' had leaked out. Brunson remained dissatisfied with the BBC's denial of responsibility because the explanation given by Bob Phillis 'raised as many questions as it answered'. If an 'improper recording' had not been made by the BBC in the first place, the whole affair would never have become as serious as it did.

Despite Brunson's bravado about being 'robust' in making sure he would never be accused of taking advantage of a private conversation, ITN finally relented in December 2005 and allowed the key footage to be broadcast in Michael Cockerell's BBC2 programme *How to Be a Tory Leader*. Brunson was in shot looking pleased as Punch as Major delivered the infamous line, 'Would you like three more of the bastards out there?'

The original leak did increase the 'bitterness and suspicion' between the Prime Minister and the Eurosceptics to the point where some of the Tory rebels began to 'glory in their isolation'. Brunson's political analysis was supported by Major in his autobiography and he devoted a chapter to an 'unhappy episode' for which he said he had only himself to blame. He was 'exhausted' after two parliamentary votes which had taken his government to the brink of collapse and 'my words and my meaning became disconnected'. The transcript suggested he was referring to existing Cabinet ministers when talking about the 'bastards' but that was not his intention as no minister had threatened to resign over the Maastricht legislation. Major took full responsibility:

> It was careless of me to have spoken to Brunson so freely. In response to his questions I should simply have told him, 'No one has threatened to resign', and left it at that. But months of posturing and off-the-record briefing from the sceptics had built up a frustration that encouraged me to be too frank. Even a Prime Minister can only bite his lip for so long.

His main regret was that his outburst had reduced the chances of a much-needed reconciliation and had kept the focus on his own attitude towards them rather switching the attention of the news media to 'a very public defeat' for the Eurosceptics.

> In itself the comment was merely a slip, not a calamity. It was one of the hiccoughs of government that are soon forgotten, and this it would have remained had some of the rebels not chosen to take affront at my words to suit their own ends. They saw my criticism of their activities as a badge of courage.

In writing his memoirs Major would have been hard pushed to have adopted anything other than a relaxed approach to the repercussions of 'Bastardgate' because, as events would demonstrate, he was soon being portrayed by political correspondents as something of a serial offender when it came to the use of unsavoury language to describe his opponents. Within two months of the media feeding frenzy over 'Bastardgate', the headline writers were pillorying the Prime Minister for 'Barmygate'. Yet again off-air remarks in between television interviews had put temptation in the way of political journalists. While visiting Japan during a tour of the Far East in September 1993, Major agreed to answer reporters' questions while at the British embassy in Tokyo. The assiduous Chris Moncrieff kept his tape recorder running as Major responded to questions from each of the main television networks.

Later Moncrieff allowed the *Independent*'s political correspondent, Colin Brown, to replay his tape and, on listening through to the whole recording,

Brown discovered that in between interviews for Sky News and ITN the Prime Minister could be heard chatting away. At one point he suddenly launched into another attack on the Conservatives' rebellious Eurosceptic MPs. Major said his intention was to outsmart his tormentors at the party conference in Blackpool the following month. In elaborating on his plans he showed nothing but contempt for the troublemakers: 'I could name eight people. Half of those eight are barmy. How many apples short of a picnic?' Brown's exclusive report about the 'barmy brigade' filled the front page of the *Independent* and it was followed up immediately by the rest of the national press, which had already given plenty of coverage the day before to the Prime Minister's colourful turn of phrase when describing former ministers. In one rejoinder to a rather pointed inquiry about their conduct, Major denounced his detractors as 'devils on the fringe living out past glories'. Some newspapers attributed these remarks directly to the Prime Minister but several correspondents sourced them to what Major had been heard 'telling friends'.

Journalists often deployed such devices to overcome the fact that they were quoting from private conversations but did not want to be blamed for a breach of privacy. Once Brown had used verbatim quotes in the *Independent*, the rest of the press followed suit and had no inhibitions about publishing an unexpurgated account of Major's injudicious small talk on the terrace of the British embassy. Another off-the-cuff remark which the newspapers took delight in attributing to him was his aside that he heard 'the sound of white coats flapping' whenever mention was made of the name of one of the leading rebels, Sir Richard Body. Moncrieff told me he could not fault Brown's initiative in listening through to the whole of the tape. 'Even though it took him thirty-six hours to file his story, he got the one quote that really mattered.' Among Downing Street officials there was some criticism of Brown for effectively having eavesdropped on what were obviously off-air remarks but most lobby correspondents considered that the Prime Minister had become fair game and that it was up to his press secretary, Gus O'Donnell, to step in and police such occasions if jibes of that kind continued to be made within earshot of reporters.

The only lobby correspondent to spring to Major's defence was Charles Lewington, political editor of the *Sunday Express*, who was subsequently appointed the Conservatives' director of communications. Lewington said Major was livid when he discovered that yet another of his private conversations had been leaked to the press. Nonetheless the Prime Minister admitted he had only himself to blame: he had 'dropped his guard' and was not aware of the 'blinking red recording light' of Moncrieff's tape recorder, which had been placed on a nearby ledge. Despite the commiserations of the *Sunday Express*, Major had become a marked man among the lobby correspondents of Westminster, who realised that leaked accounts of his off-the-cuff remarks were a sure-fire way to secure banner headlines. Within days there was news of another gaffe when it emerged that civil servants at the Central Office of Information had mistakenly played out a tape on the government's audio network which contained off-the-record remarks about the former Chancellor of the Exchequer Norman Lamont, which the Prime Minister made during an interview with Eve Pollard, editor of the *Sunday Express*.

One of the organisations fed a tape of these exchanges was the American news agency Associated Press but it refused to divulge what was said and Pollard insisted that the main emotion which Major had expressed about Lamont was 'one of sorrow'. After this false alarm the lobby had to wait until January 1994, when an accident-prone Prime Minister finally blundered into 'Dinnergate' and delighted the headline writers once more. 'Major: I'll f*****g crucify Cabinet enemies,' screamed the *Sun* over a front-page report of what it said was 'a sensational outburst which stunned guests at a private Downing Street dinner'. The story was under the joint by-line of its political editor, Trevor Kavanagh, and political correspondent Simon Walters. An identical quote appeared in the *Daily Mail* in a report filed by its political editor, Gordon Greig. Neither newspaper revealed the identity of their source but both claimed that guests at the dinner heard the Prime Minister accuse right-wing ministers of having hijacked what had become known as his 'back to basics' campaign, launched at the party conference the previous October. Greig said Major had 'lobbed a grenade at the façade of cabinet unity' by attacking them so forcibly: 'I'm going to f***** crucify the Right for what they have done and this time I will have the party behind me.' Downing Street issued a fierce denial and denounced the story as 'a malicious fiction' by two newspapers whose correspondents had fabricated a quotation. The ferocity of Downing Street's attack on Kavanagh, Walters and Greig was unprecedented because their newspapers had been such staunch supporters of the Conservative Party throughout Margaret Thatcher's premiership. But relations had cooled within months of Major winning the 1992 general election and despite Gus O'Donnell's best efforts the Prime Minister was regularly held up to ridicule by previously trusted journalists who hitherto had always been welcome visitors at No. 10. The dinner, hosted by Major, was his opportunity to say 'thank you' to O'Donnell, who was returning to the Treasury to become head of its monetary group. O'Donnell drew up the guest list, which included eight political editors and correspondents but not Messrs Kavanagh, Walters or Greig. Before Downing Street issued its denial, O'Donnell made personal telephone calls to most of the thirty-two guests, /none of whom recalls hearing these words'. He was distraught that the Prime Minister had become the victim of a deliberate attempt to sabotage a farewell dinner held for himself and his wife.

After the *Sun* and the *Daily Mail* published their stories, Moncrieff, who was among the guests, filed a personal account of the event for the Press Association. At no time, from the moment of his arrival to his departure, had the Prime Minister made 'the remark attributed to him within my earshot, or anything remotely like it'. A different slant on the evening was presented by Lewington, who was not present, but who had been told by another guest, Sir Nicholas Lloyd, editor of the *Daily Express*, that Major had spoken to a group of journalists before the dinner. During this conversation the Prime Minister had acknowledged that although he faced Thatcherite rivals within the Cabinet, he was sure the Conservative Party would not 'crucify' itself by rushing into another leadership election. In his report for the *Sunday Express*, under the headline 'Crucified by the men who did not come to the dinner', Lewington claimed that Downing Street suspected that another guest, Michael Brunson, might have given a garbled account of the dinner to Walters. ITN's political editor had vehemently denied this suggestion although other newspapers claimed Brunson had spoken to Major at the end of the dinner and that afterwards he had been seen talking to Walters.

I found it comforting to read the claim and counter-claim over who had leaked what to whom and I rather agreed with Kavanagh's assessment in the *Sun* that it was the Prime Minister who might perhaps be accused of unprofessional conduct. This was the fourth occasion when his fingers had been 'badly burned' after making ill-advised outbursts in front of television correspondents. 'Telling groups of journalists your private thoughts about political enemies . . . is like sitting a hungry man in front of a four-course banquet and asking him not to eat a thing.' Having dined and then leaked at Major's expense I knew I was being rather sanctimonious in feeling both smug about his ineptitude and relieved that a fair number of my fellow correspondents had proved just as culpable when offered a similarly tempting dish. Sir Norman Fowler had accused me of having in effect bugged the

Prime Minister's home by eavesdropping on his conversation with Brunson in Downing Street the previous July. As events over the following six months had shown, Major relished the chance to take journalists into his confidence and, despite the growing risk of being exposed in the press, he seized every opportunity to put the boot in when responding to questions about his opponents.

Even so, I knew that if my own behaviour had been held up to scrutiny I might well have been censured not only by my editors but also by my colleagues. I was in a privileged position because of my ability to monitor political interviews being recorded across the BBC's output and I had to respect the editorial rights and privacy of other journalists. In giving Major's quote about the 'bastards' to the *Observer* I had abused the trust which was expected of a staff correspondent. Leaking to a newspaper information which the BBC's management had forbidden me to broadcast was not something I intended to repeat; it was a response made on the spur of the moment and even though I had emerged scot-free, I was only too aware that I might easily have ended up putting my career at risk, especially if John Birt had not been on holiday that week.

I knew I had taken the coward's way out by passing on information to Paul Routledge rather than finding another means to defy the BBC, either by broadcasting or publishing my own story about the 'bastards'. Reporters often hear interesting gossip or pick up juicy scraps of information which they dare not use themselves. Rather than see the story go to waste they will tip off another journalist, even if this means giving an exclusive to a rival outlet. In such circumstances reporters at least have the satisfaction of knowing that their story was given an airing. Having chosen what others might have considered the easy way out, I needed no reminding that the risks I had taken hardly bore any comparison with the dangers faced by those who are so determined to get important information out into the public domain that they are prepared to jeopardise their own careers and if necessary contend with possible legal action in the courts. In the aftermath of 'Bastardgate' I had developed a new sense of respect for whistleblowers and I was determined to discover as much as I could about their motives and experiences. What I hoped to find was a serial leaker, someone who could talk me through the highs and lows of becoming a secret conduit for the trade in confidential information.

Chapter 2

It hardly needs saying that the act of leaking sensitive information is highly personal and very private; few of those who have ever breached the rules of confidentiality have any wish to draw attention to themselves. Most leakers know that if they are identified either by their employers or by the authorities they will probably be sacked and might possibly face legal action; there is also the danger that they could be shunned by their colleagues and friends. Perhaps not surprisingly, given the secret nature of this activity, most leak inquiries draw a blank; journalists are well aware of the risks which have been taken on their behalf and they will go to great lengths to protect their sources. In rare but highly publicised cases where the perpetrator's identity is revealed, those who have been prepared to make a defiant stand in challenging the state, big business or a powerful organisation are occasionally greeted with acclaim; sometimes the leaker is even hailed as a hero by the news media, because most journalists are keen to praise those whose daring exploits are considered to have been in the public interest.

The frequency with which leaks occur tends to be a useful guide to the popularity of the government of the day; the more controversial its policies the greater the temptation for civil servants and others in the know to slip out confidential data in the hope of embarrassing their political masters or of assisting in campaigns to challenge contentious decisions. While it is difficult to be precise about the motives of those who have passed on sensitive or secret material, many appear to believe they have acted for the public good, however misguided that might seem to the powers that be. In recent years the opportunities to leak confidential information have multiplied out of all recognition. Widespread use of photocopiers, which quickly came to be regarded as the 'leaker's friend', have offered a ready means of obtaining duplicate copies; the rapid introduction of fax machines, followed by a multitude of advances in computer technology, have opened up endless opportunities for the instant distribution of data. Today's office workers also have a far greater level of access to information than was ever the case for their predecessors.

With a few flicks of the finger at a keyboard, page upon page can be called up for scrutiny on a computer screen and then trawled through almost instantly; if unauthorised access can be gained, an operator with basic levels of computer literacy can easily identify and retrieve sensitive data within a matter of seconds. In years gone by, when documents only existed in handwritten or typewritten form, there were far fewer copies available and more often than not those which had been made were usually kept tucked away in a row of filing cabinets, often under lock and key. In more recent years, in order to prevent leaking and other similar abuses, the electronics industry has always given the highest priority to the task of safeguarding the security of computer networks. The flow of e-mails through the internet, telephone calls and the passage of other data by electronic means can usually be tracked with great precision, so only the most foolhardy tend to risk using that route. Although security systems can detect unauthorised leaking both within and across computer networks, the same level of protection cannot always be provided at the point where the data is printed off. Once there is a hard copy of the relevant information, a potential leaker can get to work.

Confidential data which is available in printed form can easily be slipped into an anonymous brown envelope and is then ready to be posted off at the nearest letter box. If, as a precaution, each sheet of printed paper has been stripped of any identifying marks or symbols, there may be little or no chance of identifying the source. While it may sometimes be possible to locate the printer which has been used, thus allowing any data which has been leaked to be checked against the list of items which have been printed, there may well be no way of detecting who pressed the 'print' key. For example, if a member of staff has left a desk unmanned and failed to shut down a computer terminal, all another worker in the office has to do is call up the relevant document, press 'print' and walk away with a copy of the data. Unattended computer terminals do provide a tempting prospect for prying eyes, especially if the screen is showing information which is protected by a password. Occasionally confidential data which has been printed off can be found lying uncollected beside the printer; the same goes for original documents carelessly abandoned under the lid of a photocopier. No one doubts the advances which have been made in today's computerised world but even the most sophisticated systems offer little protection against human carelessness.

Instant communication by e-mail and the rapid transfer and retrieval of data have revolutionised working practices, but just as more and more people have been able to scan a seemingly endless torrent of information, so the chances of gaining unauthorised access have proliferated, as have the opportunities to leak confidential material to politicians, journalists and the like. Once data held in a computer is in printed form, human ingenuity and frailty come into play and, as I can readily testify, the journalistic pulse quickens on spotting a strange-looking envelope in the post and then finding that it contains a set of confidential documents. Except for the handwriting or typing on the outside of the envelope, the only other identifying mark might be a cryptic line inside such as 'From an admirer', 'From a listener' etc. Faxing is another favoured route which also affords a fair degree of protection for the leaker; the sudden whirring of a fax machine often gets heads turning in a reporters' room. Each morning on early duty, when I looked through the news releases received overnight, I was always hoping that I might find a secret document or some other communication which had been sent anonymously or perhaps by mistake.

A fax, rather than the more traditional brown envelope, was the method used to deliver one of the most damaging leaks of the Blair government. A copy of the infamous e-mail in which the Labour spin doctor Jo Moore told civil service information officers that the aftermath of the attack on the World Trade Center in New York on 11 September 2001 was the moment to 'bury' controversial announcements was faxed to Barrie Clement, transport editor of the *Independent*. He received the fax a month after she had issued the instruction and his exclusive story, under the headline 'Secret ministry e-mail: Use attack to bury bad news', triggered Moore's resignation and contributed to the eventual downfall of her boss, the Secretary of State for Transport, Stephen Byers. Moore's e-mail was reproduced on the paper's front page. It listed the names of the recipients and showed the precise time she wrote it: '11/09/01 14:55:12'. Clement told me told that he assumed his source had obtained a printed copy of Moore's e-mail which was then faxed to him at the *Independent*. He refused to disclose any further details about the leak; he would not tell me whether his source had direct access to the government's computer system or was given a print-out or photocopy by someone who did.

Journalists are well versed in the precautions they should take on the receipt of leaked information: any identifying telephone numbers at the top or bottom of each page of the fax should be cut off immediately and destroyed; the document should then be photocopied so that the original can be disposed of as quickly as possible, along with the envelope, if it was received through the post. Subsequently, if challenged by the police or the authorities, journalists could truthfully say the original no longer existed; all that they possessed was a photocopy, hopefully shorn of all clues. Initially, because of the fear that there might be prosecutions for handling stolen documents, leaks received by fax were religiously retyped and the originals shredded. Later, when unauthorised disclosure of faxes and e-mails became far more commonplace, newspapers often reproduced the title or front page of a confidential document in order to prove to their readers that although they only had a duplicate copy, it was genuine. It was largely through the rapid introduction of fax machines that leaking could be said to have entered the electronic age. By the mid-1980s the fax room in most large organisations was as busy, if not busier, than the post room.

In these pre-internet days, sending faxes down telephone lines had become the fastest way to transfer documents between government departments, commercial offices and so on. Inevitably, despite its speed and simplicity, there were weak points in the process and initially, as with the development of the internet, there were few safeguards to prevent the unauthorised use of faxed material. A letter marked on the envelope as being 'secret', 'confidential' or 'private' would almost certainly have been delivered unopened to the desk of the recipient; as a result there would have been little scope for prying eyes among the sorters and messengers in the post room. The same level of protection could not be afforded to an incoming or outgoing fax which might have contained highly sensitive data. If the incoming fax ran to several pages, these would usually have been stapled together and once collated, the document would either have been delivered by hand or left for collection. However, staff in the fax room would have had every opportunity to cast an eye over any confidential data that was being sent or received and obviously the whole process relied on the workforce being totally trustworthy.

Many organisations, especially in the commercial sector, appeared to operate on the basis that low-paid employees doing jobs of this nature were unlikely to have any interest in the data which they were collecting and collating from the fax machines under their control; even if their attention had been aroused by the contents of a particular fax, it was assumed that they would not have understood its true significance, nor would they have been thought capable of putting the information to an inappropriate use. Such managerial remoteness provided the perfect opening for several of the leakers that I managed to speak during the years I spent reporting industrial and political affairs and researching this book. Out of necessity I have had to conceal their identities and disguise their places of work but, although these individuals must remain anonymous, my conversations with them do provide an insight into their techniques and motivations.

Much of the daily routine of leaker A, who was a messenger in a large organisation, was spent sorting incoming mail and collecting and collating faxes. A mechanical difficulty with one of the machines led to the chance discovery that one of its additional functions was a facility to print off a second copy of an incoming or outgoing fax. All that needed to be done once a document had been received or sent was to press the button marked 'fax' and out came a duplicate; in this mode the fax machine acted like a photocopier. This produced two identical versions of the same document with nothing to distinguish one copy from another. To begin with leaker A began taking copies of documents out of curiosity, thinking they might be of interest and were probably worth keeping; it was only later, on realising their significance, that the messenger began to post them off anonymously to journalists on national newspapers. Leaker A would give me no clue as to the type of documents which had been leaked but judging by the nature of the relevant work place, they probably related to commercial transactions involving government departments and the information had appeared to be newsworthy. Leaker B, a clerical worker, was far more focused in selecting material and had the sole intention of trying to help trade unions in their campaigns to prevent the privatisation of public services. Within a matter of months this individual had become a serial leaker, posting off countless copies of confidential government documents which gave details of the financial arrangements for the break-up of the nationalised industries and the sale of state assets.

So great was leaker B's indignation about what were perceived to be the injustices of the Thatcher years that few opportunities were missed to alert trade union leaders to the wrongdoings of an unpopular Conservative government. Great care had to be taken to make sure that recipients of the documents were never given any clues as to the identity of the sender or any other inkling as to where the leaks might have originated. 'I wanted trade union leaders to see in advance what was being proposed in the privatisations that were about to be announced by the government, so that the workers' representatives would be on an equal footing and be as well prepared as the management'. Meanwhile leaker C worked in a large outer office dealing with considerable quantities of incoming and outgoing correspondence and documentation, much of which related to the government. Again the target was Margaret Thatcher's government and leaking by this young office worker began almost as a protest against the arrogance and insensitivity of the management. Leaker C sensed that those supervising the staff thought anyone doing menial clerical duties was 'just a dumb drudge' who was not capable of having political views, let alone any knowledge or understanding of the potential importance of the information which the outer office was being required to process each day.

Leaker C gradually came to the realisation that the act of leaking had most impact when the person who had access to the information knew how to use it to the greatest effect.

> It is that deadly combination, the possession of information and knowing where best to place a leak, which turned my leaking into such a heady cocktail. Sometimes, if I was really annoyed by the correspondence which I was dealing with, I would leak a copy to a journalist or an MP. If I thought the information might be of real assistance, perhaps in helping to mount a campaign against the government, I would send it to a pressure group but I took that decision, it was entirely down to me. That was why I found leaking so addictive.

Leaker C had posted off copies of confidential correspondence for a period of several years, without detection, but would give no hint as to where or when this had taken place nor supply any clue as to the nature of the data involved. When I began looking into the psyche of leakers and asking about their experiences, I was struck by their continuing fear of being exposed, even though most of them had changed jobs and some considerable time had usually elapsed since the events they were recalling.

Leaker D remained perhaps the most fearful of those I interviewed.

> Even now if I was outed, I can imagine it could all become very, very scary. Obviously at the time I was leaking documents I must have been a bit of a loner. Part of the thrill came from knowing that none of the bosses suspected me and from sensing that I was able to exercise a kind of hidden influence, that I did have some sort of power.

I was given a precise description of the precautions that had to be taken: each sheet of paper was checked for identifying marks and any serial letters or figures were cut off; likewise any telephone numbers which might have been recorded either at the top or bottom of an incoming or outgoing fax had to be removed; anonymous brown envelopes were always used when posting off leaked documents; handwriting was varied when addressing each envelope so that it appeared they were from different sources; and as an additional precaution, addresses were purposely written with a leftward slant, rather than leaker D's usual rightward slant. Each encounter confirmed what I began to find were common characteristics: leakers usually had strong political convictions; leaking tended to become addictive; and they thought employers had only themselves to blame because the naivety of their managers had created opportunities which could easily be exploited.

Another common trait was the sense of empowerment which leakers felt on seeing the results of their handiwork reported by the news media. Leaker E developed an astute news sense and with every leak became even better at selecting the kind of documents which would hit the headlines. 'In a way I felt as if I had got to know the various reporters covering the stories I was interested in. If I saw a document which might interest them I would post them off a photocopy.' At this moment, as if to prove the point, leaker E opened a bag and revealed a sheaf of papers. Pinned to the front page of each document were newspaper cuttings of the stories which the various leaks had generated. I recognised the by-lines of most of the correspondents, some of whom I had known for many years. Seeing in print reports generated by the confidential data which leaker E had personally selected had evidently played a significant part in sustaining what by any stretch of the imagination had become a pretty reckless addiction. Although I was assured that none of the journalists knew the identity of the person sending the information, leaker E would love to have known what they thought of the leaks which they had been receiving for so long. Had the reporters ever wondered what motivated the leaker and why sometimes they were sent more than one set of documents from the same source?

I was convinced that none of the journalists who had benefited from leaker E's daring would have had any idea of the tremendous risks which had been taken on their behalf and I said I was sure they would all agree with me that having leaked so assiduously for so long, it would be wise to give it all up and get a new job as soon as possible. All the leakers I spoke to insisted they were acting out of personal conviction; they had felt a sense almost of duty to reveal what they had discovered and believed was being done in secret. Leakers A and B acknowledged that the confidential data which they had disclosed probably was commercially sensitive and that its unauthorised release might have hurt the companies involved. Leaker A was adamant that it was possible to leak from a principled position:

> In a way it was a bit like insider trading: I was trading information and in return getting stories into the newspapers which damaged the Conservatives. Sometimes it did affect share prices but I wasn't doing it to make money, I did it because that's what my conscience told me and I wanted to protect the public. But I did get a buzz from seeing my stories in the papers and finding that I had encouraged journalists to draw attention to what I thought was wrong.

Likewise leaker B considered that supplying information to the unions had been an honourable cause. 'I believed that I was leaking documents for the right reasons; someone had to help the unions protect jobs'. Leaker C, like the others I interviewed, had operated completely independently with no second thoughts about the expense involved in posting off sets of documents sometimes running to a hundred pages or more. This was leaking for a purpose, not just out of spite or devilment:

> I agree that people who do things for what they think are the right reasons aren't always angels but my return, my reward if you like, was the knowledge that the information I had leaked had been useful to MPs, journalists and pressure groups. I leaked purely for the cause I believed in, not for personal benefit or self-promotion. In my own way I was protesting about the ability of people in important positions to keep information out of sight from the public.

As I continued my researches and compared my insights into the private world of the leaker with those cases where they had been identified publicly, I was struck by the fact that many of them were in lowly positions and had often leaked over long periods without any encouragement, obvious reward or financial support. Despite the drudgery of their work and their limited knowledge and experience of how the news media operated, these committed and enterprising individuals had worked out for themselves how they could make a contribution towards countering the evils which they perceived. By carefully targeting the recipients of their leaks, they helped to bring into the open what they considered were the wrongdoings of the government or of others in authority and, whatever the opprobrium heaped on their heads, they believed they were following an honourable tradition. When I began to inquire into their psyche and motivation I had already spent some years investigating the way leaks were influencing political reporting. The frequency of unauthorised disclosures had risen noticeably during the governments of Margaret Thatcher and John Major. Both Prime Ministers became as exasperated as Harold Wilson had been in the 1960s and 1970s about the speed with which confidential documents were disappearing from offices in and around Whitehall and ending up in the hands of journalists.

Not only were Thatcher and Major having to contend with the consequences of the far wider circulation of official documentation, which facilitated the illicit distribution of data, but there had also been a significant shift in the emphasis of political journalism, with less straight reporting and far more speculative and background coverage, which meant exclusive information was at a premium. An incisive account of the steps taken by Thatcher in the early 1980s to try avoid leaks from her administration appeared in *Sources Close to the Prime Minister*, written jointly by Michael Cockerell, Peter Hennessy and David Walker. Their book contrasted the way she enlisted the help of both MI5 and Scotland Yard's Special Branch to carry out a series of inquiries into unauthorised leaks while at the same time making full use of the lobby system at Westminster to provide political correspondents with 'highly partial' accounts of Cabinet proceedings. In the view of the authors it was Thatcher's press secretary, Bernard Ingham, who became the 'anonymous provider of more stories than all the Whitehall officials and Cabinet ministers put together'; he was the ultimate 'source close to the Prime Minister' who by enforcing the rule of non-attribution turned the lobby into her 'most useful tool for the political management of news'.

Thatcher was quite capable of doing her own surreptitious briefing: in January 1981 Ingham arranged for the lobby correspondents of the *Times*, the *Financial Times*, the *Daily Telegraph* and the *Guardian* to meet her privately. Next morning all four newspapers reported that the Cabinet had ruled out an increase in income tax. It had been, in the opinion of Cockerell, Hennessy and Walker, a classic piece of news management: 'Mrs Thatcher had effectively upstaged and pre-empted her Chancellor and had been guilty of what was traditionally regarded as one of the most heinous of British political crimes: the leaking of Budget secrets.' As they observed, 'government secretiveness and news management' went hand in hand, which explained why in September 1982 an extensive leak of plans for welfare reform excited widespread attention. The *Economist* had obtained drafts of a review being carried out by the Cabinet's think tank, the Central Policy Review, which suggested that billions could be saved by scrapping the uprating of benefits. Instead of encouraging discussion among ministers and Conservative MPs, Thatcher chose to 'dissemble' and she used a sequence of leaks and briefings to castigate a section of the Cabinet as 'wets'.

Sir Ian Gilmour, one of the ministers who did not share her monetarist beliefs, acknowledged that it was Ingham's lobby briefing, to the effect that she had won the day and foiled the 'wets', which remained in people's minds because the 'early leak sets the tone for the coverage'. Ingham's ability to manipulate the government's information machine on behalf of Thatcher depended on journalists obeying the rule on non-attribution.

Such was the hostility of some newspapers to the policies she was pursuing that the lobby system began to fracture and in 1986 Ingham had to come to terms with what he dubbed the 'great lobby revolt' when political correspondents from the *Independent*, which was about to be launched, declared they would boycott the twice-daily briefings because of the press secretary's refusal to allow the origin of his guidance to be narrowed down to a 'Downing Street source'. Journalists from the *Guardian* and the *Scotsman* stopped attending the twice-daily briefings and joined the rebellion but the lobby held firm and decided by sixty-seven votes to fifty-five to retain the practice of non-attribution unless informants were willing to be identified. The three newspapers maintained their boycott for four years and only returned after Major's newly installed press secretary, Gus O'Donnell, agreed in December 1990 to allow his guidance to be attributed to 'Downing Street sources' rather than the far vaguer 'government sources' which Ingham had always stipulated.

Despite the 1986 vote to retain the rule on confidentiality, the lobby revolt had undermined the long tradition of secrecy which had always accompanied collective briefings at Westminster, and increasingly political journalists found that ministers, their political advisers and party representatives preferred to supply them with information either individually or in small, select groups. Another factor which influenced the tempo of both politics and political journalism was that there seemed to be less respect for the confidentiality of official papers, which was perhaps an inevitable consequence of the wider use of photocopiers and faxes and the difficulties which this posed for the authorities in seeking to control the distribution of government data. Thatcher's opponents took full advantage of her administration's vulnerability and, as part of their determination to try to destabilise the Tory front bench, the Labour Party began to exploit leaks in a much more calculated manner. Shadow ministers had fewer inhibitions about revealing the contents of leaked documents when speaking at the despatch box, happy to deploy unauthorised disclosures if they thought this would embarrass the government. If the material was particularly sensitive, it might be given directly to a journalist carefully selected for his or her reliability and discretion.

Some Labour frontbenchers had no desire to be implicated or questioned in any subsequent leak inquiry. Passing information direct to a reporter was usually seen as a sure-fire way to obtain news coverage which would put the Conservatives on the spot; it had the added advantage of keeping Labour's media contacts happy. Leaks excited political correspondents and by trading information and exclusive stories in this way the leadership hoped the ensuing news coverage would exaggerate the impact of whatever it was the Thatcher or Major governments were proposing and serve to highlight the appeal of the alternative policies being put forward by the opposition. Leaks of one sort or another have helped fuel political debate since time immemorial and their effectiveness as a restraint on policy makers has become all the greater the more the decision-making process has been opened up to public scrutiny. When in power politicians tend to decry the unauthorised disclosure of any information which damages their interests but in opposition, and increasingly once out of office, they have fewer inhibitions about exploiting confidential data, however surreptitiously it might have been obtained. As leaks have become part of the lifeblood of modern journalism, correspondents can hardly accuse politicians of being two faced in their behaviour.

Nevertheless, I was pleasantly surprised, within months of Labour winning the 1997 general election, to find that at least one member of Tony Blair's first Cabinet took a relaxed line on the practice of leaking. The occasion was one of the Christmas parties held in Whitehall for political correspondents and the hosts were the Cabinet Secretary, Sir Robin Butler, and Dr David Clark, the Cabinet Office minister and Chancellor of the Duchy of Lancaster. They were both said to have been embarrassed in December 1997 by a leak three days before the publication of the White Paper *Your Right to Know*, which set out proposals for legislation on freedom of information and which was regarded as a significant step forward by those who had campaigned for decades for a relaxation of the secrecy laws. Barry

Sutlieff, director of information for the Cabinet Office, was annoyed at the way certain key details had apparently leaked out from within the department and had then been used in a broadcast by a BBC political correspondent, John Pienaar. Because the BBC's report had pre-empted the launch of the White Paper, the Cabinet Office was forced to abandon arrangements for a series of off-the-record briefings for newspaper leader writers and other journalists.

Sutlieff believed the leak was designed to embarrass Clark, because the minister had been forced to apologise 'most sincerely' to the Speaker, Betty Boothroyd, for this 'premature disclosure' before being allowed to make his statement to the House of Commons. The following day the *Daily Telegraph* revealed that the minister's two political advisers, Professor James Cornford and Andrew Lappin, had spoken to Pienaar shortly before his broadcast. They denied discussing anything which was 'not already a matter of public record'. Although Clark had to apologise for the 'disservice to the House' caused by the early release of some his proposals, it was clear when discussing this with him at his reception that as Cabinet Office minister he was not really worried by what happened; the leak had not been particularly damaging and in any case the resulting publicity had generated lots of interest in his proposals. As far he was concerned leaks were part and parcel of day-to-day politics and helped rather than hindered the democratic process. 'However much politicians say they dislike them, they do keep us in check and they do keep civil servants on their toes. So in that sense some leaks are probably in the public interest because they promote discussion and can be used to bring about changes in policy.'

Clark's honesty was all the more refreshing because Blair's ministers, like their Tory predecessors, were finding it harder than they had imagined to prevent embarrassing disclosures leaking out from Whitehall and the rest of the government machine. I found their protestations hard to take seriously because during the final years of their lengthy sojourn in opposition, the Labour Party had turned the manipulation of leaks into nothing short of an art form, of which Gordon Brown and Robin Cook were the arch-exponents. In addition to being able to capture the news agenda and damage the Conservatives, Labour's leading modernisers had become equally adept at the controlled disclosure of their own strategy papers and other internal documents. By signalling in advance changes in party policy or direction through judicious leaking, they hoped to win favourable news coverage and hasten the process of modernisation. Routines perfected in opposition were put to good use once Labour won power and almost immediately the manipulation of leaks to trail important announcements became a way of life for members of Blair's government.

Advance publicity for successive Budgets proved to be a testament to Brown's mastery of these black arts: few budgetary changes came as a real surprise as most of them had been well trailed in the news media during the previous weeks as a result of careful off-the-record briefings by Treasury officials and the Chancellor of the Exchequer's advisers. Sound arguments have been advanced over the years justifying the need to prepare financial commentators for imminent changes in spending and taxation: if the City of London was caught totally by surprise this could unsettle the stock market and even lead to a run on the pound. Nevertheless by going to such lengths to massage speculative reporting about his own proposals, Brown had effectively downgraded the Budget, at least as a parliamentary event. Similarly the pressure to secure favourable publicity was so great among the rest of Blair's Cabinet colleagues that it became commonplace to trail the contents of the Queen's Speech in advance of the annual state opening. When I started at Westminster as a parliamentary correspondent for the *Times* in the late 1960s, the climate of official secrecy was very different. Civil servants needed no reminding, for example, about the precautions which had to be taken to safeguard the contents of the Budget box.

Reporters sat with pens poised in the House of Commons press gallery, ready to take a shorthand note of each announcement so that it could be phoned through to copy takers in the newsroom. As political journalists we could only dream of matching the scoop to beat all Budget scoops. In 1947, on his way to the despatch box, the Chancellor of the Exchequer, Hugh Dalton, stopped in the members' lobby to speak to John Carvel, a correspondent with the London evening paper the *Star*, and told him there would be 'no more on tobacco, a penny on beer, something on dogs and pools but not on horses'. Carvel phoned through his scoop which was published in the 'Stop Press' column before the Chancellor had time to inform the Commons of his tax changes. Because of what was considered to have been a grave breach of Budget protocol, Dalton had no option but to resign. Carvel's scoop was based on a conversation rather than a leak from a document and that reflected the care which was taken at that time to safeguard official papers. During the 1960s fears about spying on behalf of the Soviet Union, rather than leaking to journalists, tended to be uppermost in the minds of politicians.

In 1962 it was discovered that John Vassal, a junior Admiralty official, had spent seven years passing secrets to Moscow. This was followed the next year by the notorious Profumo scandal, in which the Secretary of State for War, John Profumo, was forced to resign after he admitted lying to the House of Commons when he denied having a liaison with the call-girl Christine Keeler, who had also been sleeping with a suspected spy, Yevgeny Ivanov, an assistant Soviet naval attaché. Civil servants were mindful of the penalties which could be imposed under the catch-all provisions of the Official Secrets Act, and in an era when breaches of security were viewed extremely seriously, leaks from within Whitehall departments were few and far between. Harold Wilson's election in 1964 did herald a change because, unlike the Conservative Party, factional infighting was commonplace within the Labour and trade union movement; its rival groups and sections were not averse to leaking information in an attempt to thwart or embarrass one another. These conflicting pressures emanating from the trade unions, constituency parties and various socialist societies generated ill feeling within the Labour government. Cabinet records for 1966, released under the thirty-year rule, revealed the steps which Wilson took in Downing Street to try to stem leaks to the press.

Complaints were made by the Prime Minister's principal private secretary, Derek Mitchell, and other civil servants about the 'considerable amount' of use which was being made of No. 10's Rank Xerox photocopier by Wilson's political secretary, Marcia Williams, and other staff from the party's headquarters at Transport House. Mitchell asked his assistant, Jane Parsons, to keep a surreptitious eye on their activities. In one memo it was suggested that if Transport House supplied its own photocopier to Downing Street, there would have to be 'security drills' to ensure that it could not be used 'to make quick copies of classified papers'. Another proposal, later dropped on technical and financial grounds, was to attach cameras to the photocopying machines. So great was the Prime Minister's obsession with tracing the source of leaks that several Cabinet ministers, including his security adviser, the Paymaster General, George Wigg, were required to submit memos listing the names of journalists they had or had not seen. Wilson ordered the compilation of 'source books', which indexed press cuttings by code so that 'the subject could be traced from beginning to end' by examining statements made by ministers, MPs and journalists. A source might be indicated by determining the pattern of previous stories by a reporter whose most recent 'exclusive' had been based on a particularly damaging leak; further evidence might be obtained by analysing which politician or official had most to gain in terms of publicity or political prestige.

Williams's fraught relationship with No. 10's most senior civil servant was evident within months of Wilson winning power. Cabinet records for 1965 revealed that the Prime Minister told his staff he would like her to see copies of papers for Cabinet and its committees. Mitchell challenged Wilson's decision, pointing out that the folder on which the instruction had been written included two reports from the Joint Intelligence Committee, one marked 'top secret' and the other 'secret'. Mitchell said in his memo that there was a security problem because Wilson's political secretary worked in a room which was 'often left unattended and where she often receives visitors'. He suggested Williams should be given 'an in-tray in the strong room near the duty clerk' and that she should be told 'classified papers should not be left lying about when she is not in the room; nor of course should she make copies of them, take extracts from them, or refer to them in correspondence'.

Wilson's suspicion that most leaks were the work of aggrieved or mischievous colleagues was well founded, according Peter Hennessy, Attlee Professor of Contemporary British History at Queen Mary, University of London. He told me that when studying the Cabinet records he found an MI5 review of the pattern of leaks in 1969 which showed that most of them came from ministers, not civil servants. By the late 1960s the news coverage generated by leaks related increasingly to various aspects of the Labour government's troubled relationship with the trade unions. Wilson ordered an inquiry, for example, to find the source of stories which revealed intelligence reports about the part played by Communist Party activists in organising disputes such as the 1966 seamen's strike; a leak about dock workers getting a wage deal which broke the pay norm was also investigated. By the mid-1970s I had switched from parliamentary to industrial reporting and stories about labour unrest tended to dominate the news during the final stages of James Callaghan's government in the lead-up to what became known as the 'Winter of Discontent'. Preparing news reports about the illicit disclosure of sensitive information became a regular feature of my work.

After Margaret Thatcher won the 1979 general election, her attack on trade union power generated widespread opposition. Left-wing sympathisers employed in the civil service and the nationalised industries were horrified by the sheer scale of the manpower reductions being imposed by a Conservative government. There were numerous leaks about the mass redundancies planned across the state sector in loss-making concerns such as British Steel,

British Leyland and the National Coal Board (NCB). Much of the information went direct to union leaders, who used it to strengthen their campaigns against cut-backs and closures. Sometimes it was harder to determine the source or motivation behind some of the leaks obtained by newspaper journalists; much of the press backed a shake-out in the workforce of inefficient nationalised undertakings and on occasion their alarmist stories seemed part of a wider campaign inspired by managements to persuade employees to accept the enhanced redundancy payments which were being offered in order to speed up plant closures. When it came to the exploitation of leaks, the union leader with the clearest understanding of how they could be manipulated was Arthur Scargill, president of the National Union of Mineworkers (NUM).

From the start of his struggle against pit closures Scargill used a succession of leaked reports to warn that the NCB had been given instructions by the government to butcher the industry. He did not deploy leaks in the same way as many of his contemporaries in the trade union movement, who regularly chose to work in league with the news media in an attempt to influence public opinion and apply maximum pressure on the government. Instead of co-operating with journalists by giving them information in advance and then timing its release for the greatest impact, the NUM president opted for dramatic effect and preferred to disclose the contents of confidential documents during his own speeches at conferences and rallies. Scargill's aim was to boost morale and stiffen the resolve of union members and he did so by insisting that the secret information which he had obtained proved that the NUM's industrial action was having the desired effect. As an assiduous self-publicist, he knew how to excite the media and his tactic was to tantalise journalists by quoting from confidential documents which he kept firmly under his own control, well out of their sight.

Within months of taking over the leadership of the union in the spring of 1982, Scargill lost his first pit head ballot; that year's pay offer of 8.2 per cent was accepted against the president's advice and there was a 61 per cent vote to reject strike action. Once it was clear which way the vote had gone, Fleet Street spent several days preparing for what it predicted would be the humiliation of 'King Arthur' a monarch, said the *Daily Express*, 'without a throne, a leader without followers'. When he came to make the official announcement Scargill demonstrated his acute sense of timing and his flair for understanding how the media would react. He told the reporters assembled at the union's headquarters that he had obtained a copy of a secret document, which at that precise moment he held up in his right hand, just beside his face, ready for the press photographers and television cameras. Next day the *Daily Mail* ridiculed his performance: 'Scargill had pulled out a white rabbit, a coal board briefing on pit closures. It was his only shot . . . Scargill slapped the fourteen pages of the document. "It's sensational, I'm shocked. I'm stunned." He made the white rabbit bounce again so everybody could see it.'

Despite the taunts in next day's newspapers, Scargill did succeed in diverting attention from his defeat; many of the journalists' questions at the news conference were directed towards re-examining his claim that the coal board was planning extensive pit closures. Nevertheless by quoting from leaked reports rather than releasing them for wider inspection by the media, he made it easier for newspapers such as the *Sun*, the *Daily Mail* and the *Daily Express* to dismiss his claims as scaremongering, however accurate the leaks might have been. If confidential information had been supplied in advance to newspapers on the left, such as the *Daily Mirror* or the *Guardian*, or even given to the *Times* or the *Daily Telegraph*, journalists on Conservative-supporting papers would have found it harder to ignore their rivals' exclusive stories.

Instead of thinking through ways to build up support for the NUM within the media, Scargill seemed more concerned about inflating his own importance, even if this only reinforced the mounting criticism of the way he was leading the union. Nonetheless after the devastation caused by mass redundancies in steel and shipbuilding in the early 1980s, there was considerable sympathy for the plight of the mining communities and soon after the start of the year-long pit strike in February 1984 it was obvious the dispute would become a fight to the finish between Thatcher and the NUM. Public opinion was polarised and among those who admired Scargill's stand in defence of jobs there was a strong determination to help the miners and their families. Much of the assistance was in the form of donations of money and food; there were many expressions of solidarity by fellow trade unionists, and secondary industrial action became a feature of the dispute, as did the steady flow of data leaking out from Whitehall departments, the NCB and the Central Electricity Generating Board (CEGB). Because I always needed fresh interviews with Scargill for the BBC's news bulletins and radio programmes, I often had to wait around for him at the end of union meetings and rallies, with my tape recorder at the ready.

Once the strike started I was always surprised by the number of people who approached him on such occasions, appearing as if from nowhere, and discreetly handed over envelopes or packages. Many looked as if they contained donations but he told me that he was often given confidential documents which sympathisers thought might be of use in his fight against the NCB and the government. Indeed, he frequently joked about having moles in the most unlikely places and he said they were keeping him well informed about the state of coal stocks at the power stations. As the dispute dragged on through the summer of 1984, the NUM president made regular predictions as to how long the supplies would last. At the end of June, in a speech at Llandudno to the annual conference of the National Union of Railwaymen, he warned of power cuts that autumn. His prediction was based on secret information on the latest stock position which he said he had been given a few hours earlier: 'They've only got a little over 15 million tons of coal on the ground, and I can tell you that the CEGB, in conjunction with the government, are preparing for presentation to Parliament emergency measures for power cuts on a rota basis as they go into August and September.'

Scargill delivered his unexpected warning in the middle of the afternoon, as though timing it precisely for the early evening news bulletins on radio and television, which all reported his speech. Correspondents like myself had no time to verify his estimate of coal stocks or inquire further into the likelihood of power cuts and Scargill was obviously banking on the fact that we would have had no alternative but to rely on what he had said. Although both the government and the CEGB subsequently denied that there was any threat to the continued generation of electricity, it was not until a month later that the Secretary of State for Energy, Peter Walker, felt sufficiently confident to forecast for the first time that the government would get through the winter of 1984–5 without any disruption to power supplies. Some years after the strike, Lord Marshall, the former CEGB chairman, admitted that in one respect Scargill's warning had been correct. Coal stocks were being depleted at such a rate that power cuts would have been required unless the government had agreed to compensate the board for the extra cost of nuclear and oil-fired generation. By the midsummer of 1984 Thatcher had apparently concluded there was no prospect of reaching a settlement with the NUM so she told the CEGB to take the risk of running the nuclear power stations on continuous production.

Malcolm Edwards, the NCB's commercial director, told me that in order to conserve stocks, the coal-fired stations were taken off the base load.

In effect nuclear, oil and the link-up to France kept the lights on. By the end of the strike it had cost an extra £2 billion, mostly in oil imports, but coal stocks never fell as low as Scargill was claiming. His predictions were just wishful thinking. His leak was correct about what might have happened but that changed from August onwards when Thatcher told the CEGB to spend what it takes.

Here was a case in point about how to exploit leaked documents: if Scargill had supplied the news media with copies of the secret data which had been supplied to him, journalists might well have used it to greater effect to calculate the rate at which coal stocks were being depleted; we might have had more success in exposing the steps which were being taken in great secrecy to thwart the strike, revelations which could have caused the Conservatives considerable embarrassment. Leaks about the future of the mining industry continued to make news in the decade which followed, before the eventual privatisation of the NCB, by this time renamed British Coal, in 1994.

There was considerable speculation about the government's plans in the months leading up to the 1992 general election, because warnings over the need for another round of pit closures had leaked out from a confidential report prepared by the merchant bankers N. M. Rothschild & Sons. British Coal refused to comment on the leaks but its senior press officer, Peter Heap, told me that the Rothschild report had contained a series of devices designed to prevent the unauthorised photocopying of its contents: there were anti-copying stripes across each page, some pages were blank, paragraphs were split up and the whole report divided into several parts. To Edwards's surprise the security measures appeared to have proved effective. 'We all thought the anti-copying devices were a novel departure and the management welcomed them. Nevertheless what seemed to have happened was that the gist of the report leaked out, although not the document itself.'

Another leak occurred two years later when the House of Commons finally considered the Bill to privatise British Coal. During a debate in March 1994, the shadow trade and industry secretary, Robin Cook, produced what he said was a 'secret document' from Boyds, the government's consultants, which indicated that privatisation would push up the price of coal; to publicise the leak he issued a press release which listed Boyds' key conclusions. Cook, who could not be faulted on his timing, said he had 'revealed' the 'secret document' because it 'sinks any case for privatisation'. His ability to divulge leaked information at a moment which he hoped would cause the government maximum discomfort came as no surprise to political journalists. Labour's frontbench team had developed what to all intents and purposes had become a cottage industry in handling and disseminating illicit disclosures. Within the space of a decade there had been a dramatic change in political attitudes towards breaches of confidentiality: any remaining vestiges of respect for official documents had, it seemed, all but disappeared among opposition MPs. Not only had there been a revolution in the way information was exchanged and transmitted but British politics had become highly charged as a result of the divisive policies being pursued by Thatcher.

Once Neil Kinnock was elected Labour leader after its disastrous performance in the 1983 general election, the party began a root-and-branch overhaul of its relationship with the news media. Contact with political correspondents was encouraged, even if their newspapers supported the Conservatives; after previously shunning much of the popular press, there was a friendlier approach towards some of the tabloids; journalists who were considered to be useful or politically sympathetic were offered exclusive stories, and in the process they became the conduit for the release of leaked information, which the shadow Cabinet thought might damage the Tories. While the front bench worked behind the scenes to develop their expertise in the often covert exploitation of confidential data, Labour mounted a highly visible campaign in support of the citizen's right to know. Successive administrations had indicated their backing for the reform of the 1911 Official Secrets Act but in the event the governments of Edward Heath and James Callaghan had both failed to deliver greater openness on the part of the state. The secrecy laws were eventually relaxed in 1989 and the new legislation took effect in February 1990 during Thatcher's final year in office.

Douglas Hurd, the Home Secretary, declared that it would result in 'a considerable easement' because the 'great majority of official information' would no longer be protected by the criminal law against unauthorised disclosure. But the government was resolutely opposed to the introduction of a public interest defence for leaking, and organisations such as the Campaign for Freedom of Information, which had been launched in 1984, believed the new Official Secrets Act remained as repressive as before. My return to Westminster in 1988 as a political correspondent for the BBC coincided with a sudden flurry of illicit disclosures which infuriated both Thatcher and Bernard Ingham, who had developed the habit of lashing out in all directions at his lobby briefings in Downing Street when journalists questioned him about the prevalence of leaks. By then Cook had already established himself as an extremely effective manipulator of government secrets and he had a starring role that year. In May 1988 he caused consternation in the House of Commons by revealing leaked correspondence about the impending introduction of the poll tax.

Copies of two letters from the Prime Minister's private office, which both threw doubt on the real value of concessions for the poor, were sent anonymously through the post and marked for the attention of Labour's spokesman on health and social security; Cook had the two documents retyped and the originals shredded. He used the correspondence to taunt Conservative MPs about the way he believed they had been double crossed over the poll tax by Thatcher. Cook's mischief making was said to have stiffened the resolve of the fifty Tories who rebelled against the government. Next day's newspapers were filled with lurid headlines about how counter-intelligence agents from MI5 had been called in to help trace what the *Sun* described as the 'traitor who is leaking top-secret documents from Downing Street, the very core of Mrs Thatcher's administrative headquarters'. The unauthorised disclosure of the letters, which had been written by the Prime Minister's private secretary, Paul Gray, was the third leak within six weeks and, according to the *Times*, they were being viewed with 'utmost seriousness' by the government. One of the paper's columnists, the Conservative MP Ray Whitney, who was a former diplomat and junior minister, put the blame on 'a general loosening of standards' within the civil service.

Living with leaks had become part of daily life for Thatcher; since she took office in 1979 illicit disclosures had emerged as 'a regular feature of the political landscape' due to the actions of 'a very small minority of public servants with a deep-seated intellectual and ideological opposition' to many of the government's policies. 'They see it as their right – indeed, their duty – to embarrass their political masters.' Whitney had come to the conclusion that opposition politicians and the news media, searching for an easy headline, much preferred to speak or write about an 'illicit leak' rather than spend the time and effort which was needed to assess the mass of information already accessible both to the public and to any reasonably bright and industrious journalist. He feared it was totally unrealistic to hope that one day politicians and the media might agree to 'a new concordat to forswear the use of leaked information', a sentiment which certainly appeared to be wishful thinking as far as Cook was concerned. In October 1988 he caused renewed uproar by leaking a confidential letter from the Secretary of State for

Social Services, John Moore, appealing to the Treasury for more help for pensioners who would be financially disadvantaged by the poll tax.

When asked about the leak at Prime Minister's Questions, Thatcher told MPs she had been dismayed to find that Labour's front bench 'had been a party to publishing and destroying highly classified documents'. She challenged Neil Kinnock to stand by the undertakings which she had given as leader of the opposition in 1976, when she had assured the then Labour Prime Minister, James Callaghan, that she recognised it was 'essential that confidentiality' should be safeguarded. Callaghan had been angered by the leaking of a document outlining changes in child benefit and, in an attempt to embarrass Kinnock, Thatcher quoted to the House of Commons the precise words used by a Labour Prime Minister when denouncing whoever had been responsible: 'This is a very grave matter. For, on the face of it, it could only have been brought about by theft, or by a betrayal of trust involving a breach of an undertaking voluntarily entered into, by someone with access to documents.' Having harked back to Callaghan's condemnation of the exploitation of leaks, Thatcher repeated the guarantee she had given to her predecessor on behalf of the Conservatives: 'We fully share his view about the gravity of this matter. It is essential that confidentiality of discussions and documents should be assured.'

To underline her annoyance at the opposition's refusal to follow her example, she taunted the Labour leader: 'In those days there were certain standards of conduct and integrity.' But Kinnock was determined to take no lessons from Thatcher: he accepted that the leaking of confidential information constituted a 'grave' issue but he did not respond to her request that in future Labour should co-operate fully with any investigations into leaks, nor did he undertake to stop the shadow Cabinet quoting from secret documents which came into their possession. Whenever challenged publicly about Labour's behaviour, Kinnock had always insisted that his party publicised only those leaks which could be justified on grounds of public interest; the disclosures made by his frontbench team did not put national security at risk. However, Thatcher had a point: many Labour MPs were campaigning for an easing in state secrecy and this had led to a profound change in the opposition's whole approach towards the use that could made of information which hitherto would have been regarded as confidential. Political correspondents were desperate to obtain exclusive stories and as a result there was a ready home for any confidential documents which happened to find their way into Labour's hands.

Not all Labour MPs were prepared to abandon the political standards of the past. When compiling a report for the *Today* programme about the proliferation of leaks in 1988 and the growing demands for greater freedom of information I discovered that Callaghan's views about the inviolability of official secrets were still shared by at least one former Labour Cabinet minister from the 1970s. Merlyn Rees told me that he had recently returned to the appropriate authority – without even examining it himself – a classified document which was marked 'secret' and which had been posted to him anonymously at the House of Commons. Perhaps I should not have been surprised by the fact that a former Home Secretary had been so scrupulous: Rees served on the Franks committee, which was established by Edward Heath in 1971 to review the Official Secrets Act, and, on taking control of the Home Office in 1976, he drew up plans for the possible reform of the secrecy laws. Rees was made a member of the Privy Council in 1974, on becoming Secretary of State for Northern Ireland, and although it was almost ten years since he had been a minister he assured me that he continued to respect both the spirit and the letter of the oath of allegiance sworn by Privy Counsellors, which required them to 'keep secret all matters committed and revealed' to them.

Membership of the Privy Council is mainly reserved for ministers and others involved in 'affairs of state' but it is also extended to the leader of the opposition, and it was greatly valued by Kinnock because it allowed him to be briefed in advance and in confidence on matters of government importance. In accordance with this long-standing convention, he was given a day's notice of the contents of the Queen's Speech, which opens each new session of Parliament. Within a month of his clash with Thatcher in the House of Commons, Kinnock found his trustworthiness again under attack because of a leak about the contents of the 1988 Queen's Speech. On the morning of the state opening, several newspapers revealed that the new legislative programme would include a Bill on the future of the security services. Subsequently at a briefing for journalists, Kinnock denied responsibility for the leak. As in past years he had received a copy of the Queen's Speech during the previous afternoon and he confirmed that the contents were considered by the shadow Cabinet. He had personally handed out copies but each had been numbered by himself and they had all been returned. He had since discovered that even before the meeting journalists were already aware of the contents and had apparently been contacting party officials, including David Hill, an adviser to the home affairs spokesman,

Roy Hattersley. Kinnock was adamant that both the shadow Cabinet and the party had been scrupulous in maintaining confidentiality. 'We don't leak but the same can't be said for the government . . . There are no circumstances in which I would even hint at one letter or one word about anything told me in confidence.' Nonetheless the fact that shadow ministers had been briefed in advance made them a target for journalists anxious to discover what the speech contained. In my experience Robin Cook was always keen to express an opinion on such occasions about what the government might have had in mind and he used to make a point of visiting journalists in their offices in the press gallery to see if they wanted advice or a quote. As the flow of leaks continued unabated during the final years of her premiership, Thatcher never let the Labour leader forget his public refusal to join her in trying to safeguard the security and confidentiality of official documents.

In defending himself at Prime Minister's questions the previous month, Kinnock had found that by uttering one word, 'Westland', he managed to deflect most of the protests and interruptions coming from the government benches and he succeeded in silencing Conservative MPs. Thatcher and Bernard Ingham had been badly damaged by the deliberate leaking of a letter from the Solicitor General, Sir Patrick Mayhew, at the height of the dispute in January 1986 over the future of Westland helicopters. Michael Heseltine, Secretary of State for Defence, was accused in the letter of having made 'material inaccuracies' in arguing his case in support of Westland's possible purchase by a European consortium. Thatcher and her Cabinet were thrown into turmoil when Colette Bowe, head of information at the Department of Trade and Industry, admitted that she had been ordered to leak the law officer's correspondence; his advice had been marked 'confidential'. Leon Brittan, Secretary of State for Trade and Industry, who had given his approval for the release of the letter, was subsequently forced to resign; by then Heseltine had already left the government, having walked out of a Cabinet meeting three days after the leak, in one of the most spectacular resignations witnessed in Downing Street.

An inquiry conducted by the Cabinet Secretary, Sir Robert Armstrong, determined there were no grounds under the Official Secrets Act to institute proceedings against government officials, because the leak had been authorised by a minister. Ingham was implicated because Bowe had asked if the Downing Street press office would assist her by disclosing the contents of the letter to Chris Moncrieff, political editor of the Press Association. Bowe had explained to Ingham her extreme reluctance to leak a law officer's letter, but it emerged subsequently through 'friends' of hers who were quoted in the press that she was instructed by him to do as she had been 'told'. In order to conduct his inquiry and speak to the person who had 'actually passed the information' to Moncrieff, Armstrong obtained an immunity from prosecution for Bowe in return for her co-operation. She insisted that she had been told by Ingham to leak the letter; Armstrong confirmed that she did have grave 'misgivings' and had wanted to consult her superiors about being asked to do something which she feared was unlawful. Throughout the inquiry Ingham maintained that No. 10 had given no authority or instruction regarding the leaking of a classified letter.

In his autobiography, *Kill The Messenger*, Ingham recalled that he refused 'point blank' to help Bowe but he did acknowledge, regardless of her having her minister's permission, that he should have told her to have had 'nothing to do with the ploy herself'. He accepted that because he did not 'actively object' to the leaking of the letter, he had allowed his character to be 'blackened' by the Westland affair and, in retrospect, he wished there had been a police inquiry at which he could have given evidence. In Armstrong's opinion, Downing Street had given 'cover' but not 'covering authority' to the leak; and Thatcher told MPs that had she been consulted, she would have advised that a different way should have been found 'of making the facts known'. Ingham drew a distinction in his autobiography between briefing the news media on the options that faced ministers and the leaking of classified documents or their contents. Government information officers were, in his own words, 'licensed to leak', in the sense that they could give journalists the background to policy choices and decisions but he insisted that he and his colleagues were not in the business of leaks or other 'unauthorised disclosures' from official papers.

Nevertheless Ingham found that not all his fellow information officers were beyond reproach, because there were repeated leaks from the weekly meetings he chaired to co-ordinate the presentation of the government's affairs. He concluded that during the Thatcher years the deliberate leaking of information or papers by 'a tiny minority' of officials became 'a blot on the civil service landscape'. Ingham's measured language in his memoirs was a far cry from the bombastic approach he adopted when responding at lobby briefings. He regularly denounced the 'rotten apples' within the civil service who he believed were responsible and he was scathing about the way Labour's front bench were prepared to handle information which, to all intents and purposes, had 'fallen off the back of a bus'. During my work as a BBC political correspondent I tried repeatedly, but without success, to pin him down on the reasons why the government's various leak inquiries always appeared to draw a blank.

There was to be no let-up in the flow of unauthorised disclosures in the autumn of 1988. A week after Robin Cook revealed his leaked letter about the poll tax, Labour's education spokesman, Jack Straw, brandished in front of MPs a bundle of confidential discussion papers prepared by the minister for higher education, Robert Jackson, which showed the Conservatives were considering plans to charge all university students a £500 fee. The documents had arrived on Straw's desk 'from I know not where' and he defended his decision to publish them on the grounds they did not affect national security but related to matters of policy which should be in the public domain. When asked to comment on what by then was the fifth serious leak within a year, Ingham launched into another tirade against the morals of Labour's front bench, pausing only to remind the lobby that Cook was going to be interviewed by a Cabinet Office official as part of the previous week's investigation. One of my regular lines of inquiry was to try to determine the security classification given to a particular document, as this might indicate who had access to it and the level of protection required to ensure its safety. I knew this was a highly sensitive issue: in 1982, after the *Economist* obtained a of the review on the uprating of social security benefits, Thatcher complained that the drafts had been marked 'confidential' rather than 'secret' or even 'top secret'.

When the Franks committee reported in 1972, it set out the threat posed by the unauthorised disclosure of information covered by the four main security classifications: 'TOP SECRET, causing exceptionally grave damage to the nation; SECRET, causing serious injury to the interests of the nation; CONFIDENTIAL, being prejudicial to the interests of the nation; RESTRICTED, being undesirable in the interests of the nation.' At one Downing Street briefing in the autumn of 1988 Ingham tripped up, suddenly changing in mid-sentence the status he had given to the latest leaked document. As I patiently rephrased my question, hoping to elicit something further from him, he put on a show of mock surprise and looked solemnly at the assembled journalists, saying, 'This laddie thinks he's got an exclusive.' Amid the laughter of my colleagues, he moved swiftly to the next question. Within a matter of weeks, the Prime Minister and her trusted press secretary were back on the attack, denouncing Cook yet again for his blatant disregard of the sanctity of official papers. When giving journalists copies of his leaked letter on the poll tax the previous October, Cook had been careful to protect the source by making sure the correspondence was retyped.

Any such precaution must have seemed superfluous in January 1989 when he succeeded in pre-empting publication of the government's White Paper on the future of the health service, *Working for Patients*. I described for BBC radio the scene which confronted journalists who were called to the news conference held by Labour's health spokesman:

> Robin Cook sat there with a pile of pages in front him . . . It was clearly a full draft of the White Paper, running to thirteen chapters, each of forty-odd pages marked top and bottom with the word 'SECRET' in capital letters . . . a far higher classification than for some White Paper drafts, requiring all copies to be kept locked up at night.

Cook declared that the contents were 'even more frightening' than he had previously imagined, because he calculated 320 hospitals would be encouraged to opt out of the NHS. Labour's ploy to upstage the official launch infuriated the Secretary of State for Health, Kenneth Clarke, who insisted that the document was simply an out-of-date draft; he urged Cook to 'stop larking around' and ignore what was being sent to him in 'plain brown, sealed envelopes'. At Prime Minister's Questions, the Conservative MP Paul Marland accused Cook of receiving 'stolen documents and thereby aiding and abetting a criminal offence'.

Thatcher appeared to have been well primed and once again she reminded MPs that when she led the Opposition she had backed James Callaghan in deeming it 'absolutely vital' to maintain the confidentiality of government documents. Glaring across the despatch box, she accused the opposition of having become 'so bankrupt of argument' under Neil Kinnock's leadership that the Labour Party had been forced to appoint 'an official receiver' of leaks. Kinnock was an easy and convenient political target for Thatcher when she needed to vent her fury over the government's inability to halt the unauthorised disclosure of information. By then she had completed almost a decade as Prime Minister but, as she subsequently revealed in her memoirs *The Downing Street Years*, it was her opponents in the Cabinet, rather than civil servants or Labour MPs, who she believed had caused her the greatest personal difficulty by repeatedly leaking in advance the controversial steps being taken by her government to control the economy. She outlined how, within a few months of the Conservatives winning power in 1979, proposals from the Treasury aimed at cutting sickness and unemployment benefit found their way into the newspapers in 'one of the leaks that were continually to bedevil our discussions on public spending'.

And so it went on: after the 1981 Budget, the press was full of leaks from 'dissenters in the Cabinet' expressing their 'fury and frustration'; in 1982, there was 'a media frenzy' after 'disaffected ministers' leaked 'a blow-by-blow account' of Cabinet discussions on a spending review; and in 1983, a proposal to cut public expenditure by more than £1 billion was 'splashed across the front pages' on the morning it was to be discussed at Cabinet. Because she had no wish to publicise splits on her own side, Thatcher's only option in the House of Commons was to concentrate her fire on Labour MPs, a tactic which she came to rely on increasingly when the government faced sustained criticism over a series of prosecutions which were made under the Official Secrets Act following an unprecedented upsurge in whistle-blowing. So intense was the opposition to the Prime Minister's support for the deployment of American nuclear missiles and military adventures like the Falklands War of 1982 that her government's resolve had induced a crisis of conscience among some civil servants.

Unlike serial leakers, used to acting in the shadows and covering their tracks, whistleblowers are often found to have been under considerable personal pressure for some time, suddenly reaching breaking point; they feel so aggrieved by an abuse or what they consider is unethical conduct, and they are so determined that the truth should be told, that they are prepared, sometimes on the spur of the moment, to take great risks, putting their careers and even their personal freedom in jeopardy. Sarah Tisdall, a young civil servant in the Foreign Office, spent four months in prison after she supplied the *Guardian* with documents detailing the arrangements for the delivery of Cruise missiles to the US Air Force base at Greenham Common. Her leak, in 1983, was welcomed by peace campaigners who had been staging widespread demonstrations against Nato's decision to build up its nuclear stockpile in response to the threat posed by the Soviet Union. Tisdall, who was a clerk in the Foreign Secretary's private office, believed that the Secretary of State for Defence, Michael Heseltine, intended to mislead Parliament and the British public about the deployment of Cruise missiles. After the *Guardian* was ordered by the courts to surrender its material to the police, Tisdall was said to have been identified because of tell-tale marks on the documents.

She was charged with breaching the Official Secrets Act, pleaded guilty and was sentenced in 1984 to six months in prison. Tony Benn was among the Labour MPs to stand by Tisdall, insisting she had acted honourably and had been 'motivated by conscience' to reveal the truth. He considered she had been 'betrayed' by the *Guardian* and in order to protect future potential sources the paper's editor, Peter Preston, instructed his journalists to obliterate and shred all secret or confidential documentation as soon as details had been printed in the paper. Reflecting on what happened to Tisdall after an interval more than twenty years, Preston said he still blamed himself for not having torn up the paperwork immediately. He set out the chain of events in an article for *British Journalism Review* in the autumn of 2005:

> Nobody at the *Guardian* knew, until the moment of her arrest, who had put some secret paperwork in a brown envelope addressed to our political editor and left it at head office (wrong address) so that it turned up, as though by magic, in the night news editor's in-tray. It forgets the general low intensity of the story itself: a modest lead story . . . and, when it seemed, out of the blue, that Special Branch might stage a raid and that there were too many damned copies of the vital document left in the hands of reporters on day off who were weren't answering their phones . . . Our regular, excellent lawyer suggested a legal defence which, to be activated, needed me, on behalf of the company, to pledge not to destroy the document. Sign here please . . . and I did. Some of those around me thought this was going too far. The unknown source hadn't trusted us enough to tell us who he or she was. Why try to protect someone who might already have taken every available means to disguise his or her identity? . . . The devil was that I'd signed on behalf of a company facing brutally escalating fines for non-compliance . . . You may remember what happened. The blanked-out hieroglyphics top right, which had seemed like a clue, were meaningless. But Sarah had used a Foreign Office copying machine and that helped track her down.

Although Tisdall spent only four months in jail, her sentence was widely seen as having been unjust and it heralded the start of a renewed campaign to get the secrecy laws relaxed. She had been charged under what had become known as the 'catch-all' Section 2 of the Official Secrets Act, which enabled the authorities to prevent the publication of almost any fact concerning the functions of government, and its presence on the statute book provided a spur for those arguing for greater freedom of information. Another devastating breach of security a year later put even greater focus on the lack of mechanisms within the civil service to allow government employees to express disquiet about mistakes or inaccuracies or to discuss issues which troubled them on grounds of conscience. Although by then two years had elapsed since the Falklands War, there was uproar in the House of Commons when a senior Whitehall official leaked information which contradicted the account which the British government was continuing to give about the sinking of the Argentinian battle cruiser, the *General Belgrano*, which went down with the loss of 360 lives.

In the hope that Parliament would learn the true facts and not be misled, Clive Ponting, an assistant secretary at the Ministry of Defence, sent two documents to the Labour MP Tam Dalyell revealing that the *General Belgrano* was sailing out of the exclusion zone and did not pose an immediate threat to the British fleet, thus contradicting the explanation which Heseltine had repeated in evidence to a select committee. Ponting's prosecution, again under Section 2 of the Official Secrets Act, reopened the argument over whether civil servants had a right to leak information in the public interest. Whistleblowing by government employees had always had been viewed as improper and the requirement placed on officials not to disclose information in breach of their obligation of confidence had been reinforced by Sir Robert Armstrong shortly before Ponting's trial in February 1985.

Armstrong's memorandum, *The Duties and Responsibilities of Civil Servants in Relation to Ministers*, made it clear that there had to be total loyalty; that the civil service had 'no constitutional personality or responsibility separate from the duly elected government of the day'; and that effectively this meant that a civil servant had no wider responsibility with regard to Parliament or what might be deemed to be the public interest. Therefore it was for ministers, not civil servants, to decide what information should be provided to Parliament and how and when it should be released. Ponting's defence, that his leak was in the public interest, was based on a provision in the Official Secrets Act which sanctioned disclosure of information to 'a person to whom it is in the interest of the state his duty to communicate it'. Ponting never wavered in arguing the justification for the leak: 'In my view a civil servant must ultimately place his loyalty to Parliament and the public interest above his obligation to the interest of the government of the day.' Although the judge's directions in his summing up were that Ponting should be found guilty on the grounds that he had undermined the state, he was cleared by a jury at the Old Bailey.

His acquittal was hailed as a landmark in the campaign to relax the secrecy laws because it was seen as having finally destroyed the credibility of the 'catch-all' Section 2. Freedom of information campaigners were delighted that a jury had been alive to the concept of the 'greater good' and had rejected the reiteration by Mr Justice McCowan of the long-standing convention that the 'interest of the state' was the same as the government of the day. Ponting's acquittal had shown there was legitimacy for the claim that some leaks were in the public interest, and this set-back for the government appeared to have influenced the outcome of another high-profile breach of security later that year, when Cathy Massiter, a former intelligence officer with MI5, told a Channel 4 documentary that the security services had been illegally bugging the telephones of political and human rights campaigners. Among those who had attracted the attention of MI5 were two of the Labour Party's most prominent women politicians, Patricia Hewitt and Harriet Harman, who had both been kept under surveillance when they were employed by the National Council for Civil Liberties in the late 1970s and early 1980s.

Hewitt was the council's general secretary and Harman served as its legal officer; they were classified in MI5's files as being 'subversive' and 'Communist sympathiser[s]'. In the event Cathy Massiter escaped prosecution over her disclosures but no exception was to be made in the case of Peter Wright, a retired MI5 agent, after he published an insider's account of the methods adopted by the intelligence agencies to protect state secrets. Britain initiated litigation in courts around the world in an unsuccessful attempt to stop the publication of *Spycatcher* and it was not until October 1988, at the conclusion of a three-year legal battle, that ministers conceded defeat after five Law Lords unanimously rejected the government's final appeal. *Spycatcher* was promoted as being the 'candid autobiography of a senior intelligence officer' who, along with his fellow agents, had 'bugged and burgled' their way across London. Wright, a former assistant director of MI5, painted a vivid picture of how in the mid-1970s 'half the staff were up to their necks in a plot' to get rid of the Prime Minister, Harold Wilson; he also gave a revealing account of the way in which the intelligence services were ready to supply journalists with secret or highly sensitive information.

Wilson was said to have attracted the 'attention' of MI5 after Labour won the 1964 general election because earlier in his political career he had paid numerous visits to Russia when promoting east–west trade; once he became party leader, he had also begun to surround himself with eastern European émigré businessmen, some of whom had themselves been the subject of MI5's inquiries. Wright revealed that in the run-up to the 1974 election he had reopened Wilson's file and some of his colleagues told him they wanted it passed around their 'contacts in the press and among union officials' that

Wilson was considered to be 'a security risk'; the plan was for MI5 to arrange for selective details from its files to be 'leaked to sympathetic pressmen'. On Wright's calculation up to thirty officers had already given their approval to the scheme; facsimile copes of some files were to be made and distributed to overseas newspapers. If the information that MI5 was sitting on had leaked out, it would have caused 'a political scandal of incalculable consequences' and Wright was convinced that the news that the Prime Minister, leading a minority Labour government, was being investigated by MI5 would 'at least have led to his resignation'.

Once the Law Lords had lifted the injunctions against British newspapers, allowing them to report Wright's allegations of misconduct in the security services, *Panorama* broadcast an interview with Wright in which he claimed that the conspiracy had been 'really serious' and that the conspirators had wanted to confront Wilson with the contents of his intelligence file. As it transpired, in the final months of his premiership Wilson was said by colleagues and commentators to have become increasingly paranoid about the activities of MI5 and what he believed was a possible smear campaign to destabilise his government. His sudden resignation in March 1976 fuelled speculation that the security services might have played a part in his unexpected departure, but after Wilson's death in 1995, Lord Hunt, who was Cabinet Secretary at the time, denied in a BBC interview ever having heard anything to suggest that the Prime Minister had been a security risk; he thought it was nothing more than talk and intrigue by 'two or three right-wing malcontents' in the intelligence agencies.

Needless to say, in the autumn of 1985 Margaret Thatcher and her ministers reacted with fury on discovering that Wright's publishers, Heinemann, intended to publish *Spycatcher* in Australia, where he was currently living. By publishing an autobiography which looked back on MI5's activities over a period of two decades, Wright was said to have breached the life-long duty of confidentiality which he owed to the security services and the government went to extraordinary lengths to suppress his book. Thatcher sanctioned a series of legal actions, starting in Australia, in an attempt to thwart publication but despite the best efforts of the authorities, copies found their way to the United Kingdom. In November 1986 Sir Robert Armstrong, tried unsuccessfully to persuade the Supreme Court of New South Wales that publication of the book in Australia would constitute a breach of British security and damage the national interest; at one point, when being cross-examined and asked to define what he meant by 'a misleading impression' he said it was 'perhaps being economical with the truth'. His answer seemed to suggest he was trying to admit telling a lie without actually doing so, an admission which was seized upon by the press at home and only added to the government's discomfort. Most newspapers considered that once published abroad there was no justification for preventing the book's publication in Britain, an argument which Bernard Ingham considered was entirely self-serving and 'cut no ice' with Thatcher.

Ingham tried to hold the line at his Downing Street lobby briefings, insisting that members of the secret service had to remain 'secret and silent' if their operations were to be effective, but the Prime Minister had reached the high water mark of her battle to defend the Official Secrets Act; reform of the secrecy laws could be stalled no longer.

Chapter 3

Against the backdrop of the pounding which the Conservative government had taken throughout the 1980s in the wholly unrewarding pursuit of leakers and whistleblowers, it was perhaps hardly surprising that by the early 1990s the Labour Party had succeeded in conspiring with the news media to become even more daring and inventive in the use which the opposition front bench could make of leaked information. Once Margaret Thatcher and her ministers had been forced to give ground in the face of sustained legal challenges to the Official Secrets Act, the authorities found it immeasurably harder to stem the burgeoning trade in unauthorised disclosures; and, as I picked up the threads again of political journalism, I discovered that despite the evident flair of Robin Cook, there was another up-and-coming frontbencher who appeared equally determined to establish himself as Labour's most effective trader in government secrets.

Gordon Brown's biography in Andrew Roth's *Parliamentary Profiles* for 1988 gave details of his exploits to date as the party's regional affairs spokesman. His manipulation of leaks had not gone unnoticed. Brown's entry showed that after only three years on the front bench he had made maximum use of his previous experience as a journalist with Scottish Television: 'September 1986, leaked a government report to European Regional Development Fund projecting over three million unemployed in 1990; April 1987, leaked government plans to penalize unemployed who refused training.' I had to wait a year before experiencing at first hand Brown's skill in manipulating leaked information but in the event he laid on a master class in squeezing as much news coverage as possible from his release of three confidential letters. The correspondence related to the 1988 sale to British Aerospace of the government's shareholding in the Rover Group; one letter was from the Secretary of State for Trade and Industry, Lord Young, the other two from British Aerospace. Brown released copies of the letters in December 1989 in his capacity as Labour's trade and industry spokesman, having been promoted to that position the previous month.

He argued that they proved that the government had paid hidden and illegal sweeteners to British Aerospace, an allegation which provoked an investigation by the European Commission and which it took Young's successor, Nicholas Ridley, six months to disprove. In order to sustain the news media's interest, Brown released the letters one by one over a weekend and he succeeded in keeping the story in the headlines from Saturday until the following Tuesday. I noted in my diary that it could not have been bettered as an example of the way he had learned to 'whet the appetite' of newsrooms. Once it got round the lobby that he was prepared to supply secret documents, often on an exclusive basis, Brown knew that political journalists would get hooked, would keep coming back for more, giving him every chance of securing the publicity he craved. His research assistant Paul McKinney told me that initially, when the first letter about the Rover Group was handed exclusively to the *Sunday Times*, its reporters failed to see the full significance of the correspondence, but nonetheless the story took off pretty quickly. McKinney said he did not know through what route the leaked letters had been obtained but whenever Brown was sent or given secret documents he always took great care not to reveal the source.

> If we get government minutes, then we make sure they are retyped, so as to leave no identifying marks, but when it comes to something like Lord Young's letter we give journalists a photocopy, exactly as it is, because the letter heading and signature say it all and prove it's genuine.

I was reminded on several subsequent occasions during the long build-up to the 1992 general election of McKinney's description of the precautions which Brown took to protect the identity of leakers. Under Neil Kinnock's leadership Labour was being transformed into a formidable campaigning machine. Thatcher's ignominious departure in November 1990 and the Conservatives' choice of John Major to succeed her as Prime Minister provided little respite for the government in the face of a sustained media offensive. Disenchanted civil servants continued to supply Labour's front bench with a vast array of leaked documents and secret data.

However, one important lesson had been taken on board during the Thatcher era: in the light of Sarah Tisdall's imprisonment in 1984 after the *Guardian* was ordered to hand her documents to the police, many leakers chose to send secret data direct to Labour MPs rather than to journalists, believing this to be a safer course of action as it was thought the authorities would be less likely to put undue pressure on politicians to reveal their sources. Harriet Harman, Labour's health spokeswoman, told me in July 1991 that she was surprised by the range of leaks she was receiving. Sometimes, on arriving home, she found copies of leaked documents and other confidential information 'piling up' at her fax machine. 'Once an MP's fax number gets publicised it is so easy for someone to leak a document by simply sending it off anonymously from the nearest fax machine.' In view of her legal background as a solicitor, Harman was much more circumspect than either Brown or Robin Cook in whatever use she made of unauthorised disclosures and as far as I could discover, she did not exploit them in order to generate personal publicity.

Another frontbench spokesman who proceeded with great discretion in the summer of 1991 was the shadow housing minister, Clive Soley. He was lined up to brief correspondents after the Labour Party offered the BBC an opportunity to see a copy of a leaked letter from Francis Maude, financial secretary to the Treasury, explaining why the government was prepared to provide 'a large dowry' in order to speed up the privatisation of the Property Services Agency. BBC producers tried to persuade Soley to see if the party would release the letter in time for the *Nine O'Clock News* but he refused; he insisted that the BBC would have to observe a 6 a.m. embargo which the party had imposed because the story was also due to appear in the *Guardian* the following day. Labour's tactic paid off handsomely: the row about so-called government 'sweeteners' led the morning news bulletins on Radio 4 and *Breakfast News* and the BBC's reports attributed the leaked letter to the party without mentioning Soley.

John Prescott had no such inhibitions in October 1991 when he supplied the *Sunday Times* with a draft copy of the Queen's Speech which had been sent to him anonymously in a brown paper envelope. Prescott, then Labour's transport spokesman, said that if ministers could not guard the Queen's Speech, he had no hesitation in giving it to a newspaper. 'Isn't there anything this government can keep secret? There are so many leaks it looks like a sinking ship full of holes.' An immediate inquiry was ordered by the Cabinet Secretary, Sir Robin Butler, and the *Sunday Times* took delight in quoting an alarmed but unnamed Cabinet minister who feared there was a 'fifth column' of Labour sympathisers burrowing away in Whitehall.

Timing was all important in deciding when to release leaked documents because the aim was to cause maximum embarrassment for the government and that required some astute co-ordination. At Labour's 1991 Christmas reception for the news media the party's chief press and broadcasting officer, Gerard Sagar, reflected on what he thought had been a highly successful year in keeping up the attack on the Conservatives. Sagar cited the release earlier in December of a leaked memorandum from the Secretary of State for the Environment, Michael Heseltine, which expressed concern about a split in the Cabinet that had delayed the release of £109 million from the European Commission destined for investment in the British coalfields. Cook was in an equally expansive mood about his unerring ability to expose fresh financial crises in the NHS. He had again been head and shoulders above his colleagues when it came to personal hit rates in generating stories from the contents of the confidential government documents which had found their way into the hands of the opposition.

In continuing to be such an obvious repository for illicit disclosures, Cook had amply justified Thatcher's taunt in 1989 that he appeared to have become 'an official receiver' for leaks. 'Mole shock for the Tories' was the *Daily Mail*'s headline in October 1990 over a story about Cook's release of an internal memorandum which had been circulated among only fourteen senior civil servants in the Department of Health and which revealed a likely shortfall of £400 million in the budget for the NHS; he followed up that story by giving journalists copies of confidential correspondence from the Mid Cheshire Hospital Trust revealing a £400,000 deficit. Government paranoia over leaks had grown more acute since Cook's coup in 1989 in pre-empting the official publication of the White Paper *Working for Patients*, and his skill in managing to protect leakers had ensured a steady flow of documents and data. A unnamed adviser, who was quoted by the *Independent*, attributed his success to the fact that officials who were privately concerned about NHS reforms admired the way he exploited sensitive information which was being withheld from the public. 'Cook has an attacking style. Once he gets hold of a leaked document people know he's going to go in with all guns firing.'

When I complimented him at Labour's Christmas reception on his ability to keep health so high in the news, he said the party had to be careful not to overplay its hand in publicising leaks. 'There are always ebbs and flows on stories like this but we will hit the government again on health in the New Year.' Cook was true to his word: early in February 1992 he held a news conference to publicise another leaked document from the Department of Health, which showed that eighty-six hospitals had deficits of more than £100,000; their finances were not 'in balance', as ministers had claimed. Labour's health spokesman was apparently so sure of obtaining a continuous supply of confidential data with which to go on embarrassing the government that he promised journalists that it was his intention to provide them with 'a leak a week' in the near future. Both the *Guardian* and the *Independent* gave the story considerable space but some commentators had grown weary of reporting a seemingly endless flow of what were supposed to be government secrets.

Despite the publicity which the *Sunday Times* had given the week before to a confidential report from the Department of Employment, the paper's political columnist, Robert Harris, thought Labour's revelations about 'leaked' documents were looking pretty tired: 'Cook does this so often he must have enough documents to open his own Public Record Office.' Nonetheless, instead of trying to dismiss the February leak as yet another example of the opposition's scare tactics, the Secretary of State for Health, William Waldegrave, went on the attack and used an interview on Radio 4's *The World at One* to demand Cook's resignation after accusing him of having been caught handling a 'stolen document'. An internal investigation was announced but nothing further emerged for several days until the *Daily Express* published an exclusive front page story under the dramatic headline 'Labour's NHS mole trapped'. It reported that the Whitehall official who it was believed had been 'leaking secret government papers' to Cook had been confronted by senior civil servants, summoned to see the permanent secretary, Sir Christopher France, and then escorted out of the department.

Within a few hours of the *Daily Express* revealing that Whitehall 'mole hunters' had found Cook's informer, the source was publicly identified as Stephen Pashley, an official in the Department of Health who was on secondment from the South West Thames Regional Health Authority. In its statement the department said no criminal activity had been involved; the police had not been called; and Pashley, who was twenty-nine and employed at a senior grade, had left the department having been suspended on full pay by his health authority pending disciplinary proceedings. After the abject failure of so many previous leak inquiries, Waldegrave could not resist the opportunity to vilify the shadow health secretary, especially once it emerged that one of Cook's political advisers, Gordon Best, had been Pashley's referee for his job application. Waldegrave felt 'a certain pity for the young fellow' whose career might have been damaged but he considered the moral responsibility lay with Cook, whose 'practice of touting for leaks' encouraged officials to commit a breach of faith and put their jobs at risk. 'Cook likes to have a leak a week . . . everybody in Whitehall knows he is a fence.' Not since Margaret Thatcher's accusation that he had become 'an official receiver' of leaks had there been such a hard-hitting personal attack.

Cook denied either knowing Pashley or having any idea who the source of the document might have been; his parliamentary researcher, Geoffrey Norris, said it had been received anonymously through the post and the opposition had a duty to expose the government if they had evidence to show that ministers were misleading the public by quoting health statistics which were false. Supporters of the campaign for a relaxation of the secrecy laws deplored what they considered had been the unnecessary 'naming and shaming' of Pashley and it provoked some timely soul searching both within the Labour Party and the Westminster press gallery. I heard separately from two of the *Daily Mirror*'s political correspondents, Andy McSmith and David Bradshaw, that they thought the source of the leak had been traced because Cook had given reporters a photocopy of the original document rather than taking the precaution of having it retyped. Most political correspondents took great care to protect their sources and they expected politicians to do the same. As a general rule the news media were quite prepared to regard a leak as being genuine even if the contents had been reassembled or reworked in order to avoid detection.

A fortnight after the identification of Cook's informer, the shadow local government minister, David Blunkett, published a leaked document on property values for council tax but his news release pointed out that the layout of the table of figures had been purposely changed in order to protect his source. The previous year Inland Revenue officers had questioned journalists at the *Guardian* and ITN about their use of a confidential circular from the Valuation Office which Blunkett had distributed in the House of Commons press gallery. He said a copy of that circular had arrived at his office 'in a plain brown envelope, completely unmarked and untraceable'. After Cook's experience, Blunkett was not alone in recognising that with a general election only a few months away Labour's front bench had to show at least some restraint in the way they exploited the confidential information which was leaking out from John Major's administration.

I had already been struck by the care taken by Tony Blair when he was presented with an opportunity to manipulate the unauthorised disclosure of government data. Blair was shadowing Michael Howard, then the Secretary of State for Employment; both men were barristers and Howard was a QC. I sensed that Blair was particularly anxious to avoid being accused by the Conservatives of handling stolen documents, a charge that had been levelled so forcibly against some of his colleagues. He demonstrated his discretion when holding a news conference in January 1992 to publicise confidential government statistics which revealed that over half of all youth trainees finished their training schemes without any qualifications. He was especially restrained in the language which he used in his news release, avoiding any suggestion that he was taking advantage of a leaked document. Instead he announced he was 'issuing unpublished internal data' from the Department of Employment which he said showed the 'devastating effect' of government cuts in training. By eschewing the use of words such as 'leak' or 'secret', Blair made it harder for himself to get the news coverage which he might have liked but, as I had discovered to my cost the previous summer, he was not prepared to garner publicity if there was any likelihood that in doing so he might damage his own reputation.

In July 1991 I had ended up being denounced by both Howard and the BBC's director general, John Birt, over the way I had reported the contents of a leaked memorandum which had been sent to Blair's office and which revealed disagreements within Whitehall over the operation of the newly established Training and Enterprise Councils. Labour's news release supplying journalists with copies of the document had been put out in the name of Blair's deputy, the shadow employment minister, Henry McLeish. He claimed the 'leak' revealed divisions within the Department of Employment because Howard intended to adopt a 'laissez-faire' approach, against the advice of his permanent secretary, Sir Geoffrey Holland. My report for the *Six O'Clock News* provoked an immediate complaint by the secretary of state, who wrote a personal letter to Birt demanding an apology: Howard asserted that 'the so-called leaked papers had simply been doctored' by the Labour Party and he accused me of 'a serious lapse in reporting standards' which he found deeply disturbing. In the hope of getting the backing of my line manager and other senior editors, I went to great lengths to explain to David Aaronovitch, head of news at BBC Westminster, the steps I had taken to check the accuracy of my story.

I pointed out that there had been reports for some weeks in the *Financial*

Times about the conflict Howard was facing over his plans for the training councils. In one report, in the *Independent*, Blair was quoted as saying that earlier leaks from the Department of Employment had exposed Howard's 'wilful neglect of training needs'. The following day Aaronovitch handed me a copy of the apology which he said the director general intended to send to the secretary of state. Birt's letter could hardly have been any more damning about my work. He told Howard that he was not happy with the way I had reported the story and that he considered I should have been 'very cautious of reporting detailed and substantial allegations' without independent corroboration. In what I can only assume was an act of sweet revenge emanating from within Howard's department or Conservative Central Office, Birt's apology was leaked to the *Daily Express*. Its exclusive story, under the headline 'BBC says sorry', claimed I had 'invented' the story because 'there was no such leak, no such document, no such split – and no effort made to check the story'. Graham Riddick, a Conservative MP who specialised in employment affairs, accused me and particularly the BBC of being prepared to 'swallow every left-wing tale it hears' and of failing to 'repent even when it is told the truth'.

My reprimand, administered so swiftly and so efficiently by Messrs Howard and Birt, came as no surprise to Barry Sutlieff, head of information at the Department of Employment. He considered I had been 'sold a pup' by McLeish but the shadow employment minister stood by the accusations he had made. He told me that the leaked document was one of five which he and Blair had received the previous week. 'Tony and I are both getting leaks all the time. We are not releasing them all because that could expose civil servants. We've even been sent a leaked memo about leaks within Howard's department. It says the leaks must stop.' Nonetheless, in my vain attempt to defend myself once Howard made his complaint, I had trawled through all the relevant newspaper cuttings. I found, as in the case of the previous reports about the conflict over the training councils, that Blair had only ever commented on leaked documents once their contents had appeared in the press and were already in the public domain; it was obvious that even though he and his colleagues in the shadow employment team were the grateful recipient of leaks, he had no intention of associating himself person- ally with the unauthorised disclosure of secret or confidential information.

I judged that if Blair, as a member of the shadow Cabinet, rather than his deputy McLeish, had put his name to the leak about dissent within the Department of Employment, then Howard and Birt might have found it harder to have repudiated my story so comprehensively. Although Blair preferred to keep his distance from the initial release of leaked documents to the news media, I had noted in the course of my conversations with him that he realised all too clearly how they could be manipulated and it was obvious he recognised their value to the Labour Party as a means of generating news stories which might damage the Conservatives. Journalists are always willing accomplices when it comes to mischief making at the expense of the government of the day and the culture of secrecy which Margaret Thatcher had defended for so long had played into Labour's hands. What's more, as Blair had concluded when holding his own news conference in January 1992, even if there was no leak, internal data which was unpublished or unpublicised could easily be dressed up as 'secret', 'confidential' or 'leaked' in order to grab the news media's attention.

In the aftermath of Neil Kinnock's defeat in the 1992 general election and the period of readjustment following John Smith's election as party leader, Labour took a little time to regain its previous prowess in taking advantage of illicit disclosures. But once Smith had reshuffled the front bench, the shadow Cabinet gradually went back on to the attack and were soon as determined as before to make full use of an unabated flow of leaked documents and data. Aided and abetted by the continued complicity of the news media, Labour's top traders in leaked documents were soon surprising even themselves by their ability to go on capturing the headlines. On his promotion to shadow Chancellor, Gordon Brown became one of the first to regain his flair for publicity and start generating news stories aimed at damaging the Conservatives. John Major's post-election honeymoon with both his own party and the news media had proved short lived after his victory in 1992 and while Cabinet colleagues such as William Waldegrave and Virginia Bottomley had come across as being entirely genuine in their efforts to create a more open style of government, the opposition sensed the Prime Minister's political vulnerability. And, as events would demonstrate, once Blair was elected leader of the Labour Party in July 1994, no opportunity would be missed to exploit the Conservatives' splits on Europe and a succession of sexual and financial misdemeanours which went under the general heading of Tory 'sleaze'.

However, if the choice of leader had been decided solely on the masterful manipulation of the media, Brown would have had a walk-over because of his adroitness in utilising unauthorised disclosures. I began taking an ever-closer interest in the shadow Chancellor's techniques and gained a valuable insight in November 1993 when he gave the BBC a copy of a leaked report which revealed details of a government review of social security. Brown claimed that the secret data he had obtained indicated that the Conservatives were about to tear up their manifesto commitments on pensions and child benefit. In his filmed report for *Breakfast with Frost*, Jeremy Vine, one of the BBC's political correspondents, showed viewers the leaked document, much to the annoyance of Brown, who immediately complained to the BBC. He wanted an assurance that the shot would be removed from Vine's report and not included in any subsequent news bulletins. As I was the next political correspondent on duty that Sunday, Vine left a message for me urging caution when it came to following up the story for later bulletins; he thought he had taken care to make sure that the document was not seen in close-up but looking again at the relevant sequence, he recognised that the shadow Chancellor had a point.

Vine's message revealed the steps he had taken to appease Brown:

> It's probably just a storm in a teacup but I am just about to post him a personal note of apology . . . Brown did say about seventeen times that no minister should see the document . . . he wants to make sure if Virginia Bottomley [Secretary of State for Health] is interviewed by *On the Record* that she doesn't get to see it.

Brown's fears proved groundless; there were no awkward questions from government ministers about the provenance of the document and to the great satisfaction of the Labour Party, the story played exceptionally well over the weekend. Brown's ability to irritate the Conservatives through his exploitation of leaked data had not gone unnoticed by the *Daily Mirror*'s political editor, Alastair Campbell. Next day he told me of his annoyance at the way the shadow Chancellor kept feeding stories to the political correspondents of the *Sunday Times* and the BBC rather than to a Labour-supporting newspaper like his own. Campbell described my own report for the radio news bulletins as having been a 'free hit' for Brown.

Campbell chided me for failing to tackle the shadow Chancellor about the imminent publication by the party's Commission on Social Justice of a report into the possible means testing of child benefit, which he thought could result in Labour facing the same kind of dilemma as the Conservatives. Looking back at my notes of the conversation when doing research for this book, I realised it was a possible pointer to the tensions and rivalries which lay ahead under Blair's premiership, once Brown was appointed Chancellor of the Exchequer and Campbell became the Downing Street press secretary. Nonetheless what had caught my attention about the events that weekend was Vine's account of Brown's agitation once he discovered that the leaked document was appearing on screen. I had begun to notice that although the shadow Chancellor had become totally consumed again by the urge to generate publicity about himself and the action he was taking to challenge the government, he was no longer entirely oblivious to the inordinate risks he faced in continuing to supply journalists with copies of confidential government papers and other unauthorised data.

I thought his anxiety about being exposed as a possible conduit for leaked information was well founded because if ever there was any suggestion that he was personally involved in handling documents which might have been misappropriated or even stolen, it could well have proved a considerable setback for an opposition politician hoping to gain one of the highest offices of state. Brown's dogged, do-it-yourself approach towards generating publicity had already rung alarm bells within the party leadership. Unlike his colleagues, the shadow Chancellor still insisted on dealing personally with all calls from journalists, writing his own news releases and even dictating statements to the Press Association. He was obviously over-burdened, having no filter or minder to provide him with the front line defence he needed so badly to protect himself from the insatiable demands of the news media. Within weeks of his brush with the BBC over the leaked document which he had supplied to *Breakfast with Frost*, Brown had acquired his own full-time press officer in the person of Charlie Whelan, who would scale new heights in the manipulation of unauthorised disclosures while doing all he could to insulate the shadow Chancellor from any hint of direct personal involvement.

Whelan's appointment, in January 1994, was on the advice among others of Peter Mandelson, Labour's former director of communications, who had become MP for Hartlepool but remained active behind the scenes in helping to promote the party. Whelan immediately took control of Brown's day-to-day contact with the media, supervising interviews and the distribution of press statements; from then on the shadow Chancellor was kept at arm's length from the trade in the leaked documents and data which were being released to selected journalists by Labour's Treasury team in an attempt to wrongfoot the Chancellor of the Exchequer, Kenneth Clarke, and embarrass the Major government. Brown was in an ideal position. Having hired a bluff wheeler-dealer who could hold his own and cover his tracks when negotiating with political correspondents to secure the most rewarding outlets for exclusive stories, the shadow Chancellor was able to manipulate the media from afar, safe in the knowledge that Whelan would happily take the blame should any awkward questions be asked about the sources of unauthorised disclosures.

If John Major had imagined when he championed moves to establish open government that his efforts would meet with a positive response, Brown's success in generating stories about leaks demonstrated all too plainly that Labour's frontbench team had no intention of reciprocating and would continue to exploit any confidential information which might be passed on by disenchanted or disaffected civil servants. Hiving off public services to agencies, quangos and the like had widened the scope for the unofficial dissemination of potentially embarrassing policy changes and financial data. The civil service ethos of confidentiality had, to a large extent, become a casualty of privatisation and successive Whitehall efficiency reforms. In March 1994, in a belated attempt to improve the safekeeping of secret and confidential material, Major announced new procedures for the marking and labelling of government documents which required a restricted circulation. He told MPs that the security of the government was being 'increasingly threatened by theft, copying and electronic surveillance'; the aim of his review was to reduce the number of documents which were being classified as 'secret' or 'confidential' so as to ensure sufficient protection for the data which was at greatest risk.

By identifying 'more precisely' those documents which needed to be kept secure, they could be protected 'more effectively according to their value'. There was to be no change in the four categories of 'top secret', 'secret', 'confidential' and 'restricted', but the definitions were broadened to include sensitive commercial or managerial information as well as the ever-present threat to national security. Major's assertion that the new definitions would 'drive down' the amount of data that required a security classification was challenged by the Campaign for Freedom of Information. Its director, Maurice Frankel, feared the new system would only serve to strengthen the grounds for withholding information rather than encourage greater open- ness. Nonetheless the break-up of the nationalised industries and the use of agencies to deliver public services had resulted in a vast increase in the transmission of sensitive information between government departments, merchant banks, consultants and numerous other financial companies and institutions. My own researches and discussions with leakers had indicated there was every likelihood that illicit disclosure of data had put the government at a disadvantage during commercial negotiations and had led to awkward questions about the financial viability of costly projects.

The introduction of the new security classifications had been preceded by a series of leaks blamed directly on faxed documents having gone astray. Perhaps the most embarrassing was the publication in June 1993 of a draft letter from the Secretary of State for Social Security, Peter Lilley, revealing a cut in invalidity benefit coupled with plans to force claimants to take medical tests. It had been received by fax at the Fleet Street offices of the Press Association. Initially journalists in the newsroom assumed it had been sent anonymously as a deliberate leak by an aggrieved civil servant but it then emerged that an official in Lilley's office had dialled the wrong number and instead of faxing it to government law officers had sent it to the Press Association. One of the civil servants who was present when the mistake was discovered told me that because there was no answer on the internal telephone network, the document was sent via an outside line. Without the correct prefix, it transpired that the two numbers were identical.

> The official concerned was devastated by what happened. He had even put a note on the last page asking for confirmation for the receipt of the letter and when the Press Association rang, the news agency could not believe that it was a mistake. Apparently the journalist concerned was certain the document had been sent to them on purpose.

According to the *Sunday Times*, steps were taken immediately by the Cabinet Secretary, Sir Robin Butler, to tighten security procedures for faxing sensitive material between departments. Civil servants were told they must always use the government's internal communications network rather than an outside line. A copy of the instructions was leaked to the *Guardian*, which published a Prison Service memo outlining the precautions which had to be taken:

> The email system should not be used for sending classified or sensitive material. Moreover fax machines should not be used for documents classified confidential or above, and the use of fax for the transmission of sensitive documents should always be preceded by a telephone call to ensure that the right person is on hand to receive the material and confirm safe receipt.

Political journalists were amused by the lack of any advice on what a civil servant should do on discovering that a fax had been sent to a wrong number. I was told by the *Daily Mail*'s political editor, Gordon Greig, that it was the Press Association's good fortune that a reporter had actually spotted the significance of Lilley's letter. 'Faxes spew out at such a rate in the *Daily Mail*'s office at Westminster that sometimes we hardly have time to check them all through. What we need is a fax machine which can copy-taste, spot a good story and then ring a bell!'

I was reminded of Greig's flippant aside about faxes piling up unnoticed when working late one evening at the BBC's newsroom in Millbank in October 1993. On checking through a heap that had accumulated in the in-tray, I found a copy of a private letter to Major from the Conservative MP Sir Nicholas Bonsor, warning the Prime Minister about a possible backbench rebellion. I noticed that it had been faxed from the office of the Labour MP Andrew Mackinlay. When I enquired further, Mackinlay told me he had sent a copy of the letter to the BBC and to other political journalists because he thought it might be of interest: 'My researcher found the letter lying beside a photocopier. It was on an A5 piece of paper, not the usual A4, and it looked as though it had probably been photocopied in a smaller size by mistake and then just left there, lying forgotten by the machine.' Mackinlay said he had no hesitation in disseminating private correspondence between a Conservative MP and the Prime Minister: any adverse publicity for the Tories was the political price which had to be paid for an act of carelessness. As Major's political problems multiplied, so did the number of leaks; month after month ministers found their attention being diverted as they struggled to deal with the accusations and recriminations which tended to flow from the unauthorised disclosure of confidential information.

August is renowned for being a silly season for political stories but the summer of 1994 proved to be an exception after the *Guardian* published a leaked letter from Michael Portillo rebuking his Cabinet colleague Michael Heseltine for his failure to implement cuts in government spending. An immediate inquiry was ordered by the Treasury after the finger of blame was pointed in various directions. Heseltine's supporters claimed it was part of a Thatcherite plot to boost Portillo's chances as a future successor to Major; Portillo's backers were equally adamant that the Heseltine camp was to blame; other insiders were convinced that the choice of the *Guardian* for the leak suggested it was the work of a disgruntled civil servant. Portillo had written the letter in his capacity as chief secretary to the Treasury, two weeks before his promotion to Secretary of State for Employment. He informed Heseltine, then Secretary of State for Trade and Industry, that he was 'very disappointed' at the failure of such an important department to cut back on its budget of £1.3 billion, which included state aids such as regional assistance, industrial support and other subsidies. Portillo argued that the 'best help' that could be given to business would be to 'control public spending and get taxes down' and he considered that Heseltine's response 'misses the point' and 'may risk wasting that chance'.

Revelations about the use of such forthright language in a letter from one Cabinet minister to another delighted the headline writers: 'Can Portillo slay the public spending goliath?' was the *Sun*'s take on the story, and it praised the leaker for having 'performed a great service'. Portillo must have sensed the reaction of newspapers like the *Sun* because he surprised political journalists by not only confirming the authenticity of the letter but also publicly defending the line he had taken. David Hart, his long-standing unpaid adviser, told me that as soon as they saw the *Guardian*'s story they decided it was best to stand by the letter and get the Prime Minister's deputy press secretary, Jonathan Haslam, to read out a statement to the lobby that morning pointing out that Portillo was pursuing 'a healthy and appropriate debate' about the proper level of government spending. Hart said:

> By owning up to the letter, Michael took the finger of blame off himself and it was important that he should be seen standing up for what he believed in. You can quote friends of Portillo as saying he's proud of the letter. It's not just Heseltine, other ministers are annoyed with him, Ken Clarke is just as cross and Douglas Hurd has complained about the need to end this perpetual revolution.

Hart thought the correspondence had been leaked by 'a leftie' in the Department of Trade and Industry, probably the 'same civil service trade unionist' who the previous month had slipped to the *Times* the news of an investigation by Heseltine's staff into allegations of insider share dealing against the novelist Jeffrey Archer, a candidate for the chairmanship of the Conservative Party. I was given a contrary explanation by the civil service union leader Jonathan Baume, general secretary of the First Division Association (FDA):

> We think the Portillo leak was a result of internal party feuding so there's no point the Tories looking for scapegoats in the civil service. It must have come from the private

office of one of the ministers. You can never trace the source of the leak because the letters are usually retyped and the hard copy destroyed.

Baume said that in the five and a half years he had been at the FDA there had not been a single case resulting in disciplinary action against one of his members. Patrick Wintour, the *Guardian*'s political correspondent, told Sky News that he knew the route of the leak which had generated his exclusive story but the letter itself had not been reproduced because it did contain reference numbers and code marks. His editor, Peter Preston, confirmed the following day that the original had been shredded; the *Guardian* had no intention of being forced by the police to surrender its documents as had happened in the case of Sarah Tisdall.

Robin Cook tried without success to get in on the act by issuing a succession of news releases expressing alarm at Heseltine's failure to 'come out fighting' in the face of a letter 'so dripping in political dogma and so lacking in common sense'. Most columnists were far more interested in the reported jealousies of two Cabinet colleagues than the potential loss of industrial investment. William Rees-Mogg suggested in the *Daily Mail* that Heseltine might have leaked the letter to show the world that he was having to deal with 'an insufferable young puppy' but he tended to think Portillo was responsible: 'A man with the chutzpah to write such a letter would have the chutzpah to leak it.' In his column in the *Times*, Simon Jenkins concluded that the civil servants involved must have become frustrated by the 'customary Whitehall point-scoring' which was probably why 'a bored official thought to put the letter in an envelope to the *Guardian*'. A similar conclusion was reached by the *Sunday Times*, which applauded the fact that Britain was living 'in the age of the leak', because the public interest was being served by under-the-counter disclosure:

> Whitehall leakers have had a field day under this government . . . Should Labour win the next election, it will need to remember the halcyon days when it bombarded the government with leaked Whitehall documents. Labour leaders who gripe will get short shrift. Given the opportunity, leakers can, and will, turn against them with equal relish.

Stephen Glover was equally trenchant in support of leakers in February 1995 when he used his media column in the London *Evening Standard* to praise the *Times* for scooping its rivals by disclosing details of talks between London and Dublin over the future of Ulster. Sir Patrick Mayhew, the

Secretary of State of Northern Ireland, condemned the paper for its 'scandalous irresponsibility' in jeopardising the chances for peace but Glover argued that leaks were the 'very essence of democracy' because they cast light on the workings of government which most ministers would rather keep secret. By complaining about 'a few phrases lifted highly selectively' from the Anglo-Irish framework document, Mayhew was failing to acknowledge that by their very nature leaks were selective. 'The word leak implies a trickle of information rather than a torrent.'

All the furore over the Portillo and Northern Ireland disclosures was a mere dress rehearsal for the outpouring of ministerial anger which erupted in September 1995, when Labour's media manipulators excelled themselves in their opportunism and daring. With deadly precision the party chose the morning of an all-day strategy session at Chequers to publish a leaked copy of one of the policy papers being presented to the Cabinet. Labour's education spokesman, David Blunkett, gave journalists copies of the memorandum, which had been prepared for the meeting by Gillian Shephard, secretary of state at the newly merged Department for Education and Employment (DfEE); the *Guardian* carried the front-page headline 'Leak ruins Tories' re-launch' over its report of this 'public relations disaster for John Major'. Like Portillo, Shephard had been remarkably frank when expressing her frustration at the Conservatives' failure to portray education as one of their 'major success stories'. She feared the government was politically exposed because of underfunding and that peace in the classroom was at risk: 'Insufficient resources now threaten the provision of education in the state schools sector, including grant-maintained schools.'

By releasing the memorandum to coincide with the start of the discussions, Blunkett hoped to sabotage the Cabinet's get-together at Chequers and he succeeded in diverting ministers' attention by forcing them to find ways of limiting the damage. At a news conference dominated by questions about the leak, Heseltine, the deputy Prime Minister, declared that Blunkett's portrayal of the memorandum was 'a travesty' and had been entirely politically motivated. Shephard, who was said by the *Sun* to have been 'shaking with rage', insisted she had not written the policy paper, nor did she use it in her presentation; the government was united in regarding education and training as 'vitally important'. Notwithstanding their efforts, the *Daily Telegraph* reported next day that Labour had dealt 'a devastating blow' to Major's autumn fight-back and what had been billed as the most extensive review of government policy for nearly two decades. Yet another leak inquiry was announced and the *Daily Mail* was convinced that the 'finger of blame' pointed to a 'disgruntled civil servant' in the merged DfEE. Fewer than twenty photocopies were reported to have been made of the memorandum, which was marked 'Restricted – Policy'. Blunkett refused to reveal the source of his copy but said it arrived in the morning post at his office in the House of Commons.

Labour's ability to go on releasing a seemingly endless supply of confidential documents prompted a pro-Tory think tank, the European Policy Forum (EPF), to start examining why leaks to the opposition, trade unions and the press were running at 'epidemic proportions'. It investigated a total of thirty-six 'serious' leaks from government departments which had been reported in the nine months up to March 1995 and concluded that two thirds of them were from civil servants 'motivated by political hostility' to Major's government and Conservative policies such as privatisation. The worst offender was the Scottish Office, which had been the source of five of the leaks; four had been traced to each of the Cabinet Office and the Department of Trade and Industry; and three each to the Home Office and the Department of Transport. Graham Mather, the forum's president and a Conservative MEP, acknowledged that the leakers were often sophisticated in their choice of material and timing. He was puzzled by Whitehall's failure to adopt an 'anti-leak' strategy that was commensurate with the scale of the problem, because the forum believed the Conservatives faced the prospect of 'a tidal wave of leaks until the next general election'.

Mather's dire warning was followed up by Michael Jones, political columnist for the *Sunday Times*, who discovered that after the unauthorised disclosure of Shephard's policy paper, Major had ordered his colleagues to write fewer memos and restrict their circulation. Jones found that ministers were 'paranoid' about civil servants leaking sensitive material; such was the alarm within Whitehall that some members of the Cabinet had reached the 'inescapable conclusion that Labour has a fifth column behind their lines' intent on causing maximum damage to the Conservatives in the run-up to the general election. Witch hunts to find the leakers never produced results and the Prime Minister had concluded that the only way to counter the culture of leaking which had been created by the fax and the photocopier was to commit less to paper. Jones reported that the Labour Party was delighted to be receiving leaks 'via Whitehall's fifth column' of civil servants anxious to see Tony Blair in Downing Street: 'One Labour frontbencher describes Whitehall's leakers as bitter people out for revenge, prompted by what they see as the government's destruction of civil service morale and the transfer of departmental work to anonymous agencies.'

In a second survey of leaks published at the end of December, the European Policy Forum concluded that 1995 should be described as the 'year of the leaker', as there had been an average of five significant disclosures a month from government departments, despite Major's instruction to ministers to write fewer memos and limit their circulation. Seven of the leaks were from the Department of Transport and related to rail privatisation and the sale of Railtrack. Fearing that the loyalty of the civil service was being questioned unjustly, the Cabinet Secretary, Sir Robin Butler, made a fresh attempt to assuage the anger of the Prime Minister and his colleagues. He reminded civil servants that if they were caught leaking secret papers to the Labour Party or to the press they would face disciplinary action which could result in dismissal. He announced a new code of conduct, to take effect in January 1996, which was intended to leave no room for doubt. Civil servants were told they should not seek through the unauthorised disclosure of information to 'frustrate or influence the policies, decisions or actions of the government'. When asked by journalists how many civil servants had been caught and sacked under the existing rules, Butler refused to give any figures but insisted that only 'a very, very tiny fraction' of the confidential papers in circulation at any one time were ever leaked.

One new safeguard was the introduction of a right of appeal for civil servants who felt they were being asked to act in illegal, improper or unethical ways. The Committee on Standards in Public Life, chaired by Lord Nolan, had recommended that in the event of a case which raised 'a fundamental issue of confidence' there should be a right of appeal to a civil service commissioner. Continuing pressure for the introduction of procedures to encourage civil servants to 'blow the whistle where codes of conduct or propriety are broken' had been reinforced by the EPF, which had acknowledged that frustration in the work place was probably one of the factors responsible for the prevalence of leaks. Wider concerns about the failure of management to heed safety warnings given by employees had been highlighted by a series of disasters ranging from the capsizing of the ferry *Herald of Free Enterprise* off Zeebrugge to an explosion on the Piper Alpha oil platform in the North Sea. In an attempt to provide greater protection for whistleblowers, the Labour MP Don Touhig secured all-party support in February 1996 for a private member's Public Interest Disclosure Bill. He wanted to support workers who feared lives could be put at risk if they failed to speak out.

Touhig's Bill was designed to ensure that people who acted in the public interest when they blew the whistle on serious malpractice would be able to obtain an injunction to protect themselves against victimisation and to get compensation if reprisals were taken. Touhig accepted that employers were entitled to 'loyalty and confidentiality in normal circumstances' but that that duty would be outweighed if a court found an external disclosure of information was 'lawful and justified' in the public interest; there would be no protection if the individual had not raised the matter internally first or was acting in bad faith, by 'selling the story to a newspaper' or not having reasonable grounds to believe the information was accurate. One of the Conservative MPs sponsoring the Bill was Iain Duncan Smith, who said he recognised that individuals must have the ability to raise concerns without fear of retribution. 'This is implementing existing best practice. It is not a charter for troublemakers or the disgruntled.' Like previous private member's Bills, Touhig's initiative in seeking cross-party backing for a framework to limit unauthorised disclosures failed to make progress through Parliament.

However well intentioned it might have seemed to the leadership, attempts to regularise the flow of illicit data were hardly likely to appeal to the network of Labour Party intermediaries who traded in leaked information. Their one objective during the long build-up to the 1997 general election was to win friends in the news media. The exploitation of confidential government information had become a formidable weapon in the opposition's armoury for influencing the news agenda and attacking the Conservatives. A sure-fire way of gaining patronage in a competitive market place was by supplying journalists with confidential documents and unauthorised disclosures. Despite having moved swiftly to strengthen Labour's media operation at the party's new headquarters in Millbank, Tony Blair remained as careful as in the past to keep himself at arm's length while encouraging the deployment of various techniques aimed at orchestrating the release of leaked data. Labour's burgeoning band of spin doctors had a fertile and febrile media environment in which to operate and they were being guided by the likes of Alastair Campbell, David Hill, Jo Moore and Charlie Whelan, who understood the media mindset and had few if any scruples about the lengths to which they would go to exploit journalists' craving for exclusive stories.

Frequent entries in my diaries in late 1996 and early 1997 showed how the closer it got to polling day, the more the BBC's political correspondents were being bombarded with offers which were often hard to refuse. Ringing round journalists to alert them to possible stories was usually a task left to the younger press officers, who tended to be impatient and had a habit of demanding an immediate response. One Sunday morning in late November 1996 I found messages had been piling up on my computer terminal in the newsroom asking me to contact Tim Allan, who was Campbell's deputy. Allan told me that Blair's office had obtained a copy of a leaked memo from Michael Heseltine referring to changes in the civil service which he thought the BBC should be reporting, and that he had already informed the BBC's news organiser of this. He wanted to know why this had not been followed up. An identical tip-off to the BBC had been left by the Labour Party's broadcasting officer, Dan Clifton. The tactic of blitzing the radio newsroom and programmes was having the desired effect, judging by another message left for me by the news organiser: 'Labour are in full cry about the Heseltine leak . . . Radio 5 Live might want to do a two-way with you at 11 a.m.'

When journalists were offered illicit data which had been obtained by Gordon Brown, negotiations were conducted directly by Whelan, the shadow Chancellor's personal press officer, rather than by the media department at party headquarters. Whelan operated a clearing house for leaks, dispensing the shadow Chancellor's booty with deadly accuracy. Once he had reached an agreement on the likely timing and direction of a potential story, Whelan would ask the reporter concerned to contact Brown's economic adviser, Ed Balls, for a detailed briefing on what the leaked document revealed, and it was only after these preparatory moves had been completed that the shadow Chancellor would agree to give television or radio interviews. There were many willing supplicants for Brown's largesse among Westminster's political correspondents but they were never allowed to forget the preconditions attached to use of his leaked documents, the most important of which was that when it came to the timing of any story it was Whelan who was pulling the strings.

In the final months of John Major's government his ministers were bedevilled by an unprecedented deluge of unwelcome disclosures; obviously Brown's principal target was the Chancellor of the Exchequer, Kenneth Clarke, a political street fighter, capable of absorbing punch after punch and coming back for more. Whelan considered that his greatest moment of glory in manipulating Brown's ill-gotten gains was the afternoon in November 1996 when Clarke was forced to make an emergency Commons statement at the despatch box on the eve of his last Budget as Chancellor. The lead-up to Brown's coup de grâce against the Cabinet's prize pugilist was a text book example of a Labour-inspired disclosure aimed at unsettling the government. As in so many other cases, radio and television news bulletins inevitably played a part, however unwittingly, in the orchestration which went on behind the scenes. Initially the preferred recipients tended to be newspapers such as the *Sunday Times*, the *Observer* or the *Independent on Sunday*. The advantage of using a Sunday paper as the first outlet was that it opened up opportunities for getting the leak trailed on Saturday evening television news bulletins, which were often short of hard news stories, and for then being followed up by Monday's papers. Weekend current affairs programmes, poised to follow up items from the bulletins, were usually only too delighted to clamber aboard a moving story and once interest had been aroused and mission accomplished, Labour's spin doctors would start farming out shadow ministers for as many interviews as possible. My involvement in Clarke's eve-of-Budget imbroglio began, as so often had been the case in the past, with a message on my pager to telephone Whelan. He had made contact mid-morning on Saturday and I had half-expected a call because Brown had alerted me personally the previous Thursday evening to the likelihood of there being a 'significant development that weekend involving the Chancellor'. Whelan had reinforced that warning the following evening with a tip-off to the effect that a story about the European single currency would be emerging on Saturday evening via the *Sunday Times*. 'This story is a blockbuster on the single currency . . . It's dynamite. Obviously we want to get the BBC involved. You'll be able to interview Gordon in time for the main news.' I was told that four confidential documents, which Labour believed had been withheld from MPs, had been given exclusively to Andrew Grice, political editor of the *Sunday Times*.

One of the conditions which had been imposed by Whelan was that the documents should be made available at News International's offices in Wapping at 4.30 p.m. so that they could be filmed by a BBC television crew. The precondition which I had been asked to abide by was that neither the story nor the pictures could be used until the main news bulletin at 8.50 p.m. in order to ensure that they remained exclusive to the *Sunday Times*, at least for its all-important first edition. Although I had taken the precaution, soon after Whelan made contact, of warning the bulletin editor that I was likely to be offering an important story that evening, I had taken it upon myself to negotiate a modus operandi with Whelan. Once I had given my word to follow his instructions, Balls rang to give me a personal run-down on what the documents contained. Labour were alleging a cover-up by the Chancellor because the confidential papers, drawn up by the European Monetary Institute, were said to show that the pound would have to shadow the euro even if Britain opted out of the single currency. An accompanying internal Treasury paper stated that this proposal would 'not be acceptable' to Parliament and Balls claimed this information had not been released to MPs.

Labour had a tendency to try to bounce broadcasters into accepting their spin on leaked information and my worry, shared by my weekend television producer, Julian Joyce, was that we would be presented late on Saturday afternoon with a heap of documents and have only a couple of hours in which to check out their authenticity and the validity of the story line which Brown, Balls and Whelan had successfully hawked to the *Sunday Times*. We were both well aware that this pushy triumvirate of information traders would be desperate to persuade the BBC to carry the story so as to reinforce its credibility and persuade other journalists to follow it up. When we arrived at Wapping to film the documents, Grice told me that Labour had given them to him on Friday and he had been up all night working out what they meant, researching the story, writing the front-page splash and preparing a feature for the inside pages. He showed me the story he had written. Under the headline 'Clarke in storm over cover-up', it said: 'Crucial documents about the preparations for the single currency have been withheld from MPs . . . Labour said they were "political dynamite" . . . The four documents, obtained by the *Sunday Times*, reveal that Brussels will interfere in Britain's economic policies even if the government opts out of the euro.'

Grice explained that Whelan had asked him to use the phrase 'leaked to the *Sunday Times*' so as not to reveal that Brown was the source of the documents. Subsequently, after I had taken the liberty of describing in my book *Campaign 1997* how Brown, Balls and Whelan had in effect manipulated both the *Sunday Times* and the BBC, Grice said he had not taken offence over my disclosures because he considered it was a tribute to the power of his paper that Labour regarded it as the best outlet for disseminating hot and exclusive stories based on leaked information. Once back at the studios of BBC Westminster late that Saturday afternoon, we mounted a series of checks to test the validity of the story. As Whelan had promised, Brown arrived promptly for an interview in which he claimed Parliament had not been told the full truth about Britain's stance towards the single currency. Finally, with less than half an hour to go to transmission, our telephone calls to the press office at the Treasury and to Clarke's political adviser, Anthony Teesdale, produced a short statement put out in the Chancellor's name: 'No official document properly liable to parliamentary scrutiny has been withheld.' Although my story was not the lead but the third story in the bulletin, it did give added weight to the revelations in the *Sunday Times* and the allegations of a cover-up.

Because of mounting unease among Conservative Eurosceptic MPs about the impact of the euro there had already been demands for an early debate in the Commons and, to the surprise of most political journalists, the Treasury announced at lunchtime on Sunday that Clarke would make an emergency statement on Monday afternoon in order to correct what he considered was a 'highly misleading and inaccurate' report in the *Sunday Times*. Without further ado Brown, again with his press officer in tow, was back at BBC Westminster ready for another round of interviews, this time welcoming the Chancellor's 'climb-down'. Whelan was cock-a-hoop at having scored so easily. Instead of spending the weekend going through his Budget, Labour had forced Clarke to prepare for an emergency statement. 'My job is to help Gordon wind up Ken. We never thought we'd get a direct hit like this. Our job is to try to derail the Budget and obscure the Chancellor's announce-ments. I can't believe we're forcing him to make a statement just because of our leaked documents.' But Whelan's coup in 'winding up' the Chancellor turned into something of an anti-climax for Labour because Clarke thrived in the rough-house of politics and he told MPs he had ordered the immediate publication of all documents relating to the draft legislation on monetary union. He insisted that once MPs studied the correspondence they would see that he had shown proper regard for parliamentary procedures. One of the leaked papers Brown had been 'waving about' was a briefing note prepared at the request of the two British European Commissioners, Sir Leon Brittan and Neil Kinnock, and Clarke maintained it was the shadow Chancellor, perhaps making use of Kinnock's copy, who had 'seen fit to break that confidence and put the document into the public domain'. Clarke's bullish performance at the despatch box delighted his parliamentary private secretary, Peter Butler, who told me the attempt to claim there had been a damaging leak and then use it to spark off a row about the euro had got nowhere. 'Ken can shrug off attacks like that because what he says fits completely with his beliefs. Labour just can't rattle Ken.' Whelan and Alastair Campbell, who had both been sitting in the press gallery for the statement, seemed rather miffed that Clarke had escaped unscathed but their disappointment was short lived. Within an hour of the Chancellor leaving the chamber, Labour were given a head start in deciding how best to exploit the most spectacular leak under John Major's government.

Whelan was tipped off by Kevin Maguire, political editor of the *Daily Mirror*, that his paper had obtained leaked copies of Treasury press releases explaining the background to the main tax changes which Clarke intended to announce the following afternoon. By alerting Labour to the contents of the Budget, Maguire not only gave Brown twenty-four hours' advance warning but also extended a virtual free hand to Whelan to generate an air of mayhem surrounding what was supposed to be a key event in the Conservatives' pre-election build-up. Whelan was in his element and when I met him next day he happily regaled details of his role in Labour's latest attempt to 'wind up' Clarke: 'I couldn't believe it when Kevin Maguire said on the phone, "I've got the Budget." Of course, the news of what the *Daily Mirror* was up to was so sensational it spread round the press gallery like wildfire.' From what rival political correspondents pieced together at Westminster, it appeared that the *Daily Mirror*'s editor, Piers Morgan, had been uncertain what to do but decided finally to inform the Downing Street press office of the leak and return the documents. Despite Morgan's under-taking, the government obtained an injunction from a judge in chambers banning the *Daily Mirror* from publishing the contents.

However, as agreed with No. 10, one of the paper's journalists, Anthony Harwood, was photographed handing them back to the Prime Minister's press secretary, Jonathan Haslam, at 10.30 that evening. Haslam told the lobby next morning that the leak had occurred at some point during a massive printing operation which had been conducted on behalf of various government departments. All told there were sixty-five separate news releases about the Budget and they had been bundled together at the Treasury into 2,800 press packs ready for distribution once the Chancellor had completed his speech. The news releases leaked to the *Daily Mirror* were from the Inland Revenue, Customs and Excise and the Scottish Office. After Morgan alerted the Prime Minister's office at 7.20 p.m. the government obtained its injunction by 8.05 but in the event the matter was settled by negotiation between the paper and the Treasury solicitor. Despite having agreed to hand back the documents, most political correspondents were surprised that Morgan ordered the *Mirror* to refrain from publishing any of the details about the key announcements on income tax, petrol duty and prescription charges.

Maguire told me that he found walking round the press gallery with 'the Budget in [his] pocket' the weirdest of sensations. Great care had been taken to photocopy the documents several times so that the originals could not be traced. Within a matter of hours Maguire's elation turned to torment because he then had to endure what became the most galling experience of his career as a journalist. While his editor was coming to terms with the legal undertakings which had been given to the government, he knew Labour's spin doctors were using the *Daily Mirror's* information to 'give a steer' to other journalists, including broadcasters at the BBC, and, as he accepted, perhaps not unnaturally most newspapers were only too happy to exploit Morgan's reticence. '1p off tax today' was the headline in the *Sun*, which correctly pre-empted most of Clarke's announcements. Philip Webster, political editor of the *Times*, told me the Budget contents had effectively been 'touted around' to other news organisations, most of which were able to piece together a credible story. David Hill, Labour's chief media spokesperson, conceded that Maguire's tip-off to Whelan had been invaluable because it allowed Brown to calculate that despite the 1p cut in income tax, there would still be a £300 million increase in the overall tax take:

> Because we knew the figures in advance, our Treasury team were able to start pushing the line that the Budget wouldn't leave the average family any better off. We knew if we could suggest the Budget wouldn't have any real effect, we could then say it wasn't worth waiting for and that it wouldn't change voters' minds at the election.

Notwithstanding all that I had been told by Whelan, Hill and the journalists whom Labour had helped to become the recipients of the Budget 'secrets', the shadow Chancellor could hardly have sounded any more upstanding or responsible than he did on the morning of the Budget when being interviewed by BBC radio. Brown told *Today* that if the *Daily Mirror* had offered to show him the 94-page pack of Treasury press releases he would have refused. 'Nobody can condone the leak of sensitive Budget matters the day before the Budget . . . The most important thing to recognise is that the civil servant who did this is serving no public purpose. I don't think anyone should condone the action.'

With only months to go to the 1997 general election and the near certainty of a Labour victory, Brown must have looked over his shoulder momentarily, remembered his own questionable behaviour in the past, and realised that as the likely future Chancellor it was time, at least in public, to play by the rules of Whitehall and to start attacking leakers. Had Margaret Thatcher still been in the House of Commons, she would surely have been incandescent at

Brown's effrontery and would almost certainly have delivered a sharp riposte to his belated conversion to the importance of respecting the confidentiality of official documents. Brown's condemnation of the leak enraged Lady Thatcher's former press secretary, Sir Bernard Ingham. Writing in the *Sunday Express*, he welcomed 'a sinner come to repentance' but said he would only take it for real when Tony Blair ordered his team to return 'every leaked document to the department whence it came – unread and uncopied'. The question Ingham asked himself was, 'Which opposition spokesman had not handled stolen government documents?' Robin Cook had been to government papers 'what a magnet is to iron filings' and in playing its 'long-running role of Fagin', Labour had politicised disloyal civil servants.

The Conservative MP George Walden was equally scathing in his column in the Budget day edition of the *Evening Standard*. Labour's 'shameless exploitation of every purloined document' which came their way was as cynical as it was short sighted. 'As they will discover should they find themselves in office, this is a tawdry, self-defeating game that any fool can play.' A fortnight later at Question Time Michael Heseltine said the whole basis on which documents were being leaked was severely prejudicial to the good government of the country and that it had been 'encouraged and abetted ruthlessly and remorselessly' by the Labour Party. When challenged to substantiate his claims at a hearing of the Public Services Select Committee, the deputy Prime Minister offered to show MPs 'a folder of leaks' which he blamed on 'a culture of leaking' within the civil service and which he claimed was being exploited by opposition spokesmen and by the promise of at least one member of the shadow Cabinet to 'make good use' of leaks. Heseltine was convinced Labour-supporting civil servants were largely responsible and he feared this presaged the politicisation of the civil service. 'It is the photocopier which fuels the leak culture and the network of leakers working to the Labour Party and the press.' Inevitably there was considerable speculation about the source of the Budget leak.

The press releases had been supplied to the *Daily Mirror* by a freelance investigative journalist, Peter Hounam, who had already been credited with several spectacular scoops. One theory was that the leak was connected with an announcement of 900 redundancies at a south London printing plant owned by the newly privatised Stationery Office but this was denied by the staff. Among political journalists it was considered to have been by far the worst leak during the Conservatives' eighteen years in power, and the speed with which it was exploited by the Labour Party and spread around the lobby at Westminster caused consternation in the Treasury. One possibility which was considered at the height of the government's efforts to retrieve the press releases was that the Chancellor might have to make a late-night statement announcing some of the price-sensitive tax changes in case the unauthorised disclosures caused alarm on the international money markets and allowed speculators to make a killing. In acknowledging in his *Today* interview the seriousness of the Treasury's position, Brown had certainly taken what I considered was the unprecedented step of attacking whoever was responsible for the leak.

Previously Labour's frontbench team had defended unauthorised disclosures on the grounds that they were in the public interest and had refrained from attacking the motives of whistleblowers. An insight into the extent of the shadow Chancellor's role in exploiting the Budget leak emerged in 2005 with the publication of *The Insider*, the diaries of the former *Daily Mirror* editor Piers Morgan. Morgan said his news desk told him at around midday that it had obtained the documents through Hounam, who had tried 'unsuccessfully to get more material from his source'. The paperwork confirmed that there would be a 1p cut in income tax but there was not sufficient time to verify the authenticity of all data because there were 'sheaves and sheaves' of it. Opinions were divided in the office over what do. 'Everyone agreed it was potentially a great scoop, but there were obvious concerns. Were the documents genuine? Would financial markets go into turmoil if we published them? . . . This was not an easy call.' Morgan said he came down against just 'lobbing' all of it in the paper and in the end everyone in the office agreed that the *Daily Mirror* should 'play the good guys and hand it back . . . not least because . . . we'll get loads of publicity anyway and can say we behaved responsibly, which will be a new first.'

Initially there was general praise in other papers for the Morgan's decision to return the leaked documents. The *Guardian* complimented him for having 'finally grown up and done the right thing' but the following day journalists started accusing Morgan, in his own words, of 'bottling it, fuelled by Peter Hounam, who is telling the world what a gutless disgrace I am.' What I found of far greater significance was Morgan's account of how, once he had informed Downing Street of the leak, he telephoned Brown to alert him to what the paper had obtained.

> He was desperate for information from the documents so I told him, on strict condition he didn't tell anyone else. The revelation of the Budget leak caused

shockwaves through Westminster when it broke around 10 p.m. And so did the *Sun* when it landed with what looked like an exact précis of what I had told Brown. I was not amused.

When interviewed at the time of the leak Morgan made no mention of his chagrin over Brown's double dealing and surprised friends and foes alike by his candour in taking full responsibility for returning the Budget papers to Downing Street. He told the *Observer* that his main preoccupation had been his inability to authenticate the documents: 'If I had published them and they turned out to be a hoax, I would have been sacked next morning.'

Morgan's soul searching met a largely hostile response. Paul Foot, a celebrated investigative journalist and ex-columnist for the *Mirror*, denounced his former paper's failure to publish what he considered was the biggest Budget leak since Hugh Dalton was forced to resign in 1947 after revealing the contents of his Budget to John Carvel, political correspondent of the *Star*. Morgan's action was 'an insult to the people who took the risk to leak the stuff' and broke the 'oldest rule in the book' because the leakers could have been identified. Roy Greenslade, a former *Mirror* editor, took a similarly trenchant line, accusing Morgan of 'one of the lamest journalistic decisions of all time'. Kevin Maguire, the *Daily Mirror*'s political editor, agreed: rather than handing over the leak, he thought the paper should have defied the government's injunction. Subsequently, after being awarded the 'scoop of the year' prize by BBC 2's *What the Papers Say*, Hounam told the *Guardian* that he had 'never doubted the authenticity' of the documents. He also revealed that he had remained under police investigation, an inquiry which the Metropolitan Police finally admitted had drawn a blank seven months after the original leak. Donald Trelford, a former editor of the *Observer*, was a lone defender of Morgan. He thought the ninety-four 'mind-numbing' pages of the Budget papers would have bored readers and he did not rate 'scoops' which simply gave 'brief advance knowledge' of routine matters.

Other newspapers used Morgan's discomfort to remind readers of their previous exploits: the *Daily Telegraph* had correctly predicted there would be no rise in the basic rate of income tax in the 1981 Budget after receiving a private briefing from Margaret Thatcher; and the *Independent* scooped Nigel Lawson's first Budget in 1984 by revealing he would abolish tax relief on life assurance, a leak which led to a police investigation but failed to identify a culprit. When returning the pack of Budget press releases, Morgan had pleaded with Jonathan Haslam, the Downing Street press secretary, to acknowledge in its statement that the *Daily Mirror* had acted responsibly. At Prime Minister's Questions the following day John Major told MPs he was delighted that the injunction had been honoured and that nothing had been printed in advance. Nonetheless it had been a 'disgraceful leak' by someone acting in 'an untrustworthy fashion' and Major rounded on Tony Blair and Gordon Brown the following week for continuing to rely on illicit disclosures despite their 'piety' about the unauthorised release of Treasury documents.

Major's frustration mirrored Thatcher's: the exploitation of leaks had become a key component of Labour's strategy for dominating the headlines, and with only months to go to the 1997 general election there would be no let-up in their attempts to keep the Conservatives on the defensive. Brown's post-Budget support for a tightening of the Treasury's security procedures was cast aside by his deputy, the shadow chief secretary, Alistair Darling, who taunted ministers by suggesting to the *Times* that it was time they recognised that 'leaks are a fact of life'. Darling's bravado was shared by the rest of the shadow Treasury team and as the election approached, Brown's press secretary, Charlie Whelan, continued to distribute copies of confidential government documents with gay abandon. In an attempt to persuade the media to downplay successive falls in unemployment, Labour supplied journalists with leaked figures for the monthly jobless count so that shadow ministers could then question the validity of the official statistics. In March 1997 Maguire offered me an advance copy of his story about the latest leak in the hope that it could be trailed on the *Nine O'Clock News*. When the story failed to appear in the bulletin, Whelan rang me to complain. He claimed the leak had been his 'property' and as the BBC's news judgement was so 'terrible' he would give the next one to *News at Ten*. Next morning Maguire's story was spread across two pages under the banner headline '68,200 new lies. *Mirror* exposes Tory dole fiddle'. In the event the leak proved entirely accurate, as the jobless count in February had fallen by 68,200. It was the third time in a matter months that the figures had been leaked to the *Mirror* and Maguire described with delight how a 'massive inquiry' instigated by the government after the leak of the January figures had 'got nowhere'.

Whelan was equally industrious when it came to feeding journalists with tip-offs about Brown's future policy proposals. Labour had been waiting impatiently for Kenneth Clarke to deliver his last Budget, and once the Conservatives had announced their 1p pre-election cut in income tax, the shadow Chancellor began calculating the tax and spending plans of a future Blair government. In January 1997 Brown began a series of speeches outlining proposals for his first Budget.

Whelan's brief was to generate stories to depict his boss as an 'iron Chancellor' who would be able to deliver on an unprecedented promise that Labour would not increase either the basic or the top rate of income tax for the full five years of a parliament. In order to throw the Conservatives off the scent, Whelan leaked to the political correspondent Paul Routledge the news that Labour intended to double its proposed windfall levy on the privatised utilities to at least £10 billion. Routledge's story made the front page splash in the *Independent on Sunday*. Next morning, after being briefed by Ed Balls, most of the national newspapers led with the news that a future Labour government would impose a two-year freeze on public pay. Whelan ensured an even bigger build-up to the shadow Chancellor's speech by priming the *Today* presenter Jim Naughtie to make sure that he asked about the top rate of tax when interviewing Brown that morning. As promised, the answer was delivered on cue: 'I will be making commitments for our manifesto . . . The basic rate and top rate will remain unchanged.'

Whelan was over the moon at his success in orchestrating advance publicity for the speech. 'It all worked like a dream . . . We flung out that £10 billion windfall tax to the *Independent on Sunday* just to confuse the Tories. Obviously I had to tip off Jim Naughtie.' Eliminating any suggestion of Labour's previous high-tax image remained Brown's priority and Whelan was authorised to take ever-greater risks on the shadow Chancellor's behalf. After a surprise announcement by the government that it intended to spend £60 million on building a replacement for the royal yacht *Britannia*, Whelan fed another exclusive to the *Independent on Sunday*, leaking to Routledge the decision that a future Labour government would not fund a new vessel out of public expenditure. A month later Whelan had no hesitation in leaking to Tom Baldwin, the *Sunday Telegraph's* political correspondent, news that in the hope of raising £500 million, the shadow Chancellor would be considering whether Labour should sell off the Tote, the state-owned betting organisation. On this occasion Brown and Whelan had overreached themselves because although the proposal was endorsed initially, it was then killed off by Robin Cook, who had overall responsibility for Labour policy.

Having planted, confirmed and then abandoned the suggestion within the space of thirty-six hours, it was left to the party's deputy leader, John Prescott, to explain away an embarrassing U-turn. He blamed Whelan and the rest of Labour's spin doctors for being overzealous in floating so many ideas. 'You get all these guys running round with their stories for the Sundays. That doesn't mean to say that makes it party policy.' Despite the annoyance of the party hierarchy, the debacle over the Tote had provided plenty of copy for the political journalists of Westminster and strengthened rather than weakened the value of the leaks being touted around on behalf of the shadow Chancellor. Whelan told me he had full authority to confirm that selling the Tote might become the first privatisation of a Labour government:

> I could just as easily have put it out in Gordon's name and said that Gordon himself was saying this, but I confirmed it as a 'senior Labour insider' and that meant Robin Cook could dismiss it as simply being the idea of an aide and not party policy. So it was a hit against me.

Whelan's ability to brief on the shadow Chancellor's behalf was reinforced the following week when he supplied selected correspondents with advance details of a speech in which Brown would announce that Labour was contemplating giving the Bank of England independence to set interest rates. Brown was delighted with the coverage and next day Whelan was busy congratulating himself on having leaked the story for the fourth time and still finding willing takers. However, in knocking down the story over the Tote, Cook had triggered considerable press speculation about a long-simmering feud between himself and Brown. According to the *Guardian*'s chief political correspondent, Ewen MacAskill, the ill feeling between the two men began in the late 1980s when Brown began rivalling Cook as a source of exclusive stories and appeared to have better access to unpublished government documents. MacAskill concluded that it was Brown's popularity with journalists and the fact that he was regarded by lobby correspondents as the 'King of Leaks' which had fuelled the acrimony between the two men.

As the election approached there was no doubt in my mind that Brown was the dominant figure when it came to dispensing the unauthorised disclosures and illicit data which had been acquired by the Labour Party and, as I discovered during my subsequent research and interviews for this book, while the Conservatives doubted the sincerity of the shadow Chancellor's public condemnation of any civil servant who might have had a hand in the leak of the November 1996 Budget, his denunciation of leakers did send a chill down the spine of one of my five anonymous contacts who had supplied documents and other confidential information to Labour MPs and trade unions. Until the moment Brown appeared on the radio reproaching leakers, my informant admitted never having thought about what might happen if Labour won the 1997 general election:

> It had always been my hope that some of my leaks might have helped one or two of the leading frontbenchers to establish their parliamentary reputations. I had seen how Cook and Brown had used leaked information to such devastating effect against the government but it hadn't really crossed my mind that one day they might become ministers and I suddenly got frightened thinking about what might happen if I was found out. When Brown came across on the radio that morning sounding so contemptuous of leakers, and especially of any civil servant involved, it made me think that perhaps those of us who had taken a great risk to assist the opposition in attacking the Tories might be left swinging in the wind once Labour got into government.

Chapter 4

Long before he became Prime Minister in November 1990, John Major had regularly made the point that he believed the whole of the public sector was far too secretive and was often withholding information unnecessarily in order to cover up incompetence or sub-standard performance. Once installed in Downing Street he began work on one of the main initiatives of his premiership, the Citizen's Charter, which he hoped would set higher standards for the public services. In his autobiography he explained why, if this idea was to succeed, it was so important to ensure the publication of reliable and up-to-date performance tables for schools, hospitals, transport services and so on, the very data which he believed Labour had often been misappropriating in the past and using to discredit Conservative govern-ments: 'I intended to open up the public sector to proper scrutiny and accountability.' Unfortunately Major's high hopes of ushering in a new era of open government foundered, like many of his aspirations, in the stormy waters which engulfed the final years of his premiership.

Major's plans for the Citizen's Charter formed part of the Conservatives' manifesto for the 1992 general election. Labour and the Liberal Democrats were determined not to be outdone and both parties repeated the promise they had made in 1987, that if elected they would introduce a Freedom of Information Act to open up the process of government. With all three parties promising reform, the outcome of the 1992 election looked like providing a turning point, an opportunity perhaps to start demolishing some of the restrictions which continued to deny the public right of access to information and which, over the years, had provided so much provocation and justification for a multitude of leakers and whistleblowers. Within weeks of returning to Downing Street after his election victory, he began implementing a series of measures designed to honour the Conservatives' manifesto commitment to deliver greater accountability. There was a considerable fanfare for his first significant announcement, a new presumption on the part of the state that information should always be released unless there were 'pressing public interest reasons for secrecy'.

However, as details started to emerge, it soon became evident that the scope of the Citizen's Charter fell far below the demands of those who were campaigning for a 'citizen's right to know' and it was obvious that Major's government, like previous administrations, would ultimately find it too risky and too difficult to relax Whitehall's tight grip on the deeply entrenched controls which governed the flow of information from the state to the public. For its part, Labour continued to pursue the twin track approach had served the party so well during Neil Kinnock's leadership. Support for the 'right to know' campaign was intensified, and once the Conservatives' post-election euphoria had been dissipated, the opposition front bench took every opportunity to demonstrate that through the adroit release of leaked documents and data it could undermine and even sabotage new initiatives being announced by the Prime Minister and Cabinet colleagues. In the face of the ruthlessness of Labour's media operation, the Conservatives' disarray over Europe and repeated allegations of Tory 'sleaze', it was perhaps wishful thinking to imagine that Major had even a sporting chance of introducing meaningful reforms to break down the culture of secrecy in Whitehall.

A significant first step had been taken in the final years of Margaret Thatcher's premiership. In June 1988 the government published its eagerly awaited White Paper setting out proposals to relax the law by repealing the infamous 'catch-all' Section 2 of the 1911 Official Secrets Act. Replacing Section 2 had been a Conservative commitment ever since being promised by Edward Heath in the party's manifesto for the 1970 general election, and the Home Secretary, Douglas Hurd, set about the task with enthusiasm. Throughout the 1980s pressure had been building up within the party to limit the risk of criminal prosecution for the unauthorised disclosure of official information and at last there seemed to be a chance to bring the secrecy laws up to date. Richard Shepherd, one of the Conservatives' leading libertarian MPs, became an indefatigable campaigner for reform. In January 1988 he attempted to revise the Official Secrets Act through a private member's Bill which would have replaced Section 2 with a 'narrower, better defined and better targeted' definition of those disclosures which could lead to prosecution; this would have been coupled with a public-interest defence for the improper release of information.

Despite being admonished by Thatcher and advised that revising the secrecy laws was not a job for a backbencher, his Bill attracted considerable support on second reading; it was defeated by only thirty-seven votes after the Tory whips took the unprecedented step of imposing a three-line whip against a private member's measure. Shepherd argued that the Franks committee had recognised in 1972 that criminal sanctions should only apply to clearly defined classes of information whose release would result in serious injury to the nation's interests. He thought the risk of prosecution for disclosing 'every piece of official information', whether harmful or not, had cast 'an appalling pall over our national life'. Without access to information no executive or minister could be held to account and Shepherd was 'outraged' by the prospect that civil servants would continue to be bound by a life-long duty of confidentiality which prevented them from revealing information which went to the very heart of the democratic process. In his reply to the debate Hurd sought to reassure MPs that after so many false starts the Home Office was about to complete yet another review of the Official Secrets Act; a White Paper setting out ways of reforming the 'oppressive' nature of Section 2 would be published within a matter of months.

Like previous administrations, the government recognised that it was 'wrong in principle' that the criminal law could in theory result in prose-cutions against civil servants who 'disclose the colour of the carpets in their offices or what was on the menu in the staff canteen'. However, the government had yet to decide which categories of information it would be unlawful to disclose. The opposition were also impatient for change: Roy Hattersley, the shadow Home Secretary, called instead for a Freedom of Information Act, which would require the publication of material which was not damaging to national security, a demand which had been attracting strong support on the Labour benches. Tony Benn urged that any future law should provide protection for civil servants such as Sarah Tisdall, Clive Ponting and Cathy Massiter who had been 'motivated by conscience to reveal what they thought should be in the public domain'. Benn's suggestion infuriated Michael Heseltine, who feared it would encourage a regime under which public servants would think it was 'reasonable and legitimate to leak, sometimes publicly and sometimes covertly'.

During the three years he was Secretary of State for Defence, Heseltine had been 'close to the events' which surrounded the Tisdall and Ponting prosecutions.

> If the views of Tony Benn ever gain sway, the standards of the British civil service, who I happen to think are world leaders, will be destroyed, because they will become politicised . . . I treasure the fact that a minister could say more or less whatever he liked to civil servants. He could even make a stupid mistake in front of them and they would remain confident to him and would not abuse that trust. The day that one feels that, every time one is indiscreet or one makes an error of judgement or is plain wrong, it will be in the public domain, that day we shall recruit people who are politically loyal to us and we shall not have the wider discussion on which the proper government of the country depends.

Hurd was determined to keep up the momentum and a fortnight after the private member's Bill had been defeated he told the *Analysis* programme that the government would honour its undertaking to lift the threat of prosecution from most civil servants. Routine information would cease to be included under the Official Secrets Act and civil servants who were found to have leaked sensitive material would, except in certain cases, be subject to disciplinary procedures rather than prosecution.

When the White Paper was published it specified six categories where the unauthorised disclosure of official information would remain a criminal offence: defence, international relations, security and intelligence, the interception of communications, inter-government communications and criminal investigations; in addition, members of the security and intelligence services would continue to face prosecution for disclosing any information without authority. By defining the areas where disclosure would be harmful to the public interest, the Home Office believed it would be easier to provide 'effective and fair protection' of that 'very small area' of information which it was in the nation's interest to keep secret. Many Conservative MPs welcomed what they were convinced was a much-needed liberalisation of the law, but it failed to satisfy either Hattersley or Shepherd. They both remained highly critical of the government's continued refusal to establish a public-interest defence for unauthorised disclosures. Without a balancing factor allowing a leak to be justified on the grounds that it was 'necessary for the public to know about something', Shepherd contended that the secrecy laws would remain repressive and illiberal. Experience in the United States, Canada and Australia had shown that it was unreasonable to 'bind up' civil servants so that they could never speak about the duties they had performed.

The White Paper acknowledged that there were some public servants who might make unauthorised disclosures for 'altruistic reasons and without desire for personal gain' but the government believed that proposition to be equally true of people who committed other criminal offences; the courts had to consider the criminality of what people did, not their ultimate motives. Therefore the aim of a new Act would be to concentrate the application of the criminal law on information which demonstrably required protection in the public interest; it could not be acceptable to 'lawfully disclose information' which might lead to loss of life simply because the person concerned believed there was 'a general reason of a public character' for doing so.

In assessing the White Paper for the *Guardian*, Clive Ponting predicted that Britain would remain the 'most ill-informed democracy in the world'. Ministers would still retain 'illiberal and sweeping powers' which would give them 'greater and more effective' sanctions to stem the flow of information from the state. Ponting feared that the sole objective was to bring in a law which was enforceable, and in his judgement he could still have been prosecuted under the revised Section 2 for the secret information which he divulged about the sinking of the *General Belgrano* during the Falklands War. What it meant for the future was that a civil servant who was caught leaking an embarrassing minute from the Prime Minister would be quietly sacked rather than prosecuted and would have no chance of defending his or her action in public. Ponting's concern about the lack of a structure through which civil servants could raise issues which ministers were 'concealing from Parliament' was shared by the Association of First Division Civil Servants. Its general secretary, John Ward, said he accepted that it was 'unprofessional to leak' and that civil servants who betrayed trust should be disciplined. But if the disciplinary code was to provide the means for dealing with most of the leaks which originated from within the civil service, the association felt there should be an 'outside avenue of appeal' because it was unreasonable to expect public servants to choose 'between keeping quiet or putting their jobs at risk'.

The government's determination to remain as vigilant as before in punishing leakers had been underlined by the Cabinet Secretary, Sir Robert Armstrong, four months before the White Paper was published. In order to remind civil servants of the duty they were under to 'keep the private confidences of citizens and others', Armstrong had strengthened the advice he had issued in 1985. His new memorandum was explicit about the penalties for leaking:

> Any such unauthorised disclosures, whether for political or personal motives, or for pecuniary gain, and quite apart from liability for prosecution under the Official Secrets Act, result in the civil servant concerned forfeiting the trust that is put in him or her as an employee and making him or her liable to disciplinary action.

Armstrong's memorandum, like the White Paper, rejected the concept of a public-interest defence and it was the lack of any recognition of a 'citizen's right to know' which was seized on by groups such as the National Union of Journalists and the Campaign for Freedom of Information (CFI). Des Wilson, co-chairman of the campaign, insisted in the *Times* that a public-interest defence would only apply where there was evidence of fraud, abuse or neglect of authority, or equivalent serious misconduct; he was confident it would not become 'a leaker's charter'.

When the government's Bill was published in November 1988, the Home Office had not budged on the fundamental principle that it would be ministers who would determine which unauthorised disclosures would harm the public interest. Douglas Hurd tried to reassure his critics by explaining that the Crown would have to argue that 'actual and serious harm' had been done and it would be for a jury to consider whether that test had been met; alternatively a defendant could argue that the disclosure had caused good and not harm. But the Home Secretary conceded that this apparent lifeline to leakers and whistleblowers would have its limitations:

> What a defendant could not argue is that his disclosure did cause this degree of harm but, because it also did some good, then the harm didn't matter . . . We see no reason why any person should be able knowingly to cause any of the forms of harm to the public interest which Parliament has decided are unacceptable and yet escape penalty.

Hurd's confirmation that it would still be impossible for anyone accused under a new Act to plead that on balance the public interest had been served was a disappointment to the *Independent*. 'An ounce of theoretical "likely harm" would, it seems, be enough to outweigh a tonne of actual public good. Yet there cannot be no-go areas in which the behaviour of public servants is beyond scrutiny.'

Right-to-know campaigners detected a hardening in the government's position and a sudden sense of urgency on the part of the Home Secretary, which no doubt reflected the anger of his Cabinet colleagues at the Labour Party's growing expertise in exploiting leaks from disenchanted civil servants in the wake of the government's humiliating defeat the previous month in the *Spycatcher* case. On the eve of the Bill's second reading in December 1988, Wilson declared that the CFI had to 'destroy the myth' that the new legislation was a liberalising measure. Cross-party support was marshalled and rallies were held around the country. Roy Hattersley accused ministers of accumulating even greater powers to prevent the public learning about corruption and maladministration. A blanket of secrecy was being perpetuated because if any information was classified by the government as relating to security, then anyone who repeated it, for whatever reason, would have committed a criminal offence.

Once the Bill entered its committee stage, a group of Conservative MPs led by Richard Shepherd launched a concerted attempt to protect whistleblowers. Their amendments were along the lines of those outlined by Wilson: a person accused of disclosing secret information could mount a defence on the grounds that he or she had 'reasonable cause to believe that it indicated the existence of crime, fraud, abuse of authority, neglect in the performance of official duty or other misconduct'; another justification for leaking would be disclosure where public safety was threatened. Unless a public-interest defence was built into the legislation, Hattersley claimed that a revised Act would remain authoritarian. He said Clive Ponting had been prosecuted for 'telling the truth', for correcting a deception that had been perpetrated by the government, yet he was acquitted in 1985 because the jury decided that it was in the public interest that the truth should be told. If the law was changed in the way that was proposed, it would be impossible for a jury to acquit him because the information which Ponting disclosed would have prejudiced 'the capability of . . . the armed forces of the Crown to carry out their tasks' and therefore he would have been found guilty. Eighteen Conservative MPs joined the opposition in voting in favour of a public-interest defence, and the unexpected imposition of a guillotine on the remaining stages provoked a second revolt, which was led by Edward Heath and attracted the support of fourteen Tory backbenchers.

The rebels' failure to amend the Bill in the House of Commons produced some dire but perceptive predictions from its detractors: Heath feared that Britain would remain the 'most secretive country in the world' and another of the dissenters, the Conservative MP John Gorst, was convinced that the 'draconian and obnoxious clarity' of the 1911 Official Secrets Act was being replaced with a regime of uncertainty which would suppress publication of much information which was previously entirely legitimate. Labour peers made a renewed but unsuccessful attempt in the House of Lords in March 1989 to persuade the government to provide a safety net for civil servants who exposed malpractice. The former Home Secretary, Lord Jenkins of Hillhead, proposed an even tighter definition of a public-interest defence: an official charged with making an unauthorised disclosure would have to prove that the leak revealed serious misconduct and that the benefit of revealing any scandal outweighed any harm done to national security. Once these challenges had been defeated and it received Royal Assent, the Home Office declared that the new Official Secrets Act would take effect in March 1990.

Steps were taken almost immediately to honour Hurd's repeated undertakings that repeal of the previous 'catch-all' Section 2 would lead to 'a considerable easement' in the secrecy laws: his successor as Home Secretary, David Waddington, announced that the number of employees who held office under the Crown, and who were subject to the legislation, would be reduced substantially. The secrecy laws would no longer apply to information emanating from organisations such as the National Health Service, the Post Office and British Telecom; only a 'comparatively small number' of concerns, such as the Civil Aviation Authority, the Atomic Energy Authority and British Nuclear Fuels would remain protected by the Act. But as the Parliamentary debates had shown, the removal of vast swathes of official data from the scope of the secrecy laws went nowhere near meeting the objectives of the CFI. Its monthly newspaper *Secrets* continued to deplore Margaret Thatcher's refusal to allow a public-interest defence for unauthorised disclosures affecting security, intelligence or defence. Even if a leak was regarded as the only way to prevent 'gross wrongdoing or impending public danger', that benefit to the public could never be taken into account, a position which the campaign considered intolerable.

Despite considerable publicity surrounding her government's action in narrowing the reach of the Official Secrets Act, Thatcher continued to be plagued by leaks during her final months in office. According to figures released in October 1989, breaches of confidentiality by civil servants which resulted in disciplinary action had averaged ten a year since she became Prime Minister. In January 1990, at the start of what turned out to be a catastrophic year for her, Labour's education spokesman, Jack Straw, published a leaked copy of a confidential minute which revealed that she was 'absolutely fizzing with fury and promising retribution against the banks' because of their decision to withdraw from the student loans scheme. In July Thatcher was so infuriated by a leak to the *Independent on Sunday*, disclosing details of a private seminar she had held at Chequers to discuss Britain's future relationship with a reunified Germany, that she ordered an inquiry in an attempt to discover who was responsible. A confidential memorandum written by her foreign affairs private secretary, Charles Powell, criticised the Germans for their 'aggressiveness, bullying, egotism . . . and a tendency to over-estimate their own strengths and capabilities'. Under the headline 'Find the No. 10 German mole', the *Daily Express* claimed that Scotland Yard had been asked to help detect the source of what Thatcher's press secretary, Bernard Ingham, told the Downing Street lobby was a 'totally unacceptable leak'. There was no shortage of advice: Thatcher was advised by the *Times*'s columnist Woodrow Wyatt to institute civil proceedings against the *Independent on Sunday* for breaching government copyright rather than try to mount a prosecution under the Official Secrets Act. If the case wasn't settled out of court, the newspaper could be forced under the process of discovery to reveal the source of the leak or justify why its silence was in the public interest. Either way Wyatt thought it would be difficult to establish that publishing a government document was not a serious breach of copyright. Other newspapers would be put on notice that they too could face similar actions and although it would be 'less glamorous' than a charge under the Official Secrets Act, breaching copyright would be 'more painful to the pocket'.

Thatcher's continuing irritation at the mischief being caused by leakers and whistleblowers paled into insignificance in November 1990 after the devastating resignation of the Leader of the House, Geoffrey Howe, and Michael Heseltine's bid for the leadership of the Conservative Party. John Major's subsequent victory in the second round of the contest, after Thatcher felt she was left with little option but to resign, heralded the start of what her successor hoped would be a new era of openness. As soon as he was installed in Downing Street, the new Prime Minister began work on his plans to 'force the pace' in driving up standards in the public services. At his first meeting with the Downing Street policy unit in January 1991, he asked for work to begin on the introduction of the Citizen's Charter, which he announced in a speech in March that year. An 'information revolution' would be at the heart of the charter and Major believed it would help deliver proper scrutiny and accountability in the public sector which had suffered for so many years through being 'too secretive'. Initially the reaction was positive. Both the CFI and a cross-party group of MPs tried to encourage Major; newspapers such as the *Guardian* and the *Independent* sounded upbeat and renewed their demand for better access to official information.

When the government finally published its White Paper on the Citizen's Charter in July 1991, it was obvious that Major had concluded this was a step too far. Francis Maude, financial secretary to the Treasury, defended the government's decision to retain control over the flow of information from the state. He said that establishing a public right of access would 'undermine the traditional concepts of ministerial responsibility under the Crown and accountability to Parliament'. Major's refusal to countenance fundamental reform of the secrecy laws triggered a new offensive at Westminster with the publication in November 1991 of a Freedom of Information Bill. It was sponsored by the three MPs who had become the CFI's co-chairmen – Archy Kirkwood (Liberal Democrat), Richard Shepherd (Conservative) and Chris Smith (Labour). The Bill proposed a general right of access to all official records held by public authorities and Kirkwood introduced it in the House of Commons in January 1992 after winning seventh place in the ballot for private member's Bills.

As its supporters had feared all along, the Bill was talked out by Conservative MPs and failed to get a second reading after the government argued that freedom of information was impractical and would conflict with the 'open government' provisions within the Citizen's Charter. Tim Renton, minister for the civil service, said Major's aim was to create the conditions for an informed democracy through the voluntary action of the state: 'Freedom of information is a good public relations term for a general right of access. It might provide a temporary relief for the inflamed political imaginations of those who are inclined to see evil behind all government confidentiality . . . but candour and self-criticism within government would be impaired.' Renton's claim that the Prime Minister and his colleagues were genuinely seeking to cultivate open government was derided by opposition MPs, who predicted that ministers' complacent and negative response would only serve to mobilise cross-party support and assist the efforts of the CFI to turn the excessive secrecy of the state into an election issue. Paddy Ashdown, leader of the Liberal Democrats, promised that in the event of a hung Parliament in the general election of April 1992, his party would use whatever power and influence it had to ensure that legislation was included in the first Queen's Speech.

Not to be outdone, Labour published proposals for a Right to Information Bill to establish a statutory right of access to official papers. When the election was declared both opposition parties made manifesto commitments to introduce a Freedom of Information Act. The Conservatives responded by giving pride of place in their manifesto to the Citizen's Charter, which the party claimed was the 'most far-reaching programme ever devised to improve the quality in public services'. Each of the eighteen individual charters gave 'new information and rights' to the public and the Conservatives promised that if they were re-elected the Charter would give 'even more information about standards and performance'. One specific pledge related to increased access to information about the impact of pollution on water supply, air quality and food safety. Because of the secrecy surrounding environmental protection, the CFI had argued that the public were being exposed to hidden dangers. Major was determined to find additional ways to break down Whitehall's reluctance to embrace open government and, to the surprise of the 'right to know' campaigners, the Tory manifesto promised a review of what were described as the eighty or so 'statutory restrictions' on the disclosure of information; only those needed to protect 'privacy and essential confidentiality' would be retained.

Wherever possible the government would provide greater access to personal files, such as tax records, an initiative hailed by the *Today* newspaper, which said the quicker Major lifted the veil of secrecy the better. While his victory in the general election inevitably set back hopes of achieving a Freedom of Information Act, the commitments which the Conservatives had given were regarded by the *UK Press Gazette* as having provided an important platform from which journalists and other campaigners could keep up pressure on the government to be less secretive. In a series of announcements that followed, the election ministers set about honouring their pledges. In May 1992, William Waldegrave, who had been given ministerial responsibility for the Citizen's Charter, declared that there would be a new presumption on the part of the state that information should be released unless there were 'compelling and substantive reasons of national interest to withhold it'. A review which Waldegrave had been carrying out had identified 150 statutory restrictions on disclosure of information, almost twice the estimate given in the party's manifesto, and wherever possible he promised to root out the 'use of secrecy for administrative convenience'.

In another initiative, the Secretary of State for Health, Virginia Bottomley, announced that her department would be issuing new guidance aimed at 'preventing the gagging of whistle blowing staff' who publicly voiced their doubts about developments taking place within the NHS. She said she recognised the understandable fears of health care professionals who wanted to express genuine concern about health reforms. In future managers would be expected to provide a channel for complaints to 'reach the highest levels', and confidentiality clauses in new contracts of employment would need to respect the rights of staff. Both developments failed to satisfy the opposition and two Labour MPs introduced private member's Bills in a renewed attempt to force the pace. Mark Fisher presented a Right to Know Bill, which was intended to ensure access to all official records, and his colleague Derek Fatchett published a National Health Service (Freedom of Speech) Bill, which would protect staff who blew the whistle on malpractice and ensure they had 'freedom of speech on patient care and fraud'. Fisher's Bill, like some of its predecessors, had strong cross-party backing and despite its making considerable progress and reaching the committee stage, the government withheld its support, arguing that a public right to know would conflict with the greater openness promised in the Conservatives' manifesto.

When a White Paper on open government was eventually published in October 1993, it proposed a statutory right of access to information in a limited number of areas affecting the environment, health and safety and personal records. Waldegrave acknowledged its limitations but said that a balance had to be struck between the government's aim of giving information in specific cases and the demand for a general right of access. Where it was thought appropriate, departments would supply information contained in the files and although the actual documents themselves would not be released, there would be a code of practice to guide civil servants; any appeals would be considered by the parliamentary ombudsman, who could rule on whether the data which had been given was 'laundered or otherwise inadequate'. Having been conditioned by the draconian standards of official secrecy during the Thatcher administration, Labour had been rather caught off guard by Major's determination to champion the cause of open government, but the restricted nature of his code of practice gave fresh impetus to the attempts by backbench MPs to support the far-reaching changes being proposed by freedom-of-information campaigners.

Tony Blair's election as party leader in 1994, following the death of John Smith, pushed the demand for a legal right to information higher up the political agenda. New Labour promised support for a comprehensive programme of constitutional reform and in a speech in March 1996 at the annual awards organised by the CFI, Blair declared that disclosure was in the public interest and that a right to know was 'absolutely fundamental' to the way his party would seek to govern. There was still 'far too much addiction to secrecy' and a wish to conduct government business behind closed doors.

> We want to end the obsessive and unnecessary secrecy which surrounds government activity . . . It will signal a new relationship between government and the people . . . which sees the public as legitimate stakeholders in running the country. A Freedom of Information Act is not just important in itself. It is part of bringing our politics up to date, of letting politics catch up with the aspirations of people.

Going hand in hand with Blair's undertaking that Labour would be far bolder than Major's code on openness was the same ruthless and unspoken determination as in previous years to exploit every possible leak that might discredit the Conservatives.

Labour's ability to claim the high ground, by promising to open up the flow of data from the state, while the shadow Cabinet was simultaneously showing total disregard for the confidentiality of official documents, was highlighted in December 1996 by the publication of the European Policy Forum (EPF)'s third review of leaks by civil servants. It identified eighty significant illicit disclosures during the previous twelve months, twice as many as in its 1995 survey, and the forum believed the volume of leaks reflected the 'proximity of the general election'. Its president, the Conservative MEP Graham Mather, was convinced that most of the leaks were from civil servants who were 'politically hostile' and seeking to 'awaken public hostility' to the government's proposals. He noted that the 'mother and father of leaks' in 1996 had been the *Daily Mirror*'s coup in obtaining the Budget press releases, followed a week later by disclosures from a confidential document on Budget cuts in the road programme which, according to the *Evening Standard*, 'fell into the hands of the shadow Chancellor Gordon Brown'. Mather believed that one of the most worrying leaks related to the Conservatives' latest plans for curbing public sector strikes; a draft of the Green Paper had been obtained by the TUC, which had then released it to the Press Association. He had detected a shift away from the usual practice of passing information anonymously direct to journalists that indicated leakers had become more sophisticated. 'They have realised that they will obtain more exposure if they pass them to opposition politicians or to trade unions. These agencies make better use of the material by adding expressions of outrage'.

Political objections to Conservative policy were seen as the most likely motive for half the leaks surveyed by the forum and, although reluctant to admit it, the Cabinet Secretary, Sir Robin Butler, was forced to concede that the closeness of the general election was having a marked influence. His pre-election advice to ministers on the need to avoid asking civil servants to do work which could threaten their political impartiality was leaked to the *Independent on Sunday* and, when questioned subsequently by a House of Lords select committee, he acknowledged that politics was playing a part. Many of the most recent leaks were designed to 'sabotage' new policies and there was no other apparent motive than a desire to embarrass the government and assist the opposition. While Labour were 'very often the recipients of such leaks', Butler said that did not necessarily mean the party had requested or encouraged them but he could not hide his frustration; at one point he remarked, 'I wish the opposition would condemn them.'

When questioned by the Commons Public Services Committee, Butler reflected on the 'uphill task' which his officials faced in trying to track down leakers. Since 1980 there had been a total of 430 unofficial disclosures, averaging twenty-five a year over seventeen years, and the Cabinet Secretary blamed the increased frequency of leaks on the 'arrival of the photocopier'. Butler's appearance before the two parliamentary committees had been given an added edge because of the publicity which the forum was attracting for its survey tracking the number of leaks from each Whitehall department and also because of Mather's assertion that their estimate of eighty leaks during 1996, compared with the thirty-four admitted by the government, showed that the civil servants' code of conduct on the need to observe the confidentiality of official documents was being 'widely ignored'. Labour's election victory in May 1997 had the impact on leaking which Mather suspected. Initially the number of unauthorised disclosures fell away dramatically and although this slowly increased, the forum's fourth survey showed there had been only twenty leaks during Blair's first eight months in office, well down on the rate during on the final year of Major's government.

Mather detected another significant shift, namely that the purpose of the leaks seemed to have changed: instead seeking to inflict political damage on Conservative ministers, the aim appeared to be one of trying to influence policy decisions. Another surprise was that the new Labour ministers seemed far more upset about minor leaks than their predecessors. Blair had been annoyed by unauthorised revelations about his family's living arrangements in No. 10; the Chancellor, Gordon Brown, was said by aides to have expressed his irritation about the leaking of his brother's job application to the Scottish Office; and the Cabinet Office minister, Dr David Clark, complained when it was revealed he had flown first class rather than as a business passenger as the civil service advised. Mo Mowlam, the Secretary of State for Northern Ireland, was the first member of the Cabinet to voice her concerns publicly after a series of damaging disclosures in October 1997. She told the *Guardian* she feared the leaks were damaging her relationship with her civil servants. 'You get wary. The leaks unnerve you, because you get to a point when you say "this machine and I are working together, we are chugging along" – and then there is another leak.'

By chance, some years later, I discovered that the EPF's annual surveys of leaks had angered Butler. He finally lost his patience and asked for them to cease. Mather described his somewhat frosty meeting with the Cabinet Secretary:

> He accused me of grossly exaggerating the number of leaks and said I was besmirching the whole of the civil service. I was also interviewed by the Cabinet Office's security adviser. He was especially interested in our list of possible sources. He said that even when a leaker was detected it was very difficult to do anything about it, because the civil service unions got involved very quickly and brought in their lawyers. Often all the security staff could do was tell leakers that their card was marked, that the Cabinet Office knew what they had done and that they had no future in the civil service.

Mather thought that instead of just keeping quiet, the government should have led by example; some well-publicised dismissals and even prosecutions would have had a deterrent effect. On the other hand, he felt the civil service was at fault for not having done more to help whistleblowers and for failing to support the demand for a legal right to information. Senior civil servants could hardly continue to resist 'meaningful freedom of information' while their colleagues persisted in abusing their position by leaking information to further their political views and embarrass ministers.

Mather might just as easily have levelled the same charge of double standards against the shadow Cabinet but amid all the allegations of 'sleaze' which dogged the final months of Major's government, Blair was out in front setting the agenda; his promise to bring in a Freedom of Information Act was one of the many pledges contained in Labour's 1997 manifesto. Within eight months of winning power, the new government published its White Paper *Your Right to Know*, which Dr David Clark, the new minister for the Cabinet

Office, said marked a 'watershed' in the relationship between state and people because at last there was an administration which trusted the public with a 'legal right to know'. The aim was to bring about 'more open government' and Clark believed ministers had struck a 'proper balance between extending people's access to official information and preserving confidentiality where disclosure would be against the public interest'.

Maurice Frankel gave a guarded welcome on behalf of the CFI. Notwithstanding the exemptions for national security, defence, international relations and the law enforcement functions of the police, he considered the government had adopted a 'surprisingly radical approach' and he hoped it would pave the way for an 'outstanding' piece of legislation which would give the British public a right to know which was stronger than in many overseas laws. Frankel said he could not help but observe that on a day when Clark should have been receiving the acclaim of MPs he was having to apologise to the Speaker, Betty Boothroyd, for the premature leaking of his own proposals to the BBC.

Heady euphoria surrounding the launch of the White Paper slowly dissipated as the campaigners began to realise Blair's government had only taken a tentative step towards honouring a pledge which had been made in every Labour Party manifesto since 1974; supporters of the right to know did not know it then, but few measures would take as long to reach the statute book and start functioning as the Freedom of Information Act. Set-backs came thick and fast: first the consultation process took far longer than expected and then, because of a disagreement among ministers, the legislation failed to find a place in the 1998 Queen's Speech.

Frankel was appalled by the 'backsliding'; the *Guardian*'s columnist Hugo Young deplored the 'rearguard action' by 'the revisionists, the anti-freedom faction' which was ranged against Clark and which was led by the Home Secretary, Jack Straw. Clark was sacked in the July 1998 Cabinet reshuffle; Straw took on the responsibility for drafting the legislation; and it was not until the following February that the Home Office announced that the Bill would be ready in May 1999. When the legislation was published Straw told MPs the government had faced a 'difficult balancing act' but the public would still get a 'general and robust' right of access. Freedom-of-information campaigners were deeply disappointed and detected a 'major retreat' from the White Paper; Labour's much-promised right to know had been so watered down it had ended up being weaker that the openness code introduced by the Conservatives in 1994. Frankel was at a loss to understand how deeply, once in office, Labour ministers had absorbed the culture of secrecy they purported to be demolishing. 'What can have blinded conscientious ministers to the abysmal nature of these proposals?'

In the face of sustained cross-party criticism Straw made a series of concessions: he strengthened the role of the new independent information commissioner and lifted the blanket ban on access to investigations into fatal accidents such as rail and ferry disasters. After so many false starts the Bill gained a place in the Queen's Speech, secured its second reading in December 1999, and began its long and tortuous path through the two Houses of Parliament. The worst news was yet to come: during many months of debate and several rebellions along the way, no mention was made of when the right to know would be in place. The Bill stipulated that all its provisions 'must come into force within five years' but the assumption was that although it might have to be implemented in stages, it would take immediate effect. Instead of clarity there was uncertainty and it was not until June 2001, seven months after Royal Assent, that the Lord Chancellor, Lord Irvine, who had taken over responsibility for the legislation, was forced to concede in the House of Lords that there was still no timetable other than the 'outer date' for implementation of November 2005.

Another battle was underway in the Cabinet: Irvine favoured adopting the advice of Elizabeth France, the first information commissioner, who wanted the public's right to know phased in over three years, starting with Whitehall in the summer of 2002 and applying to public authorities such as local councils, health trusts, schools, universities and other services at six-monthly intervals until the end of 2004. To the disbelief of the CFI, Irvine's advice was ignored and the government imposed a four-year delay; the right of access would not take effect until January 2005. Frankel condemned ministers for obstructing implementation of the new law. Political commentators and opposition MPs pointed an accusing finger at Tony Blair and reminded him of the opening sentence of the 1997 White Paper: 'Unnecessary secrecy in government leads to arrogance in governance and defective decision-making.' Irvine struggled to defend a five-year wait from Royal Assent: 'We collectively concluded that it would create an unsatisfactory state of affairs where rights existed in relation to one organisation and not another . . . Our collective judgement was that a single right-of-access day across all public authorities would be better understood by the public.'

Fellow peers commiserated with the Lord Chancellor's misfortune in having been overruled by the Prime Minister but they were forced to accept his argument that the January 2005 start date would give all public authorities enough time to make the necessary changes in 'procedure and culture'. France decided she was not prepared to wait so long and announced she was standing down. Her sense of frustration was shared by the parliamentary ombudsman, Sir Michael Buckley, whose most recent ruling on the release of information by the Home Office had been ignored, the first time one of his findings had not been complied with since John Major introduced the code on open government. Buckley feared that the flouting of the ombudsman's advice reflected the 'harder line' which government departments were taking over requests for disclosure. In July 2003, his successor, Dr Ann Abraham, reported facing similar obstruction: unless the government dropped its policy of non-compliance and Downing Street ceased its 'political interference' in the work of the parliamentary ombudsman, she let it be known she would withdraw from monitoring the code and might even resign.

In the hope of resolving the conflict, the new Lord Chancellor, Lord Falconer, promised Abraham he would apply strict deadlines for the release of information. Falconer had assumed responsibility for the mammoth task of ensuring that 70,000 separate public bodies prepared publication schemes which met the approval of the new information commissioner, Richard Thomas. Growing impatience on the part of those who had spent more than twenty years demanding a right of access kept resurfacing and campaigners continued to express disquiet about the thirty-one exemptions from disclosure. Documentation relating to the preparation of government policy was one area excluded from access; the research organisation Democratic Audit feared this would allow Blair's 'cadre of political advisers' free rein to continue leaking information without fear of the full facts being made available. Professor Stuart Weir, the Audit's director, told me that the secrecy laws had always been used by the state to control the flow of information and it was through leaks and tip-offs that Blair's government had become so adept at spinning its policies. Therefore the tighter the 'firewall' remained around official information the easier it would be for special advisers and government information officers to pursue a 'hard-sell strategy' in an attempt to influence public opinion.

Wider concern about the continuing ability of ministers and their aides to manipulate the media through the partial disclosure of official information was voiced in January 2004 in the report of the Independent Review of Government Communications. It said full disclosure would be a 'disincentive to spin' and the review group recommended that ministers should voluntarily forgo the veto they retained to overrule the information commissioner and stop disclosure. Thomas added his support, warning that if ministers deployed the veto he would ensure their action was scrutinised in Parliament, but Falconer was in no mood to accept last-minute changes to the regime which had taken so long to introduce. By the autumn of 2004, with only weeks to go, there was a flurry of action: town halls were reminded they had to be ready by January; journalists up and down the country were urged by their editors to get know how to use the Act; and the CFI feared that a new code of practice introduced by Falconer might allow authorities to ignore the guidance that information should normally be supplied within twenty working days.

A series of leaks to the *Daily Telegraph* in November provided an unexpected twist to the final build-up to the start date: 'Records being shredded before Information Act' was the headline over an exclusive report that anonymous government officials had revealed that vast numbers of files were being destroyed to frustrate applications for access. According to another report in the *Times*, the 2,000 civil servants under the control of the Cabinet Office had been ordered to delete all e-mails which were more than three months old; any e-mails which had been printed and filed would be subject to disclosure. Within a matter of days the Conservatives were demanding an inquiry after parliamentary answers obtained by their spokesman, Dr Julian Lewis, revealed there had been a huge acceleration in shredding: most departments had doubled the normal rate at which they disposed of files and the Department of Work and Pensions had destroyed nearly 37,000 files during the preceding twelve months, well over twice the usual number. Lewis feared the frantic activity within Whitehall could deprive academics and historians of potentially vital information: 'It looks like there has been a bonfire of historical records.'

Maurice Frankel accepted that government offices and public authorities had been forced to get their records management into shape but the campaign feared that the wrong emphasis had been given and that there had been a temptation on the part of officials to destroy documents so as to avoid disclosure. Although Thomas told *The World at One* that he was not aware of 'wholesale destruction deliberately' to avoid the legislation, he insisted he would use his authority as commissioner to intervene if he found that was the case, and as from the beginning of 2005 it would become a criminal offence to destroy information where a valid request had been made. Thomas was more alarmed by the report that e-mails were being deleted and he reminded government departments that the guidance under the Act was that they should be retained unless they served 'no current purpose'. In the face of predictions by newspapers such as the *Observer* that 'chaos' loomed because Whitehall departments feared they would be 'swamped' with requests for information, Falconer spent the final days of the year giving a series of interviews to reassure the public that the 'long transition period' had given officials full opportunity to prepare for a 'giant step forward' in honouring the government's commitment to 'transparency and openness'.

At the latest count 100,000 public bodies ranging from government departments to doctors' practices would find there was 'no hiding place'; organisations which failed to meet requests within twenty working days would find that the information commissioner would not accept excuses such as lack of time or poor records management. Falconer told the *Today* programme that any proposal by a minister to veto the release of documents would have to be approved by the Cabinet; Parliament would have to be informed; and the decision would be subject to judicial review. However, when asked whether the government would release the Attorney General's conclusions on the legality of the Iraq war, the Lord Chancellor said no organisation was being required to release legal advice; there had to be space to allow conversations to take place when collective decisions were being made. Falconer's send-off for the Act had a sting in the tail for journalists: he revealed in an article for the *Guardian* that answers given by the government to requests for information which was considered of general interest would be published simultaneously on departmental websites. He knew that members of the news media had argued that their freedom-of-information enquiries should be kept secret for their own use rather than be made available for general release. Falconer, tongue in cheek no doubt, found it hard to fathom the journalists' argument:

> Surely media organisations, for so long campaigners for open government and for freedom of information, cannot be suggesting their own commercial interests are of greater importance to them than the public's right to know? They cannot be suggesting that the stories their commercial rivals would not otherwise have are more important to them than openness and transparency?

Thomas had agreed with the government that the public should have same rights as reporters and be able to see the information on which newspapers based their stories. The prospect of having to share scoops with its rivals upset the *Guardian*, which warned in an editorial that newspapers would be reluctant to mount labour-intensive investigations if the fruits of their investigations were released at the same time to every other journalist. 'This is not a wish to keep information "secret for journalists". No editor would object to all the documents being placed in the public domain immediately after publication . . . This sly little announcement reeks of Lord Falconer having been nobbled by a Sir Humphrey. He should think again.'

Determined not to be outdone by the Lord Chancellor, the *Guardian* led the pack by publishing its first story based on a freedom-of-information request on Monday 3 January 2005. It obtained briefing papers from the Department for Culture, Media and Sport which showed that during the passage of the Communications Bill through Parliament, representatives of Rupert Murdoch's media empire had lobbied ministers on six occasions about the possible purchase of Channel Five. In order to pre-empt media requests, the Ministry of Defence was among the departments which took the initiative and immediately began publishing files on its website. 'Whitehall's secret plan to let the IRA hunger strikers die' was the main headline in the *Times* over a page of reports based on documents released from the archives. Before the month was out the Department of Constitutional Affairs gave the answer which journalists had been waiting for: forty separate requests for disclosure of the Attorney General's advice on the legality of the invasion of Iraq had all been rejected on the grounds that it was exempt because of 'legal professional privilege' and the public interest in 'protecting the confidentiality of communications between lawyers and their clients'.

With the approach of the May 2005 general election, the Freedom of Information Act was on the point of facing its first political test: surprise disclosure was about to become a weapon in the propaganda battle which was hotting up between Labour and the Conservatives. 'Cover-up row over £27 billion secret of Black Wednesday' was the front page headline over an exclusive report by Philip Webster, political editor of the *Times*. He quoted anonymous 'senior Treasury officials' as having told him that highly sensitive papers which should have been released that week were 'being kept secret' at the request of the former Prime Minister, John Major, and the former Conservative Chancellor, Lord Lamont. Major was furious that a leak to the *Times*, which had been so steadfast in support of the Labour Party, was being used to make false accusations against himself and Lamont when they had both made it clear they had no objection to the publication of the papers, which dealt with Britain's withdrawal from the European exchange rate mechanism in September 1992.

Sir Andrew Turnbull, the Cabinet Secretary, was equally forthright in denying that he had intervened to block the release of the documents. His involvement had been entirely proper: 'As Cabinet Secretary I have oversight of the propriety rules on access to papers from a previous administration. Both Major and Lamont asked for time to review the papers. This was entirely reasonable and was agreed without hesitation by Treasury officials in consultation with me.' When interviewed on *Today*, Major claimed he was the victim of a dirty tricks operation which had been orchestrated by Alastair Campbell, who had been recalled by Tony Blair after his resignation in 2003 in order to help with Labour's election campaign. The former Prime Minister accused his successor of presiding over the 'worst period of political chicanery I can remember at any time in my political life'. In a further unexpected twist to the story, when the documents were finally released to the *Financial Times* the following week, unflattering comments about Major, and a remark to the effect that he was engaged in 'open warfare' with Lamont, were e-mailed to the BBC's newsroom by mistake. None of the personal excerpts were due to have been released and they had been blanked out in the version being published officially; the Treasury was forced to apologise for what it said had been a 'genuine error'.

Turnbull's explanation, and the Treasury's apology, failed to satisfy the Conservatives. Oliver Letwin, the shadow Chancellor, complained about the way their requests for information about sensitive episodes during Labour's eight years in office were constantly being rejected, yet the Cabinet Secretary could decide independently whether to release information about events before Labour won power. All the cards were stacked in the government's favour and the rules for disclosure should apply in the same way to past and present administrations. 'This is supposed to be a Freedom of Information Act, not a Freedom of Propaganda Act.' Major suggested the government should consider a moratorium on the release of information during the run-up to polling day. Although his request was turned down, Falconer issued a new protocol for the publication of papers relating to previous administrations; former Conservative ministers would in future be given five days to review the papers.

Nevertheless in order to outflank Labour and demonstrate that he had nothing to hide, the Conservative leader, Michael Howard, asked the Home

Office permanent secretary, Sir John Gieve, to authorise the publication of documents relating to high profile incidents during his time as Home Secretary, including his handling of prison break-outs and his much-publicised disagreement with the former head of the Prison Service, Derek Lewis. After all the dire predictions about the inability of 100,000 public bodies to process a flood of enquiries, the figures for the first six months showed that over eighty per cent of requests were being met within the twenty-day limit. The biggest logjam was in the office of the information commissioner, Richard Thomas, whose staff were struggling to cope with complaints about non-disclosure. In September 2005 the *Times* revealed there were 1,200 unresolved cases; three quarters of the appeals lodged since of the start of the year had not been settled. By the end of the year decisions were still awaited in half the cases before the commissioner.

Delays of six months or more were considered unacceptable by the CFI, but its director, Maurice Frankel, told the *Independent* that the 'good news' was that Britain had a functioning system which was producing a substantial amount of previously undisclosed information, most of which had been released without charge. In his end-of-year report in the *Guardian*, Falconer hailed what he believed had been a real change: 'The culture of secrecy in Whitehall, and beyond, is cracking open.' From central government alone 16,000 pieces of information had been released in the first nine months and the 'deluge of detail coming into the public domain' allowed the citizen to hold the public servant more fully to account. Although there were no official figures, one estimate put the total number of requests at 130,000, of which 36,000 were directed to Whitehall departments. When giving his own round-up, Falconer could not resist taking another swipe at journalists: the government was reviewing procedures to ensure that the central purpose of the right to know was being honoured. 'Freedom of information is about giving power to the people, not about declaring open season for the wilder fevers of journalistic wish-lists.'

Frivolous inquiries, such as how many windows a department had, were 'clogging up the time of some of Britain's most senior civil servants' and the Lord Chancellor's Department was not going to allow the right of access to be discredited by 'being turned into a vehicle for news ideas dreamt up at news desks' morning conferences'. He could hardly have been surprised at the fury he provoked: 'Falconer accused of "sinister" Freedom of Information curbs' was the *Mail on Sunday*'s headline over its report that civil liberties campaigners had been 'enraged' by the government's threat to clamp down on 'trivial requests'. To set the record straight, the *Mail on Sunday* claimed it had gained access to secret Whitehall papers which secured unknown details about the death of the Princess of Wales in a car crash in Paris in 1997; another successful inquiry which Falconer would no doubt have considered 'irresponsible' was the request by the Liberal Democrat MP Norman Lamb which forced the release of the list of guests entertained by Tony and Cherie Blair at Chequers, the Prime Minister's official country residence.

Other newspapers adopted a similarly lofty tone: the *Independent's* tally of successful requests also included the Chequers guest list; among the paper's 'failures' was the refusal of the Cabinet Office to release information either about the resignation of Alastair Campbell in 2003 or the precise nature of his new role in the government, which began at the start of December 2005. Falconer acknowledged that there was a backlog in appeals against the refusal to release information but he thought that was hardly surprising in the first year; and he believed that the information commissioner and the Information Tribunal were determining the limits of a legally enforceable process. Sometimes they agreed with the government, sometimes not; but the boundaries would be set case by case. One decision hailed as a victory by campaigners was the tribunal's finding in December 2005 that the public had the right to see e-mails which civil servants had deleted; the ruling stipulated that e-mails and papers which had been erased but were still stored on back-up systems were still subject to the right of access. The *Times* reported that thousands of people who had previously been told by the government and the information commissioner that such material was exempt from disclosure were being urged to resubmit their requests.

Securing legal protection for whistleblowers was an objective which over the years had gained as much cross-party parliamentary support as the long-standing demand for a law on freedom of information. Richard Shepherd, the Conservative MP who had campaigned so valiantly to stop such workers being victimised or sacked, found to his great surprise and satisfaction that newly elected Labour ministers were far more receptive to the possibility of legislation than in previous administrations. Unlike many of the measures proposed by MPs, his Public Interest Disclosure Bill won the backing of the government and went through both Houses of Parliament, receiving Royal Assent in July 1998. Shepherd benefited from what he said at the time was 'an unprecedented consensus' between the CBI and the TUC to ensure that whistleblowers who lost their jobs for exposing serious malpractice obtained full compensation. His Bill protected employees from being penalised or dismissed for disclosing information which they reasonably believed exposed financial irregularities, miscarriages of justice, dangers in health and safety, abuse in care, breaches of the civil service code, risks to the environment and cover-ups.

The strength of the government's commitment to support workers sacked in such circumstances was reinforced shortly before the new law took effect in July 1999, when whistleblowers were exempted from the limits on compensation for people who had been unfairly dismissed. Stephen Byers, Secretary of State for Trade and Industry, decided that employees who had the courage to expose corruption, life-threatening practices and other abuses deserved more protection than the rest of the staff, for they were the brave people who had put their entire careers at risk by speaking out. Such was the impact of the legislation that within less than a year the charity Public Concern at Work, which had helped Shepherd prepare his Bill, was able to point to a 'significant increase' in the number of frauds which had been uncovered in government departments through whistleblowing by civil servants. Guy Dehn, the charity's director, thought that if whistleblowers were already responsible for stopping two out of every three bogus payments being identified by the Treasury, then the rest of the public sector should move just as swiftly to set up proper channels to give workers the confidence to expose malpractice without fear of recrimination.

In its first in-depth review of the compensation payments received by employees who had been sacked or victimised, Public Concern at Work found that by 2003, tribunal awards to whistleblowers who had lost their jobs were averaging more than £100,000 per case. Dehn believed the size of the pay-outs showed that employers who ignored the safeguards which had been established did so at their peril. 'It's no longer whistleblowers who are paying a heavy price, but those who victimise them. These cases show how much we need whistleblowers if we are to turn the tables on crime, complacency and cover-up in the workplace.' However, most claims were still being settled privately by employers and the TUC was more concerned to ensure there was a system which prevented whistleblowers being sacked in the first place. In the five years since the legislation took effect, 1,500 workers had lost their jobs for raising health and safety issues with their employers and the TUC's general secretary, Brendan Barber, believed the situation was far worse than the official statistics suggested. Casual and migrant workers who were forced to choose between risking their jobs or their personal safety stood little chance of redress if they blew the whistle on hazardous working practices.

If employees were unable to disclose their concerns to prescribed regulators such as the Health and Safety Executive, they were advised to ring a helpline which Public Concern at Work established in 1993 and which by 2002 was receiving over well over 500 calls a year. Like the Freedom of Information Act, the Public Interest Disclosure Act did change attitudes and what Dehn found so encouraging was that their statistics showed that workers were twice as likely to disclose wrongdoing in the work place as they had been a decade earlier, when most whistleblowers were branded as 'traitors'. Despite the best efforts of both legislators and campaigners to bring some order to the unauthorised flow of information, they have been powerless in the face of human carelessness and incompetence; as events have shown, some sources of illicit data could not have been regulated against even by an Act of Parliament. Some of the leaks which have aroused the greatest interest in the news media have been the result of nothing more than forgetfulness. During the last few decades secret files, private correspondence and a great variety of other confidential documents have had a nasty habit of turning up in the most unlikely places. If the papers were handed over to journalists rather than returned to the authorities, the consequences have often turned out to be highly unpredictable.

In recent years absent-minded civil servants have usually suffered no more than a reprimand for losing official documents but in 1982 an employee of the government's Central Office of Information suffered a double humiliation. Robin Gordon Walker, son of the former Labour Cabinet minister Patrick Gordon Walker, left a bundle of documents on a London Underground train and when the papers ended up at the offices of the weekly magazine *City Limits* instead of the lost property office, the outcome was nastier than he expected. His misfortune, according to Michael Cockerell, Peter Hennessy and David Walker in their book *Sources Close to the Prime Minister*, was to have fallen foul of Margaret Thatcher's determination to bear down on leakers, with the result that he felt the full force of the Official Secrets Act. The documents revealed Foreign Office attitudes towards the Israeli invasion of Lebanon. On the advice of the Attorney General, Sir Michael Havers, Gordon Walker was charged with the careless handling of official documents and fined £500 at Bow Street magistrates' court. The point of using the Official Secrets Act was to 'frighten and deter' and with Whitehall suitably cowed, Thatcher hoped 'a new security consciousness was abroad'.

Experience proved otherwise: as the photocopiers of Whitehall churned out more and more copies of the same document, the likelihood of official papers going astray seemed to increase pro rata and so did the levels of carelessness. Twenty years later the threat of terrorism required unprecedented levels of security but even they could not cope with an absent-minded police protection officer. 'Security shambles' was the front page headline in December 2004 for the *Daily Mirror*'s exclusive account of how a secret file found in the street in London had revealed Scotland Yard's plans to protect the Pakistani President, Pervez Musharraf. Only hours before the President and his wife were due to arrive at Heathrow Airport from Washington, a seventeen-page document marked 'confidential' was seen lying on the pavement in Curzon Street, Mayfair, outside Marco Pierre White's Mirabelle restaurant. A delivery driver spotted the A3-sized brown envelope and passed it to the *Daily Mirror*, which claimed that if the file had got into the hands of Al-Qaeda it could have been a 'death warrant' for Musharraf, who was the 'world's no. 3 terrorism target'. The file was returned to the Metropolitan Police and in reproducing parts of the document the paper blanked out all the key details such as travel arrangements and the items which would have identified the plain-clothes protection officers, who were carrying firearms.

Even the introduction of the supposedly paperless world of the computer failed to provide the answer, since ministers and civil servants found they were never more than a click away from an embarrassing disclosure. A leak to the *Sunday Times* in December 2003 which disclosed the reasons for thirty-eight of the awards in the New Year's honours was traced to a civil servant's computer error. An e-mail intended for eight officials was sent by mistake to eighty people. As the *Financial Times* pointed out at the time, civil service mandarins and ministers yearned for a return to the days of 'paper documents and carbon copies', when leaks were so much rarer. The electronic revolution meant that whether by accident or design the risk of leaks had hugely increased. Laptop computers also had a habit of getting mislaid or stolen. When six disappeared from the Cabinet Office in July 2003, the *Daily Mail* claimed that it had sparked off a 'security crisis at the heart of government'.

Sensitive information found on discarded computers was another source of news: the *Sunday Times* carried the headline 'Top secret SAS records put up for auction on eBay' over a report of an inquiry by the Ministry of Defence into how minutes of an SAS meeting marked 'top secret' had been mislaid. Recycling discarded confidential information became a money-spinner. Purveyors of illicitly gained data inhabit a subterranean world in which thousands of pounds can change hands when tabloid newspapers buy up hitherto unknown details about the private lives of celebrities, politicians and other public figures. To lawyers, music promoters and public relations consultants the name Benjamin Pell used to spell one thing: trouble. 'Benji the Binman' earned himself the kind of notoriety that put professionals on their guard. During the 1990s he exploited with great cunning a weak link in commercial life – the habitual carelessness of office workers and their bosses, who gaily set off for home having left their waste paper bins full of private correspondence and other potentially valuable or incriminating documentation. Rubbish bags left outside business premises rarely get a second glance from most passers-by; seeing them being collected and loaded into a van was hardly likely to arouse suspicion.

Pell preyed on the naivety of most executives and their secretaries. Once confidential letters or documents had been finalised and retyped, the drafts got thrown away. Who could be bothered to shred every bit of waste paper chucked into the bin? Who could have imagined there was someone out there rummaging through other people's rubbish on a systematic and targeted basis? When I interviewed Pell in 2002 he told me that at the height of his business as a trader in other people's secrets, he was earning around £25,000 a year. He abandoned the practice of rummaging through bins after being fined £20 for theft. The long list of those whose lives were disrupted by Pell's disclosures about their business dealings or private affairs reads like the 'Who's Who of Showbiz': Sir Elton John, Sir Richard Branson, the former BBC director general Lord Birt, the All Saints singer Nicole Appleton and Robbie Williams. Mohamed al-Fayed, the owner of Harrods, and two disgraced politicians, Jonathan Aitken and Neil Hamilton, were among the other victims of the conduit which Pell had established for the onward transmission of illicitly gained information. Nonetheless 'Benji the Binman' insisted he was a man of principle:

> Of course, it is a method of obtaining stories that involves sifting through refuse sacks that can be dirty and unpleasant . . . I cannot expect solicitors and judges to approve of what I did, but there is a difference between morality and legality. I have always behaved impeccably when using the information I acquired. Being a journalist involves activity that many people would consider to be invasions of privacy and breaches of confidence. Newspapers are not interested in information of which the public is already aware. That would not be news. I would consider myself to have been an extremely industrious investigative journalist who rattled a few cages but acted at all

times in the best traditions of journalism . . . I should also point out that all the information I acquired was passed on to journalists.

His nocturnal adventures began in a small way and initially his snooping through other people's rubbish was simply a way of trying to identify new clients for his office cleaning business. By searching through chartered surveyors' waste paper, he found highly confidential paperwork which provided the basis for tip-offs which were of interest to rival surveyors and estate agents. In the hope of getting a good price, he went to inordinate lengths to ensure his clients were ahead of the game. Pop music had always been one of his great obsessions, and he hero-worshipped Elton John, which led on to looking at the rubbish left outside the star's agency, John Reid Enterprises. Pell was about to get sucked into an unscrupulous underworld which feeds the constant craving of the tabloids for bizarre and sensational revelations; the turning point in his career was in October 1997, two months after the death of the Princess of Wales, when he discovered correspondence which included a letter from Sir Richard Branson asking permission to reproduce the version of *Candle in the Wind* which John had sung at the princess's funeral in Westminster Abbey. Reid Enterprises refused the request on the grounds that John had received enough publicity and did not want to make money out of his tribute to Diana. After failing to interest the *Sun*, Pell contacted the public relations consultant Max Clifford, who suggested the *Daily Mirror* might buy the correspondence for £10,000.

In the event he received £2,000 for the correspondence. His story filled the first five pages of the paper and Pell told me that he became hooked: 'You cannot imagine how I felt on reading the paper that morning. It was a remarkable feeling. There were the fruits of my endeavours, filling five pages of the *Daily Mirror*. It was my first story in a national paper and my biggest.' Pell's reaction seemed so similar to the sense of empowerment experienced by the anonymous serial leakers whom I had met and interviewed: purveyors of illicitly gained information found that the ability to influence the news media could become highly addictive.

Chapter 5

Labour's expertise in exploiting illicitly acquired data in order to damage successive Conservative governments was matched during the late 1980s by the development of equally sophisticated techniques within the party leadership for deliberately leaking confidential information about their own policy initiatives and intentions. Labour's long years in opposition coincided with a rapid expansion in the output of newspapers, television and radio. One consequence of this heightened competition among news outlets was a significant change in the balance of power between journalists and those who sought to manipulate the flow of information from a vast array of public, private and commercial sources. So great was the demand for fresh material that there were plenty of opportunities to develop the practice of leaking in a purposeful, controlled and co-ordinated way. Trading confidential data with trusted journalists and broadcasters became one of the principal means through which hidden influence could be exercised by spin doctors, public relations consultants, information officers and an assortment of anonymous individuals.

Under Neil Kinnock's leadership, and with the help of his new director of communications, Peter Mandelson, Labour began to take advantage of these competitive pressures within journalism as it refashioned its relationship with the media. Sympathetic contacts in advertising and public relations advised the party on how best to exploit the information which it had at its disposal. During the course of my own career I experienced at first hand many of the advances which took place in the development of press and broadcasting, a transformation which would facilitate the growing deployment of these manipulative techniques. When I left school in the summer of 1959 new opportunities were opening up across the media landscape. There was no longer any limit on the size of newspapers following the ending of wartime restrictions and an easing of shortages in the supply of newsprint. On the back of a steady growth in advertising, the employment of journalists had increased and once they had been hired they found they had more and more editorial space at their disposal.

My first job was on the trade paper *Advertisers' Weekly*. As an editorial assistant, one of my tasks was to compile a page giving details of the new campaigns being undertaken by advertising agents and PR consultants. Public relations had nothing like the profile it has today and seemed at the time to be mainly concerned with the promotion of new products and services. Government information offices were well established but corporate public relations, and especially the public affairs departments which now promote all manner of services and undertakings, were still in their infancy. Nevertheless the whole industry was expanding at a rate of knots and I recall writing frequent reports about the new PR accounts being signed up by the big London agencies and consultancies; of American companies establishing bases in Britain; and of new PR firms opening up offices in the provinces. This expansion reflected the rapidly changing dynamics within the news media. As the economy improved and the number and size of newspapers and magazines increased, so did the appetite for the good things in life. Instead of just hard news, there was much more editorial space for lighter stories and features about entertainment, fashion, foreign travel, expensive foods and so on. Job prospects at the time were good and after eighteen months as an editorial assistant I joined a local evening newspaper, becoming an indentured apprentice on the *News* in Portsmouth in early 1961.

Regular supplements and special editions reflected the continued growth in local advertising; weekly newspapers in Hampshire and West Sussex in the towns neighbouring Portsmouth were enjoying a similar upturn in editorial space and sales. Broadcasting was expanding with equal vigour, not just nationally but also in the regions; commercial television was so popular it had already become what was later to be described as a 'licence to print money'. Journalists had so much editorial space to play with, and broadcasters had so much airtime to fill, that we became eager to develop new sources of information; big business was just as anxious to take advantage of new opportunities to promote its goods and services. Throughout the 1960s the pace quickened: the task of extracting information from commercial and public organisations became more organised because enquiries from journalists were increasingly being directed towards press departments, public relations officers or publicity consultants; many government services and local authorities followed suit. Within our community of local reporters we all knew of journalists who were leaving the profession and were being hired as press officers.

Public relations had become a growth industry: newsrooms and district offices began receiving many more press releases and, as the competition for attention intensified, news conferences became far more commonplace, not just in London but also in the provinces. Thinking back to my days as a local newspaper reporter, then as a parliamentary correspondent on the *Times* in the late 1960s and finally joining the BBC in 1972, starting as a news producer at BBC Radio Leicester, I personally always felt fairly comfortable about my relationship with press and information officers. I understood their role as a conduit for communication between the news media and those public and commercial undertakings from which I and my colleagues needed information and access. However, once I joined the BBC's team of labour and industrial correspondents in the late 1970s, I came face to face with covert attempts to shape the coverage of industrial news and especially to influence the way stoppages and disputes were reported. Increasingly the strikes of that era were being played out in the news media as much as on the picket line and it was my insight, in seeing how the trade unions were outmanoeuvred by government and managements, which prompted me to write my first book, *Strikes and the Media.*

What so fascinated me when conducting my research for this book was discovering that it was not only political and industrial correspondents like myself but also financial journalists who had been among the first to be subjected to the manipulative techniques which have become the hallmark of the modern public relations industry. By the late 1980s, after the privatisation of many of the nationalised industries and the massive share flotations of the Thatcher era, financial news was regularly commanding far more space and airtime than industrial coverage. The sale at knockdown prices of shares in privatised utilities such as gas, electricity, water and telecoms had resulted in a phenomenal increase in the level of personal share ownership. Instead of just reporting the latest share prices from the Stock Exchange, television channels and radio stations developed separate news sequences and programmes devoted entirely to business news and to the latest developments in the City of London. Company takeovers and mergers had become front-page news. Most newspapers expanded their financial coverage to reflect both the rise in share ownership and a growing interest in personal finance, which in turn was generating extensive press advertising for the launch and promotion of new financial products.

What was emerging was an ideal market place in which to trade information: journalists had empty columns to fill and they were desperate to obtain the kind of insights and tip-offs which they knew would interest their readers. By taking advantage of sharp fluctuations in share prices, companies could transform their size and value during the course of mergers and takeovers and it was perhaps little wonder that astute public relations practitioners began to perfect ways to influence financial journalists in the hope that their news coverage might have an impact on trading in the Stock Exchange. Once I began interviewing some of the leading figures of that era I was struck immediately by the extremely close links between financial journalists and those upon whom they relied for information. A high proportion of public relations consultants had themselves previously been employed on the business and City pages of the national press, either as reporters or columnists, and they had an intimate knowledge of the working practices of their former colleagues. Of all the factors which were responsible for pushing financial journalists towards the open arms of PR advisers with clients in the City of London, perhaps the key phenomenon was the growing prevalence of hostile takeovers.

The company being targeted and the group which constituted the raiding party were in a fight to the death and the outcome almost always depended on whether it was prey or predator which had succeeded in exerting the greatest influence over movement in their respective share prices. With so much money at stake, shareholders and investors turned increasingly to the City pages of their newspapers for insights and advice; the race was on to capture the best headlines and secure the most favourable reaction in the comment columns. Brian Basham, himself a former business journalist, was one of the hidden persuaders in the key takeover battles of the 1980s. After leaving the City diary of the *Times* he spent a couple of years as a fund manager before moving into PR when he joined John Addey Associates in 1973. Addey, an ex-barrister, was considered by many seasoned business journalists to have been the inventor of modern financial public relations and was credited in his obituary in the *Times* as having been 'an adroit practitioner of the "hunches and lunches" school of PR'. Basham went on to form Broad Street Associates in 1976 and it became a leading consultancy, advising on a string of daring, hostile bids.

Because he had personal experience of the changing nature of financial journalism on the *Times*, and before that on the *Daily Telegraph* and the *Daily Mail*, Basham told me that he knew instantly how to exploit the opportunities which were opening up for the public relations industry.

> Gone were the days which I had enjoyed on the *Times* when as long as you came back with a decent story every couple of months, it was possible to go off for several days at a time and dig around for something interesting. Because newspapers were cutting costs, there was a fundamental change in the way that journalists operated. Reporters were finding themselves overworked and that was why they became increasingly dependent on the information which they could only obtain from PR advisers. What every newspaper wanted to achieve was the largest possible circulation at the lowest possible cost and because exclusives tended to push up sales, the journalists were under constant pressure to get stories which differentiated their papers from their competitors. But at the same time they were having to cut costs and as a result reporters did become less discriminating; they were forced to rely more and more on the information which we could provide.

Pressures which Basham identified in the 1970s had become ever more intense by the mid-1980s because of a revolution in production techniques and the defeat of the printing industry's trade unions. Eddie Shah's unprecedented confrontation in 1983 with the National Graphical Association over the introduction of labour-saving technology at his Warrington newspaper printing plant paved the way for a mass exodus from Fleet Street. Rupert Murdoch's audacious move to a new printing plant at Wapping in 1986 was followed in turn by the departure of other major groups and within a few years the camaraderie of Fleet Street, for so long the home of press reporters, was dissipated. Instead of working cheek by jowl, the journalists ended up in editorial offices spread across central London. Not only were they working in relative isolation from their compatriots on other newspapers, but they also found their freedom to leave the office had been curtailed even further by the insatiable demands of the cost-saving computerised techniques which heralded greater editorial flexibility but which were necessitating extra news and feature pages to be filled under ever-tighter deadlines.

Instead of going out to meet their contacts and gossip with fellow reporters, editorial staff had to spend much more time on the telephone collecting information and increasingly they found themselves tied to their computer screens. Yet again it was the public relations industry which became an unexpected beneficiary of a technological upheaval which it had been promised would widen the horizons of editors and journalists. George Pitcher, a former industrial editor of the *Observer*, witnessed the demise of Fleet Street at first hand and described in his book *The Death of Spin* how the dispersal of financial journalists made the staff of the City and business news desks more vulnerable to vested interests:

> Fleet Street émigrés . . . removed geographically from where the action was and demoralised by mismanagement and rationalisation . . . were like a scattered herd of wildebeest – and the lions and lionesses, jackals and jackalesses of the public relations industry recognised that. In their new technological palaces, the newly remote journalists were grateful for visits from outsiders with information.

Pitcher identified another unforeseen consequence of the revolution in newspaper production. Initially journalists found 'screen-based wizardry' exciting but new technicians, expert in page make-up, began replacing the traditional sub-editors who had previously acted as copy tasters and had checked what the journalists had written. In removing a layer of editorial management, the quality of journalism suffered. Young and inexperienced reporters got more stories into their newspapers 'unchecked than they could before the Fleet Street diaspora . . . and that made the British press far more susceptible to the spin culture of such vested interests'. Pitcher, who left the *Observer* in 1991 to co-found the public relations consultancy Luther Pendragon, believed it was media proprietors rather than journalists who should shoulder much of the blame for falling standards. Once the newspapers began publishing separate sections containing business and financial news, it was obvious the reporters were 'never going to find enough from their own resources' to fill the available space. Pitcher's assessment was shared by Basham, who had put his journalistic expertise to immediate use.

One of his first tasks when he became a public relations advocate for clients in the City of London was to identify what he considered were the 'space barons', the feature and diary editors, who controlled significant amounts of editorial space and who were under the greatest pressure to deliver exclusive stories.

> Yes, my job did become easier, not because individual journalists were corrupt, but because they were desperate. Instead of checking five sources, they began to contact only two. Their editors were determined to push up circulation with scoops yet at the

same time the journalists had even more columns to fill. That was how a space baron emerged, an editorial executive who was in a panic and had blank pages to fill.

In Basham's experience, the financial journalists who were often in the direst straits were those employed by the business sections of Sunday newspapers.

We didn't have to push for this, they would come to us. They would plead with us to leave an announcement until the weekend when they promised they would give it a good show in Sunday's paper. After an offer like that we would go back to the client and sometimes a company would change its timetable or even what it intended to say; that reflected the influence which the journalists could exercise. What we could get in return from the reporters was control over the way the story might be presented and especially control against the wilful distortion of our message. Admittedly some reporters hadn't been as well trained as their colleagues and we had to make sure the journalists didn't get it wrong. But by giving it to them the day before, and by making them an insider, we made sure they got it right. We had to proceed carefully. We might have been up against people in the City of London who were from the other side and who might have had an axe to grind or perhaps a journalist who owned shares and who might have taken a contrary view.

Basham worked particularly closely with Sunday paper journalists during protracted takeover battles such as the bitter struggle in 1986 between Arthur Guinness and Argyll for control of the drinks group Distillers.

I was advising Jimmy Gulliver of the Argyll group and I remember telling him that if he chose a Thursday to put out an announcement it might get picked up in the press in an unpredictable way but if we held it back until a Saturday, we would get a page to ourselves in one of the leading Sunday papers. Gulliver was delighted with this advice. He realised he had a better chance of getting a full exposition of his case if he gave it to one of the Sundays. We wouldn't seek to mislead anyone and obviously there are two sides to any story but naturally the side which initiated it got a heavier weighting in their direction. So yes, as a result of the editorial pressure on journalists to deliver exclusives, there was a trade off for us.

Inevitably in exchange for the advance information which had turned the reporter into an 'insider', there was an expectation on the part of Basham and his fellow PR consultants that they would, as he explained, retain 'control' over the way the story appeared in print. Patrick Weever, who spent almost two decades as a financial correspondent, including a lengthy stint on the *Sunday Telegraph*, described to me the force of the obligation which was placed upon the journalist who had been offered and had accepted exclusive information in advance of an official announcement, a practice which became known in the PR trade as the 'Friday night drop'.

> Think of it this way: you are a City journalist on the business section of a Sunday paper. It is 9.30 p.m. on Friday night and there is no worthwhile story around. Then a PR man comes in and says, 'I've got something for you.' He hands you a document, you look at it and your eyes pop out. He has just shown you details of a bid worth hundreds of millions of pounds that is due to be announced on Monday morning. The journalist asks only one question: 'Will this be going anywhere else?' The PR man replies, 'No, it's just for you.' Do you expect that journalist when he dons his commentator's hat on Saturday morning to write a column for Sunday's paper saying why this bid is bad for Britain? If you think that, you don't live on the same planet, the extent of the favour is too great. Imagine how hard it is too put the boot in. You've been given information about a multi-million-pound bid in breach of Stock Exchange rules and the principles of insider dealing. It's asking more than a human being can deliver to write an objective assessment.

After leaving the *Sunday Telegraph* in 1999, Weever started to campaign against a culture which he believed had enabled financial public relations consultants to manipulate the media and in 2003 he founded the website anti-spin.com. He had wide experience of business reporting, having worked on the *Daily Mail*, the *Birmingham Post* and the City desk of the London *Evening Standard* before joining the *Sunday Telegraph*. In his opinion it was a hostile bid by Tube Investments for British Aluminium in 1959 which probably began the era of unwelcome takeovers and which provided a launch pad for some astute public relations consultants who realised that by orchestrating one or two well-placed stories, there was a chance they could swing the outcome of a bid.

> These PR guys were all former journalists themselves and their friends were mostly journalists and media people. The difference was they were the ones who could dish out the stories. People outside the media don't understand the sheer pressure on journalists to get exclusives. It's all about maintaining the editor's approval. The PR guys understood that pressure and they realised they had the power to choose which journalist got the story. So in reality they had an iron grip.

When it came to granting access and interviews to journalists, Weever said it was the PR advisers who became the gate keepers for company chairmen and chief executives:

'When business journalists were required to write a profile of a City high flyer, they soon realised they couldn't put in anything too hostile because the PR gatekeepers might not let them in next time. They had the last word on which journalists went in and out. Initially many of the captains of industry didn't understand how the press could be controlled in this way. Admittedly, by the 1970s, it did lead to a breakthrough because, with the help of the PR guys, journalists found their calls got through and they managed to start talking directly to chairmen and chief executives. What had changed was this understanding within the City of London of the pivotal role which the press could play in the outcome of hostile bids, but the journalists knew the access they had achieved could just as easily be withdrawn.

Weever's description of the systematic way in which the public relations industry developed ever-tighter control over the distribution of financial information was mirrored by Brian Basham's account of the incremental changes which the consultants managed to introduce. As the number of highly publicised hostile takeovers increased, news conferences held by one or other of the protagonists often became difficult to control. There was always a danger that an unhelpful story line might emerge which obliterated the message which it had been intended to convey.

Basham said the problem with such headline-grabbing occasions was that they regularly attracted journalists who might be abusive or who showed off by asking provocative questions.

Our aim was always to exercise as much control as we could over the message, while maintaining our integrity, so in the end I just banned press conferences for our clients. I knew that the really good journalists, such as those from the *Financial Times* or the BBC, didn't like them anyway. They had almost always thought through their questions in advance; they didn't want to reveal to their colleagues what they were interested in; so they would just sit there and then afterwards they would huddle round in a corner and through me put the most important questions direct to the chairman or chief executive. Once I introduced that concept of control into financial PR, by banning press conferences, no one else held them and then they became redundant anyway because of the break-up of Fleet Street. With the journalists ending up having been spread across London, from the *Daily Mail* in Kensington High Street over to the *Daily Telegraph* in Canary Wharf, they found press conferences difficult to get to.

Basham's expertise in developing new techniques for influencing the press coverage of mergers and takeovers helped his consultancy, Broad Street Associates, attract considerable new business.

When companies were in difficulty they needed the best possible advice. John Coyle, another former journalist turned PR adviser, sought Basham's help in 1979 when the Myson Group, of which he was public affairs director, required urgent financial restructuring following a slump in sales of its heating, ventilating and air conditioning equipment. The management feared a collapse in its share price once the news got out that Barclays Bank were taking 30 per cent of the equity in return for £23 million.

> Bob Myson called me in and told me about their appalling trading conditions. He wanted to know how I thought I could explain to the media that Barclays Bank were taking a stake in the company. I consulted Brian immediately. I wanted advice on how to get across the positive side rather than see the share price decimated. Brian was keen to give the story to a Sunday paper, before the announcement the following Monday. I wasn't keen, nor were my directors. They didn't want to go to London either to answer journalists' questions but again, at Brian's suggestion, rather than hold a press conference, I went round to speak personally to the leading City columnists such as Lex and Questor. I presented it as a triumph rather than a defeat that Barclays were getting 30 per cent of the equity. Because of informed comment, the share price didn't move at all, although we'd expected it to drop. So Brian's tactic of going individually to journalists, rather than holding a press conference, had worked. It was being able to give advice like that, and knowing when and how brief Sunday papers in advance, which explained why in his heyday Brian was the best in the business.

In fact Coyle was so impressed with the advice the Myson Group had been given that he and Basham began to work together and in 1981 he became managing director of Broad Street Associates. Coyle recalled that in the 1960s, when he was a financial journalist on the *Sunday Telegraph*, the only effective way to obtain information was via banking and broking sources, or sometimes through investment houses, and at that time there was 'none of the hands-on financial PR' which developed in later years.

What was the norm in the 1960s was for the financial PR consultant to sit outside the boardroom and wait for the directors to make a decision. Only then would a statement be issued. Most of the press releases that went out were pretty turgid and there was nobody around to answer questions.

Coyle made his switch from print to PR when he went to work for Stanley Gale, a former deputy City editor of the *Daily Express* and the *Evening Standard*, who had established Shareholder Relations.

We were more proactive than previous PR consultants because we didn't just disseminate announcements and company results but tried to market the information to the relevant newspapers. Originally leaking sensitive information in advance was not on our agenda. Often we weren't told anything at all until the last minute. One day I remember getting a call from Jimmy Goldsmith at 10 a.m. and he told me that later that day he was bidding for Bovril. I then made sure I had the press release ready on my desk, ready to go.

When Coyle joined Broad Street Associates in 1981 the practice of trading exclusive information with the Sunday papers was well entrenched, especially during hostile bids. He believed the 'Friday night drop' was a justified tactic.

In my view leaking information to the Sunday papers was ultimately to the benefit of the shareholders. If there was suddenly a bald announcement about a takeover, shareholders would wonder what was happening. But if there was a logic behind a bid or a merger and if the story was written in the right way by a grateful journalist, thankful for the exclusive, then the City of London would be forewarned and when the announcement was made on Monday morning, the stock market would take it in its stride. Shareholders and investors would have seen the story, they would be prepared for something to happen and no one would lose out. To my mind that is the justification for selective leaking: it is the shareholders who gain because their shares are protected.

Coyle acknowledged that during the 1980s, when he was regularly supplying financial information to selected journalists, a close relationship tended to develop between leaker and recipient. After giving one tip-off about a bid to the *Sunday Telegraph*, the journalist suggested, half as a joke, that Coyle might like to write the story himself.

He said to me, 'You know our style.' He was right, I could just as easily have written the story myself. Indeed some of my colleagues got pretty close to doing that. We all made a habit on Saturday evenings, once the first editions had been printed, of going round as many Sunday newspaper offices as we could. We'd have a drink with the City team to make sure our message had got across. If the story wasn't being written up the way we wanted, we would try to get it changed for later editions. I knew financial PR consultants who have actually been found on the printing room floor, subbing proofs of the first editions. We'd then be able to tell clients that the story was being changed, that we had the press under control. In that way we could justify our high fees. They were paying for that power.

Coyle found that handling public relations for a hostile bid was so hectic it was rather like running a marathon. During the sixty days between offer and closure, Broad Street Associates charged £10,000 a week minimum, rising for example to £40,000 a week in 1986 when defending the glass makers Pilkington against a bid by the industrial conglomerate BTR.

Companies would hire Broad Street Associates just to keep us on side because press coverage and comment were so important. The clients could not ignore us, nor could the journalists. Typically, in the course of my work, I would leak information about new share issues, perhaps a change in management or the direction of a company. I would only brief one reporter at a time and that paper always knew it was an exclusive. I still thought of myself as a hack, not a PR man, and that was an important mindset when dealing with journalists. They thrive on scoops and would give a story greater prominence, which obviously helped us prepare the market. They'd go out of their way to be nice to us, to cultivate us, because they were sometimes in a state of terror about not getting our stories. Obviously in return for a real exclusive, I could say to a journalist, 'Now you owe us one.' So yes, we could pull in favours and a story that was not very strong would get a good show.

Coyle considered the *Sunday Times* and the *Sunday Telegraph* easily the most influential in helping to ensure that trading went as smoothly as possible once the stock market opened for business at the start of a new week.

Those two papers had the most powerful weekend readerships in the City of London. Our targets were the traders and investors we wanted to reach before shares could be bought or sold again on Monday morning. Journalists on newspapers like the *Financial Times* got very brassed off about missing out on so many exclusives. We went to lunch with their team in 1986 and I remember they told us they wanted the same sort of inside information.

Coyle's recollection about the irritation felt at the *Financial Times* was reinforced by Brian Basham, who recalled being taken to lunch by one of the paper's senior executives.

> When he complained to me about his journalists being excluded, I explained that the Sundays were desperate. I named one Sunday journalist, who I knew, who called a list of twenty-five senior people every Thursday to see if any announcements were coming. Instead of expecting the *Financial Times* to be spoon fed, I suggested he should ask each of his journalists when they'd last taken the trouble to call me up.

The ability of Sunday newspapers to deliver a captive audience strengthened the hand of their journalists. David May, who worked on the *Sunday Times* business pages in the late 1970s and early 1980s, told me it was not surprising that close relationships developed with financial PR consultants:

> They we well aware we had a big city readership, influential people all at home over the weekend, looking at the Sunday papers. They also knew that with the right information a Sunday journalist could write a brilliant story, which did a lot more work for a city client than a report in a daily paper.

May, who went on to become head of strategic communications at the BBC, said in his experience the Friday night drop usually took the form of a tip-off or a chat over a quiet drink rather than the actual delivery of a document. 'The general consensus in financial PR was: Why bother with a press release when a well-timed telephone call can get the story out much more effectively? Ring the *Sunday Times* with a tip-off and it ends up as a front page story.' However, there was one daily newspaper which Brian Basham believed it was vital to brief in advance: the *Evening Standard*. When there were controversial takeovers and mergers the City desks tended to look at the *Standard* to see how the story was developing, especially when the correspondents came back from lunch and wanted to get themselves up to date before writing their own reports.

As it was so important to have as much influence as possible over the way in which such stories were being covered, Basham said he offered to alert the *Standard*'s business desk the day before an important announcement.

I agreed to brief them after 4 p.m. once the stock market had closed so as to avoid any hint of insider trading and on condition that no calls were made to any other organisation. This meant that by 7 or 8 a.m. next morning the City desk could have the story done and dusted ready for the first edition. The *Standard* tended to set the agenda for the national papers the following morning so it was vital their City desk got the story right. At the time I was running the biggest PR company in the City and once I started briefing the *Standard* at 4 p.m. it became common practice.

Not every attempt to manipulate the media had the desired effect: one story planted by Broad Street Associates which did not go entirely to plan involved the opening stages of the highly acrimonious takeover battle for Distillers. News that Jimmy Gulliver of Argyll intended to launch a hostile bid was given exclusively to the *Sunday Telegraph* and Coyle said 'all hell broke loose' once the story appeared.

> Exhortations were made immediately by Distillers to the Takeover Panel and Argyll were told to put up or shut up, either to put in a bid or be forced to wait for three months. Jimmy Gulliver couldn't go ahead straight away and that gave Ernest Saunders at Guinness time to digest its takeover of the whisky firm Arthur Bell and come back with a counter-offer for Distillers. I think that was a leak which went wrong because the premature publicity did not help Gulliver and Argyll failed to acquire Distillers.

Although the Guinness bid ultimately succeeded, the struggle for control of Distillers ended disastrously for Saunders because his conduct prompted an investigation by the Department of Trade and Industry (DTI), resulting in him and two others involved in the takeover receiving prison sentences for a number of offences. Coyle said the drawn-out fight to the finish between Gulliver and Saunders became a feeding frenzy for the news media, not least because of determined attempts to leak damaging information. In order to answer the claim and counter-claim, rival news conferences were regularly held by the two sides, often within half an hour of each other and in adjoining rooms.

> On one occasion, when reporters were going from room to room, I saw a PR consultant from the other side give brown paper envelopes to two journalists. That afternoon I had a call from one of the reporters, who was from the *Sunday Times*, asking if I was aware that Gulliver's entry in *Who's Who* was incorrect. Apparently he

had not graduated at Harvard but had just been there for a three-week marketing course. When I notified Argyll's management they were distraught and thought Gulliver would have to go. A resignation letter was prepared. I was told that journalists at the *Sunday Times* were dancing around with delight. I didn't want Gulliver forced out, so at 10 p.m. that Saturday evening I leaked to the *Observer* the news that a resignation letter had been written. I thought that was the only way to get the management to think again. There was a tremendous row that Sunday at the merchant bank. I denied all knowledge of the leak but then I succeeded in persuading Argyll's management to stand firm and insist that one inaccurate entry in *Who's Who* should not deter them from bidding for Distillers and attempting to restore confidence in the Scottish whisky industry. I am proud of that leak. It did the trick at that precise moment.

What I had found so illuminating about my interviews with seasoned financial journalists and public relations consultants was the more I discovered about the techniques which had been fine tuned during the takeover battles of the 1970s and 1980s, the more I realised these were the very same practices which had been applied with increasing vigour in an attempt to influence industrial and political journalists. I needed no reminding of how often as a broadcaster I had been upstaged during the strikes and stoppages of the Thatcher years by the careful placing of exclusive stories with anti-trade union newspapers such as the *Sun* and the *Sunday Times*. Nor was I surprised to hear from the inside how public relations consultants identified and selected journalists who were to be given the access and interviews which would be denied to their colleagues. Nonetheless I was intrigued by the intricacies of the trade in leaked information, especially by the development of the Friday night drop and the reasons why it proved so attractive and so addictive to both leaker and recipient; and why, instead of providing equal access for all journalists, financial PR consultants began to avoid holding news conferences in all but exceptional circumstances.

Much has already been written in an attempt to expose the hidden machinations which took place within the City of London and the stock market during controversial takeovers and I acknowledge that the insights I had been given by Basham and Coyle about their role in promoting Gulliver and his bid for Distillers were simply a couple of snapshots from countless such covert manoeuvres. Also working behind the scenes during that epic struggle was Tim Bell, another high profile public relations consultant. He had a close and enduring relationship with the Conservative Party, having given advice and assistance during successive general election campaigns; he was knighted by Margaret Thatcher in 1990 and eight years later made a life peer. In 1986, during the battle for Distillers, he was chief executive of the advertising agency Lowe Howard-Spink, which had been hired by Saunders the year before to promote the earlier bid by Guinness for the whisky firm Arthur Bell. In the wake of the subsequent investigation by the DTI into the takeover of Distillers, Tim Bell insisted that he had been responsible for advertising during that bid and had not given advice on public relations.

However, in *The Ultimate Spin Doctor*, an unauthorised biography written by Mark Hollingsworth, Bell was credited with having had a much more influential role. Several of the key figures who were involved in promoting the Guinness takeover praised the strategic PR advice given by Bell; Saunders was quoted by Hollingsworth as saying that what he valued most of all was Bell's guidance on presentation and communications and his 'real involvement when things became rough'. Saunders's assessment mirrored that of Sir Ian MacGregor, chairman of the National Coal Board (NCB), who relied heavily on Bell's advice during the 1984–5 miners' strike. It was in the summer of 1985, within a few months of the ending of the pit dispute and a resumption of coal production, that Guinness turned to Lowe Howard-Spink and asked the agency to prepare its takeover advertising. Bell, who had done so much to marshal media support for Thatcher, was ready to play his part in yet another of the memorable business confrontations of her premiership.

In his autobiography, *The Enemies Within*, MacGregor said he was attracted to Bell because of his realisation that ultimately the NCB's confrontation with the National Union of Mineworkers (NUM) and its president, Arthur Scargill, would have to be fought out not only on the picket line but also through the news media, and that would require an 'offensive in PR terms too'. He was convinced that the dispute could not be handled simply through 'cosy chats' with industrial correspondents, which he realised had been the traditional response of the NCB's public relations department. 'This had all the makings of a gloves-off job and I wanted a man who could handle the rough and tumble.' Bell, who at that time was chairman and managing director of the advertising agency Saatchi and Saatchi, was appointed MacGregor's personal adviser on public relations and advertising in May 1984, two months after the start of the strike. By July of that year, when serious negotiations had begun with the NUM, the management felt ready to launch a £1 million advertising campaign to explain its case and MacGregor said that it was at this point that Bell 'came into his own'.

Later in the strike, working in co-operation with the property developer David Hart, a political adviser to Thatcher and subsequently to Michael Portillo, Bell helped to devise a strategy aimed at encouraging a return to work, an initiative that would be fronted by the National Working Miners' Committee. As was only to be expected, in the light of the many media contacts he had established during his work for the Conservatives in the 1979 and 1983 election campaigns, Bell's great strength was that he could provide a direct link with the editors and executives of those newspapers which were urging the Prime Minister to stand firm and defeat Scargill. Once the dispute developed into an all-out confrontation between the mine workers and the state, many of the labour and industrial correspondents such as myself found it increasingly difficult to obtain inside information about the initiatives being taken behind the scenes by the management and the government. Because we were regarded as being too close to the NUM and the rest of the trade union movement, we were effectively being bypassed by MacGregor's advisers and also by ministers such as the Secretary of State for Energy, Peter Walker, who preferred to give personal, off-the-record briefings to selected political correspondents and other sympathetic journalists. These two alternative news management operations, orchestrated by Bell and Walker, were deeply resented by the NCB's much-respected director of public relations, Geoffrey Kirk, who found that his own advice was no longer being accepted and his department was being ignored when it came to day-to-day arrangements like fixing media interviews with MacGregor.

Bernard Ingham, the No. 10 press secretary, who had known Kirk since his own earlier days as a labour correspondent on the *Guardian*, became equally exasperated when he found his Downing Street lobby briefings were being upstaged by these rival sources of information. Matters came to a head in October 1984 when the NCB unexpectedly changed its advertising agency during a renewed campaign to persuade striking miners to return to work. Press advertisements had already been prepared by the NCB's long-standing agency, CM Partnership, but after being presented with alternative copy, MacGregor decided that all future advertising during the strike should be prepared by Lowe Howard-Spink, which, three months later, hired Bell as its chief executive. Kirk protested at the change in agencies but without success and departed next day, or, as MacGregor put it, went 'on vacation'.

Ingham was visibly upset by the news that a valued acquaintance had been ousted in such humiliating circumstances and he told lobby correspondents at his daily briefing that he would have preferred MacGregor to have made greater use of Kirk rather than rely on public relations consultants such as Bell, who, he was forced to acknowledge, had after all been appointed on the personal recommendation of Margaret Thatcher. Her readiness to listen to the opinions of party rather than government advisers when formulating media strategies was a frequent source of irritation for Ingham. One idea put forward shortly after her victory in the 1983 general election was that Bell and the Conservatives' former director of publicity, Gordon Reece, should meet the Prime Minister at 8.50 each morning to advise on public presentation. Plans for what would in effect have been rival briefings to those given to the lobby correspondents at Westminster were apparently 'firmly scotched' by Ingham and her chief whip, John Wakeham. According to the freelance journalist Rodney Tyler, who revealed details of the proposal in his book *Campaign!*, Thatcher was 'very keen on the idea'.

Tyler, who subsequently co-wrote MacGregor's autobiography, *The Enemies Within*, was well placed during the miners' strike and his exclusives included a controversial interview in May 1984 with the NCB chairman, which filled a page in the *Sun* under the headline 'Scargill doesn't scare me'. Neither the *Sun*'s industrial correspondent, Tom Condon, nor Kirk had been informed of the interview and the first either knew of it was when they opened the paper that morning. Condon's experience was not unusual. Donald Macintyre, labour editor of the *Sunday Times*, asked on more than one occasion for his name to be removed from stories which he felt had been changed and given an incorrect slant because of copy submitted by the paper's political staff or as a result of information obtained by the *Sunday Times* editor, Andrew Neil. A report by Macintyre in April 1984, which accurately predicted that the NUM would hold a special delegate conference rather than a pit head ballot, was given a new introduction suggesting it had been 'a disastrous week' for Scargill and carried the headline 'Government scent victory in pit battle', which bore little relation to reality, given that the strike was only a few weeks old.

Sunday papers apart, dailies such as the *Sun*, the *Daily Mail* and the *Daily Express* were unstinting in their support for Thatcher, during both the pit dispute and other industrial struggles, and their backing was rewarded in later years with a clutch of knighthoods and peerages for sympathetic newspaper editors and proprietors. The Conservatives' seemingly effortless ability during the 1980s to exercise so much influence over news reporting and press comment provoked deep anger and resentment within the Labour Party. Soon after his election as party leader in 1983, Neil Kinnock took his first steps on the long and tortuous path towards modernising Labour's image and what for him personally would ultimately prove to be the fruitless task of trying to establish a more positive relationship with the news media. Help was at hand because Labour had well-placed sympathisers within the communications industry who were impressed by Kinnock's determination to take on Thatcher and also by the depth of his commitment towards rebuilding the party after two disastrous election defeats. Labour needed assistance not only in marketing and publicity but also in devising strategies to counter the Conservatives' superiority in communicating via broadcasting and the press.

Kinnock took a risk in backing Peter Mandelson to fill Labour's vacant post of director of campaigns and communications because he was untested in the cut and thrust of briefing political journalists at Westminster. However, he had one vital attribute, experience of television production, having spent three years at London Weekend Television under the director of programmes, John Birt. After starting as a researcher on *The London Programme*, Mandelson joined the production team of the weekly political programme *Weekend World*, where one of his duties as a producer was to help with research and other preparatory work for the presenter, Brian Walden, who on occasion used Mandelson as a dummy interviewee in order to practise his questions. Mandelson had impressed the party hierarchy during the Brecon & Radnor by-election in July 1985 when he spent his summer holiday acting as minder for the Labour candidate. On hearing of the vacancy at party headquarters, he applied for the job and was appointed communications director the following October. Anxious to seize the initiative, Mandelson immediately sought ideas on ways to strengthen the party's publicity. He commissioned a report from the marketing and advertising executive Philip Gould, who proposed that Labour should adopt a new corporate identity.

Kinnock favoured having a red rose as Labour's new symbol and it duly appeared at the 1986 party conference. As the modernisation process gathered pace under Kinnock and his deputy, Roy Hattersley, the party attracted increased financial support, especially from the business community. Brian Basham, whose public relations consultancy, Broad Street Associates, was benefiting from substantially higher fees, joined those who were donating money to help rebuild the party and to prepare for the 1987 general election campaign. At the request of the Labour life peer Lord Williams, a former chairman of the Price Commission, Basham was asked to advise Mandelson on the latest public relations techniques. Although much of his expertise in briefing journalists related to takeovers and mergers, Basham knew that many of the same pressures applied to political reporting as well. He was sure lobby correspondents were as desperate for scoops and tip-offs as were their colleagues on the City desk. The challenge for one of the country's leading PR consultants was to work out how that pent-up demand for exclusive information could be exploited for the benefit of a political party which for so long had been so derided and demonised by much of the press.

> I was the one who coached Mandelson. I had to explain to him that news and information had become a currency, which could in effect be traded with journalists in return for sympathetic treatment. Within financial PR we had identified a rather unpleasant vulnerability about newspaper reporters. Certain stories really did have a monetary value when you related them to journalists' salaries. Their earning power did depend to a degree on the number of exclusives they could deliver, so news had become a currency, a bribe if you like, with which it was possible to buy favourable coverage. Someone in authority in a public organisation, political party or business who had control over the flow of information could easily pick out a young journalist, hand over exclusive stories and turn that reporter into a star, perhaps earning a salary that had been quadrupled along the way. That is what Peter Mandelson learned from me . . . that, yes, there were useful strategies which had been developed in the City of London and the world of the hostile takeover bid. They were techniques which had been used to influence financial journalists and in the end there was that same kind of economic integration at Westminster, but in this case it was between politicians and political journalists, and it was the political correspondents who were ultimately delivered into the hands of the political spin doctors.

Basham advised Mandelson to adopt an equally calculated approach when trying to appeal over the heads of journalists direct to the executives of media companies:

> You have to remember that the ball being aimed at the Labour Party by the Tory press was coming with such a heavy right-hand spin that it was essential for the leadership to find a way to reach the very source of this. The party had to get to the heart of the matter, by trying to convince the newspaper proprietors that Labour deserved a fair

hearing. Rupert Murdoch, like the other proprietors, knew only too well the real value of news. He knew that it was a commodity, that there was a trade in information which was there to be taken advantage of, and if the opportunities were exploited, then the leaks and tip-offs which were on offer would allow his journalists to get more scoops and exclusives than their rivals.

Basham had other political roles behind the scenes: in the run-up to the 1992 general election he advised the Labour Party on ways to start building a positive relationship with the City of London. The following year he became embroiled in the media firestorm which engulfed British Airways when it was accused of engaging in a 'dirty tricks' campaign against Richard Branson and his airline, Virgin Atlantic.

What had been heralded as the most explosive libel case in corporate history collapsed in January 1993 when BA apologised unreservedly and paid damages of £610,000 plus £3 million in costs. Branson sued for libel following a prolonged dispute which began in 1991 after he heard that Basham, who was BA's public relations consultant, was attempting to plant 'hostile' stories in the press as part of a wider campaign to discredit Virgin and poach its passengers. When BA capitulated, Basham's counsel tried unsuccessfully to get references to him deleted from the agreed High Court statement on the grounds that they were inaccurate and that he had not circulated smear stories. Basham insisted that the report he prepared for BA, which was entitled 'Operation Barbara' and was seen by some journalists, was an assessment of Virgin businesses and their financing and was based entirely on publicly available sources. One of the 'discreditable' stories which surfaced related to allegations about the management of a nightclub owned by Branson. Basham believed at the time that he had been 'bugged', a claim which was confirmed in October 2005 by the journalist Chris Hutchins, who described in his autobiography, *Mr Confidential*, how he made a surreptitious recording of a briefing Basham had given him about the way Branson operated Virgin Atlantic and his other business interests.

Campaigns of press disinformation were not uncommon in commerce or politics and over the years one of the easiest ways to discredit an opponent has been to leak information to well-placed journalists. Basham, who was once described by the Observer column in the *Financial Times* as the best-known 'street fighter' in City PR, played another important role behind the scenes in the 1997 general election campaign when he was on stand-by, ready to advise Labour on possible counter-measures should the Conservatives have been tempted to mount a dirty tricks campaign. Labour believed, erroneously as it transpired, that it might have to face a much-feared political opponent, Dr Julian Lewis, deputy director of the Tories' research department. There was concern that under his direction, Conservative Central Office might possibly have accumulated potentially damaging information which could have been leaked to Conservative-leaning newspapers to embarrass Tony Blair and his colleagues. Lewis acknowledged subsequently that his brief could 'loosely be described as negative campaigning' but he strenuously denied at the time ever having had any intention to fight a war of disinformation against the Labour Party or of having been involved in 'dirty tricks'. In the event Lewis had his own campaign to fight, having been selected as Conservative candidate for the constituency of New Forest East, a seat which he held for the Tories after a close fight with the Liberal Democrats.

When I met Basham in June 2003 and he outlined the type of help and guidance which he had given over the years to both the Labour Party and its newly appointed director of communications, I found myself fascinated by his revelations. Mandelson must have been a star pupil, because by the time I returned to Westminster in 1988 he had already established a legendary reputation in the dark arts of media manipulation. Basham admitted that in later years he did become increasingly uneasy about the way he believed Mandelson had failed to heed the warnings he had given him about the need to proceed with a degree of caution:

> I remember talking to Peter about how to control the message but I kept saying to him, 'You must maintain your position in this business with integrity.' I think that is where he went wrong. The trouble with him was that he had no brakes and sometimes in this business you do need to stop. I cannot stand behind Mandelson over what he did in his dealings with some journalists, his screaming strategy of threats and manipulation, when he used to say to reporters, 'I know your boss. Your job is on the line.' That kind of tactic, especially when it was applied in politics, brought the whole political spin thing into disrepute.

Whatever might be said in hindsight about Mandelson's behaviour, there was no doubt that his dogged determination to back Neil Kinnock's efforts to rebuild the party had begun to pay handsome political dividends and there was much praise for the way in which Labour fought the 1987 general election. That campaign was one of the main events of my final year as a labour and industrial correspondent and what I found so noticeable about the election was the degree of self-discipline shown by leaders of the trade union movement. They were determined to behave reasonably and responsibly; they wanted, above all else, to minimise the risk that trade union militancy might get the blame for another defeat. In many ways 1987 was the forerunner of the tightly controlled campaigns which in later years became the norm under Blair's leadership. No longer would Labour be vulnerable, as it had in the past, to the claim by the Conservatives that it was the unions which had a dominant role in deciding party policy. I found that switching from industrial to political reporting did have its advantages, because a knowledge of the mechanics of the trade union movement often held the key to understanding the inner workings of the Labour Party.

Needless to say it was this inside knowledge, and a professional acquaintance with influential union leaders, which Mandelson saw as a potential threat. He told me repeatedly that he did not trust former labour correspondents; Blair was equally disenchanted with our work and accused me of 'living in a time warp' by seeking to wind up stories about 'meaningless' trade union resolutions. So great was the level of suspicion and hostility that I was the last person that Mandelson would have chosen to use as a conduit for leaked information or tip-offs. Nonetheless, as a BBC political correspondent, I was in regular contact with him over day-to-day political events. He relished his role as the party's principal spokesman and had a hands-on approach when dealing with journalists. We knew that until we had spoken to him directly we could not be entirely sure either about the latest line in party thinking or the action which the leadership might take. Mandelson was especially assiduous in maintaining contact with corres-pondents on Sunday newspapers. Each Thursday and Friday he could regularly be seen briefing them, usually one by one, in and around the offices and corridors of the House of Commons press gallery.

After his defeat in 1987, Kinnock was resolute in his determination to accelerate the process of modernisation within the party and Mandelson appreciated the potential news value of information about the policy changes which Labour was making across a broad range of controversial issues, including the switch from unilateral to multilateral nuclear disarmament and the gradual acceptance of the trade union and employment laws which had been introduced by the Thatcher government. Mandelson was convinced that one way of hastening that shift in thinking was to win the support of newspapers which were traditionally hostile to Labour. If the party was getting praise from unexpected quarters for taking bold initiatives, the leader-ship thought they were more likely to win the approval of the membership. A well-placed exclusive story in the *Sunday Times* was seen as an ideal vehicle for helping to promote the process of political change, an almost identical task to that performed by the Sunday papers on behalf of financial PR consultants seeking to influence the outcome of hostile takeover bids. Mandelson was probably at the height of his powers as an information trader during the late 1980s, in the years immediately before his unexpected and rather awkward departure from the party's staff in October 1990 after being selected as Labour candidate for Hartlepool.

Because I frequently had to work on Saturdays and Sundays I tried towards the end of each week to keep a close eye on which journalists were being briefed by Mandelson or his deputy, Colin Byrne, Labour's chief press and broadcasting officer. I often saw either one or sometimes both of them locked in deep conversation with Andrew Grice, who was then a political correspondent for the *Sunday Times* and who almost a decade later, after being promoted to political editor, would become a favoured recipient of confidential government information being leaked to the media by the shadow Chancellor, Gordon Brown. Grice soon established a remarkable reputation for the accuracy of his stories: his exclusive front-page splash that Kinnock would sack his employment spokesman, Michael Meacher, and move him to another job, proved to be entirely justified although it took six months for the demotion to take effect. Because I had often observed Grice being briefed in advance, I knew his copy was likely to be correct and I always found it rather ironic when urged by Labour to pay special attention to his exclusives.

Late each Saturday evening or alternatively early on Sunday morning, Mandelson and Byrne made it their practice to give me a run-down on those Sunday newspaper stories which they considered were accurate and which they were urging the BBC to follow up; Paul Bromley, then a political correspondent with the Press Association, told me that he received a similar run-down when he was doing weekend duty. Mandelson and Byrne were vouching for the accuracy of stories which they themselves had leaked; they could call the shots because they not only controlled the flow of information but also knew that the journalists involved were prepared to be manipulated, albeit in some cases rather reluctantly. Grice needed a constant supply of exclusive stories, for which the *Sunday Times* provided an ideal platform for the Labour Party; and correspondents such as myself who were on weekend duty at the BBC and the Press Association, and who were having to decide what to do about a plethora of 'exclusives' in the Sunday papers, were only too willing to take guidance on which of the various stories were reliable and worth developing further. Favourable follow-up reports broadcast on Sunday news bulletins or appearing on news agency wire services were often considered as important as the original story because they ensured wider publicity and helped to set the agenda for political journalists preparing their copy for Monday's newspapers.

Leaking advance information in order to build up publicity for a policy change or announcement was not without risk. There was always a danger reporters might treat the story in an unexpected or damaging way. Disclosures about tactical disputes and assorted internal disagreements were particularly hazardous and could easily backfire, not least because reporters often had their own suspicions about the true motives of those who were doing the leaking, especially when it was obvious that one aim was to harm a political opponent or discredit a party rival. Although Mandelson has insisted repeatedly over the years that his objective when dealing with the media was to promote the interests of Kinnock, and in subsequent years Tony Blair, he was a compulsive leaker and he did become addicted to the power and influence which he could exercise through his ability to feed information to journalists and broadcasters.

I experienced at first hand the deadly accuracy with which he could select a newspaper which was likely to make the most effective use of a planted story. In January 1996 I was told by the BBC's management to write a note of apology to the shadow health secretary, Harriet Harman, after Mandelson had complained on her behalf about the distress which I was said to have caused to her children when filming outside her home after it emerged that her son was going to an opted-out grammar school. I was anxious to 'apologise unreservedly' and I went to her office to deliver my handwritten note, which was in an envelope marked 'personal'. Next day Jon Craig, the political editor of the *Daily Express*, asked me to explain why I had apologised. He said the contents of my letter had been leaked to him. Several days later, when discussing my put-down with BBC colleagues, Mandelson could not resist taking the credit. My letter had been leaked because it had only been marked 'personal' and was not stated as being 'private and confidential'. The *Daily Express* had been chosen because it was known to take an anti-BBC line but he insisted that my apology could just as easily have been 'put up in lights for the Sunday papers' if that had been thought more appropriate. Mandelson's ability to exploit the media marketplace was in great demand because of the New Labour mantra that it was essential to think through in advance how the public might react to decisions taken by the leadership.

Presentation could not be divorced from policy making; public opinion had to be tested by floating various options in the media; and once a new programme had been agreed to, it had to be trailed ahead of the official announcement so as to generate interest. Few information traders applied themselves to their craft with anything like the intensity of Labour's director of communications, and references to his ability to manipulate the media peppered the pages of *Mandelson*, Donald Macintyre's biography of 'one of the most intriguing and least understood figures in British post-war politics'. Macintyre, who at the time of writing the book was chief political commentator for the *Independent*, described in admiring terms the numerous occasions when Mandelson leaked confidential or sensitive data to a select band of journalists. Having been given what he acknowledged was unequalled 'direct access' to Mandelson, his papers and former colleagues, Macintyre has provided an invaluable insight into the mindset of a political fixer whose clandestine activities trading information with journalists were highly valued by Kinnock and subsequently by Blair but distrusted by the late John Smith, who kept Mandelson at arm's length during his time as leader because of his own 'innate detestation of trickiness with the press'.

Although Smith told me that he believed the 'value of personal publicity was highly overrated', Kinnock and Blair were both preoccupied by their desire to secure what they called 'a good press' and most of the plaudits for Mandelson's news management acknowledged his gift for manipulating journalists and what Macintyre says were his 'darker media skills'. Charles Clarke, formerly Kinnock's chief of staff, believed that one of Mandelson's most significant contributions during his period as the party's director of communications was his 'key quality, his brilliant quality . . . managing the media'. Shortly after Mandelson left party headquarters to become the Labour candidate in Hartlepool, Glenys Kinnock urged her husband to recall him in order to 'get a better press'. Four years later, after Labour's 1992 defeat and Smith's death, Blair defended Mandelson's behind-the-scenes role in the 1994 leadership election because his 'semi-clandestine media handling' had been crucial in securing a decisive victory. In one telling example Macintyre described how the leaking of Blair's campaign themes to Andrew Grice backfired initially because of concern over the headline printed by the *Sunday Times* – 'Blair reveals SDP mark II' – but later Mandelson was congratulated because the reaction to Grice's exclusive had been 'very good'.

Mandelson was equally adept at leaking information in order to promote himself and to bolster his own image as a 'brilliant' election strategist. Macintyre recalled that during a period of soul searching following Labour's 1987 defeat, the *Times* 'saw fit to splash across its front page' selected extracts from the latest policy paper 'leaked by Mandelson, of course'. Among Colin Byrne's contributions to the biography was a vivid description of how his boss spent Saturday evenings 'speaking to journalists in the run-up to Sunday newspaper deadlines' with his ear glued to what in the late 1980s was a 'suitcase-sized' mobile telephone. Byrne was a willing pupil and in an article for the London *Evening Standard* he said that although his four years as the party's chief press officer were 'a searing experience', he emerged 'battle hardened', having learned from Mandelson the importance of 'constant, proactive media management'.

After being passed over for the job of director of communications, Byrne left the party's staff in October 1991 to become a press officer for the Prince of Wales's business leaders' forum. He rose rapidly through the ranks of public relations consultants and after becoming deputy head of public affairs at Shandwick at the age of thirty-eight, he went on to be appointed joint chief executive and then, in September 2003, took sole UK control of what had become Weber Shandwick, Britain's largest PR agency. Byrne was a firm advocate of the 'focused and disciplined communication' regime which became the hallmark of New Labour. Just as the Conservatives had been assisted in the 1980s by the successful strategies of 'corporate men in smart suits from advertising and PR', so he believed Blair's government had benefited from the media management routines which had been developed by his mentor, the 'greatest political strategist of his generation', techniques which had then 'revolutionised corporate communications'. In an interview for *PR Week*, Mandelson was equally effusive about his pupil's abilities and on Byrne's promotion to chief executive at Weber Shandwick, he praised his 'knowledge of where to pitch his message'.

On becoming MP for Hartlepool in the 1992 general election, Mandelson hired Derek Draper, an up-and-coming young lobbyist, as his political assistant. Before long Draper was describing himself as Mandelson's 'chief political adviser' and five years later, despite having left to become a lobbyist with the public affairs consultants Prima Europe, Draper's insider status gave him the opportunity to write his first book, *Blair's Hundred Days*, which chronicled the 'breakneck pace' at which the new Labour government began implementing its manifesto commitments. After a long career break following his entanglement in July 1998 in what journalists dubbed the Labour lobbyists' 'cash for access' scandal, Draper turned his back on the world of politics and re-emerged as a psychotherapist. In an article for the *Guardian* in July 2005, he reflected on the time he spent as Mandelson's spin doctor and gave an insight into his boss's predilection for leaking. He described what happened when Mandelson started 'cosying' up to a journalist who would not normally have been seen as New Labour: 'For six halcyon weeks Peter could slip him stories undetected to the consternation of Westminster. Then they were spotted having lunch, and the secret was out.'

Draper had come to the conclusion that the purveyors of anonymous leaks did not always blow their own cover out of carelessness or stupidity:

> The frequency with which the briefer makes the headlines is, I believe, down to something that even the protagonists themselves aren't conscious of: a secret desire to be recognised and seen to be important. I have rarely known a back-room boy (or girl) who didn't want to be recognised – not necessarily walking down the street but certainly by their peers. That is why, so often, the spinner becomes the story.

Once Mandelson began climbing the ministerial ladder after Labour won the 1997 general election, he found it as difficult as before to forsake his 'darker media skills'. Paul Routledge, chief political commentator for the *Daily Mirror*, described in *Mandy*, billed as 'the unauthorised biography', how even on his promotion to Secretary of State for Trade and Industry in July 1998 he could not 'slough off his spin doctoring self'. Mandelson was still in regular contact with his 'captured castles, as he derisively called his key contacts in the press'. Routledge's hostility to Mandelson was legendary among political journalists at Westminster and he had no qualms about identifying colleagues who he believed were relying on information being supplied by 'a manipulative spin doctor'. He claimed that staff in the Westminster office of the *Independent* noticed that 'Mandelson spoke "two or three times a day" to political editor Andrew Grice, newly arrived from the *Sunday Times*'.

Further corroboration of Mandelson's inability to kick the habit of leaking information to journalists was provided by Alastair Campbell's deputy, Lance Price, in his book *The Spin Doctor's Diary*, published in September

2005. In his entry for 14 July 1999, Price revealed that leaks about an imminent Cabinet reshuffle had been blamed unfairly on Gordon Brown: 'It's clear Peter has been doing his usual trick of talking to a lot of journalists and letting them think he knows TB's mind. He's been talking on the summer reshuffle, in particular, which everyone is paranoid about.'

Earlier that month Mandelson had escaped punishment after the House of Commons Select Committee on Standards and Privileges decided to take no further action over the home loan scandal which had forced his resignation in December 1998. No doubt one of his aims in claiming that he was privy to inside information would have been the hope that the journalists whom he had briefed would help him rebuild his image, a strategy which finally paid off with his return to the Cabinet in October 1999 on being appointed Secretary of State for Northern Ireland.

Price's insight into the often strained relations with Campbell's team of spin doctors, and Paul Routledge's claim that the relationship did get off to a 'shaky start', were apparently not what Mandelson hoped for or intended. In his account of Campbell's appointment as press secretary in 1994, Donald Macintyre said Mandelson was delighted that Blair had at last found 'someone who was even better at spinning than he had had been'. Campbell, then a political commentator for the short-lived *Today* newspaper, was in a similarly upbeat mood and used his column to declare that he intended to exploit Mandelson's expertise, 'which in some areas is second to none'. Nevertheless, when it came to mastering the skulduggery involved in leaking confidential documents, the Labour Party's former director of communications had finally met his match. Macintyre described Mandelson's admiration for one of Campbell's 'notable stings' in February 1997, when he manufactured 'an almost entirely synthetic row' by leaking to the *Sunday Express* and the *Independent on Sunday* draft Labour Party advertisements depicting the Prime Minister, John Major, as 'Mr Weak'. Macintyre concluded his account by observing that 'if Mandelson was ruthless at times, Campbell was hardly less so'.

Under Mandelson's direction, and with the encouragement of Neil Kinnock and subsequently Blair, Labour's burgeoning band of propagandists had clearly developed considerable expertise in manipulating the flow of sensitive data to selected journalists in return for favourable coverage. Campbell's arrival gave the party's media machine an even sharper edge when it came to the all-important task of influencing the news agenda. Trading leaked information was not a new weapon in the fight for tactical political advantage but Labour were operating in a far more sophisticated and systematic way than had been achieved even by the Conservatives during the height of the Thatcher years. The 'focused and disciplined' communication regime which Colin Byrne had found so instructive was a key factor in helping to defeat Major and propel Blair to victory. In my election diary *Campaign 1997*, I suggested that 'Labour's relentless and imaginative efforts to guide and shape' political coverage in the news media were 'partly responsible for turning their already near-certain victory into a record-breaking triumph'.

What I had not appreciated then was that the practice of leaking, which had become a way of life for Labour when in opposition, was about to become institutionalised in government. Long-standing conventions about the confidentiality of documents were about to be abandoned, civil service rules would be changed and under Alastair Campbell's guidance, and with the all-important approval of the Prime Minister, servants of the state would become the most effective leakers in the land.

Chapter 6

When long-established political propagandists argue that there is nothing new about the art of spinning they have a point. Putting the best possible gloss on a new policy or event has been the aim of politicians down the ages. The same goes for the practice of leaking information for party or personal advantage. Kite flying has long been the favoured sport of the political opportunist, a chance to float an idea or raise the stakes if controversy is afoot. A well-placed, well-timed story, planted in the right newspaper, can be just what is required when a flagging politician is in need of a little restorative publicity. Alastair Campbell's supreme value to Tony Blair was that his greatest professional attributes were two of the essential requirements for a modern-day spin doctor: an instinctive nose for political intrigue and an innate understanding of how best to exploit the thought processes of today's journalists. Campbell not only knew how low tabloid reporters could stoop in their search for sensationalism but he could also forecast with a fair degree of accuracy the likely treatment and potential impact of a great variety of political stories. What he longed for was the opportunity to exercise control over the flow of information from within the Labour Party, a chance to influence and even to dictate the news agenda. Once Blair had been elected party leader in July 1994 and Campbell had been signed up as press secretary, he immediately put his personal stamp of authority on Labour's media offensive.

The depth of his commitment to Labour, his wide experience of journalism as reporter, political editor and columnist on the *Daily Mirror*, *Sunday Mirror* and *Today* newspapers, together with the party know-how he had acquired during a close working relationship with Neil Kinnock, meant he was tailor-made for the job. From the moment he took command of

Blair's media relations, political correspondents at Westminster were aware of the change which had taken place. No longer was there a danger of news emerging from the party in a haphazard way. Instead information was being released in a manner and at a time which suited Blair, almost always being distributed in advance and on a selective basis to favoured journalists, so as to secure the best possible coverage. Within a matter of weeks he had become the party's most influential information trader. Choosing where best to place a story came as second nature to Campbell. His flair was infectious and to begin with most political journalists were anxious to win his confidence in the hope that one day they might be the recipient of an exclusive story or be afforded privileged access to Blair's inner circle. Initially, as far as Campbell was concerned, the controlled leaking of news about changes in Labour policy or personnel was simply part and parcel of the everyday process of news management, just one of the many techniques at the disposal of a political party which was fighting back after years in opposition and which had been traduced for so long by a largely belligerent media. Campbell had few scruples when it came to deciding what to leak and to whom, his sole objective being to boost Blair and get Labour into power. If the only way he could influence the news agenda was by feeding the media's obsession with stories about leaked documents, then so be it.

He had the same matter-of-fact approach when dealing with hostile leaks. Rather than complain or get diverted into a fruitless witch hunt for a likely culprit, Campbell would focus his attention on seeing if there was any way that an unauthorised disclosure could be turned to the party's advantage. Being so single minded was a great bonus and his brilliance in exploiting stories about the splits and 'sleaze' that had dogged John Major allowed Labour to maintain a continuous offensive against the Conservatives, which helped turn the certainty of Blair's victory in the 1997 general election into a landslide of historic proportions. Labour were so convinced that a key factor in their success had been the professionalism of the party's communications staff that, once in power, Campbell and his aides pushed through sweeping changes in Whitehall's information services. Long-standing safeguards designed to keep civil servants at arm's length from the manipulation of the news media were cast aside; the requirement that ministers should make significant statements in Parliament before informing the press was frequently ignored. Of far greater importance to Campbell was the need to grab the media's attention and that meant doing everything possible to trail forthcoming announcements in advance.

'Trailing' was in effect leaking by another name, the systematic release of information and data about a decision or change in policy immediately before an official announcement. Ministers of various political persuasions had been indulging in such practices for many years, with varying degrees of success, believing it was essential to tease out their proposals bit by bit in order to engage the media's interest and prepare public opinion. What changed after the 1997 election, when Campbell became the Downing Street press secretary, was that civil service information officers were freed from the constraints which had previously been applied to their work. Instead of refusing to comment for fear of pre-empting a parliamentary statement, as had been the long-standing convention, they were increasingly being instructed to confirm what the minister intended to announce and then offer more details. Political journalists had been briefed regularly in previous years on the background to important decisions, occasionally by ministers themselves. More often than not the task would have been left to senior information officers whose off-the-record guidance was trusted by journalists; the correspondents knew that their well-established contacts could be relied upon to give an impartial insight into the considerations that would have been in the minds of ministers and their officials. Nonetheless in my experience, if a parliamentary statement was imminent they invariably refrained from revealing precisely what it was that the government had agreed to, and in my years at the BBC I was certainly never given sight in advance of any of the documents which accompanied a ministerial state-ment. By changing the rules, by giving civil servants the authority to release confidential data ahead of an announcement, the Labour government blurred the dividing line between party propaganda and public information and it was hardly surprising that Campbell took full advantage of the latitude he had established in order to help Blair gain a tactical advantage through the early release of information. Leaking had to all intents and purposes become institutionalised, an everyday occurrence in the affairs of government.

Instead of seeking to ensure a level playing field for all journalists and equal access for every section of the media, servants of the state were required to distribute information on a selective basis, to those news outlets deemed most likely to deliver favourable coverage. Eventually the advance leaking of the contents of ministerial statements became so commonplace that the opposition parties and ultimately the Speaker grew increasingly tired of complaining. Labour's conviction that the government had to be forever competing for attention in a crowded media marketplace, that it always had to take the offensive, even if that involved politicising the flow of information from the state to the people, were beliefs and practices which became embedded within the culture of Whitehall. The pressure from Downing Street was relentless: there had to be a constant stream of new initiatives. Typically, by the middle of each week, ministers in the main departments were required to think through with their political advisers and information officers how they intended to trail the announcements that were to be made the following week. Invariably the first target for planting stories was next Sunday's newspapers. Critical decisions had to be taken: which journalists could be relied upon to give the best showing for the exclusives that were on offer; which weekend television or radio programme would provide the most positive platform for the minister. As soon as the strategy had been agreed, the hard sell would begin. Servants of the state had been given a free hand to distribute on a selective basis information and data which hitherto would have been considered secret or confidential within the machinery of Whitehall.

Once the relevant story had been published or broadcast by the chosen news outlet, civil service information officers were authorised to brief the rest of the media. During Neil Kinnock's leadership, Peter Mandelson and his deputy, Colin Byrne, had concentrated much of their efforts on using the Sunday newspapers to influence the news agenda in the hope of turning each weekend's reporting to Labour's advantage, thus encouraging and hastening the process of change within the party. Campbell put Mandelson's endeavours into the shade. He took the orchestration of weekend news coverage to new heights, demonstrating time and again both his ability to co-ordinate stories which would capture and dominate the headlines and his sure touch in picking off those newspapers and programmes which were only too happy to be manipulated in return for an exclusive story or interview. Within a year of joining Blair as his press secretary, Campbell laid on what I considered was a textbook example of how to synchronise a devastating body blow to a political opponent; it would be the first of many inflicted on the Conservatives. John Major, who had comfortably defeated John Redwood after forcing an unexpected leadership election in June 1995, was desperate to ensure that his party conference that autumn became the launch pad for a new Conservative fightback against a reinvigorated Labour Party. However, unbeknown to the Prime Minister, the Conservative MP Alan Howarth had been having private discussions for some weeks about possibly defecting to Labour and, after a meeting with Blair at his home in Islington, it was agreed he would wait until the eve of the Tory conference before announcing that he intended to cross the floor of the House of Commons and join the Labour benches.

At this point Campbell swung into action: news of the first-ever defection to Labour by a Conservative MP was far too important to be left to chance and was held back for the Sunday papers. It appeared under the by-line of Anthony Bevins, political editor of the *Observer*, whose front page splash had the headline 'Exclusive: Tories rocked as senior MP defects to Labour'. Bevins had clearly been given ample time to assemble the material he needed; Howarth was photographed at his office in Westminster and the *Observer* also reproduced the letter he had sent to the Stratford-on-Avon Conservative Association explaining his 'profound disagreement' with Tory policy. An arrangement had also been made behind the scenes with the BBC for Howarth to be interviewed that Sunday morning on *Breakfast with Frost*, which Bevins predicted would provide the 'first sparks of a politically dramatic week' because the defecting MP would be appearing alongside the newly installed Conservative Party chairman, Dr Brian Mawhinney. Howarth's defection dominated the pre-conference coverage and the head-lines were horrendous for Major. Next day the *Daily Telegraph*'s columnist Boris Johnson complimented Labour's spin doctors on their 'vicious timing'.

When managing a fast-moving story of this nature there is not always an opportunity to trail each development in advance and, rather than leak information ahead of an announcement, Campbell was sometimes forced to adopt the more customary practice of issuing a statement for general release by the Press Association, so that all news outlets could be informed simultaneously. On several celebrated occasions he was not just a spin doctor but also an active participant in devising and shaping political sagas which captured the headlines for days.

A Good Friday newsflash from the Press Association in the lead-up to the 1997 general election marked the start of just such a drama: Campbell was pulling the strings and preparing the ground for the defeat of Neil Hamilton by the former BBC war correspondent Martin Bell, by far the most entertaining story of the whole campaign. To begin with, the one-sentence newsflash from the Press Association gave journalists little to go on: 'Labour's candidate in Neil Hamilton's Tatton constituency, Jon Kelly, is to stand down tomorrow in a bid to force the Tory to resign.' Hamilton was the Conservative MP at the centre of what had become known as the cash-for-questions affair and, despite a continuing investigation into his financial affairs by the House of Commons Standards and Privileges Committee, he was determined to seek re-election. Although Gordon Brown's press secretary, Charlie Whelan, claimed subsequently that it was Brown's idea to put up an anti-sleaze candidate against Hamilton, it was Campbell who did all the early legwork, as I discovered after Hamilton lost the seat. He telephoned Kelly to persuade him to stand down as Labour candidate and, while not mentioning Tony Blair by name, assured him that the request that he should step aside came 'right from the top' of the party. Campbell's next move that Good Friday morning was to contact the Liberal Democrats' campaign director, Chris Rennard, to see if their candidate could be persuaded to join the plot. Rennard promised to help and a week later he arranged for the local executive to meet Bell, who by then had agreed to stand as an Independent.

Bell's statement, setting out how he intended to campaign on an anti-corruption platform, was approved by Campbell. Rennard told me that he co-operated with Labour because the strategy was simply brilliant.

> Campbell described to me how desperate the newspapers were, how the journalists were really hungry for a good story. He knew how to feed them and the way Campbell prepared the ground for Bell to emerge as an Independent anti-corruption candidate made sure that sleaze dominated the first fortnight of the campaign. John Major thought six weeks might be enough to turn it round for him, but thanks to Campbell he lost the first two.

Even when he had been elevated to the status of a civil servant on becoming the Prime Minister's press secretary and should not have engaged in party political activities while working in Downing Street, Campbell had the same hands-on approach whenever an opportunity arose to derail the Conservatives. In December 1999 he helped arrange the defection to Labour of the Conservative MP Shaun Woodward, who was sacked from the opposition front bench by William Hague for refusing to support legislation that prohibited the acceptance of 'homosexuality as a pretended family relationship'. After being told by his openly gay deputy, Lance Price, and the Labour MP Ann Keen that Woodward had become so alienated by the Conservatives' intolerance towards the gay community that he might defect, Campbell took a leading role in a series of clandestine meetings. Woodward paid four visits to No. 10 and met Blair twice in the Prime Minister's flat.

In his book *The Spin Doctor's Diary*, Price described how Blair thought

Campbell and Mandelson 'would be best at judging what would look credible in the media'. The news that the MP for Witney was defecting, which had been hinted at exclusively that morning in the then pro-Labour *Daily Express*, was released at noon on Saturday 18 December, and as Campbell predicted, it dominated the weekend's news coverage, causing Hague maximum discomfort. In a signed article the following Monday, Woodward complimented the *Express* on its 'proud record of campaigning against bullying in our schools' and said that New Labour was now his natural home. Despite sustained complaints by senior Conservatives that Campbell had broken the rules by using Downing Street to plan the defection of a Tory MP, he escaped with nothing more than a gentle reminder from the Cabinet Secretary, Sir Richard Wilson, that in future he should conduct his political activities 'away from No. 10, either at lunchtime or outside office hours'.

Wilson's reluctance to criticise him reflected the enhanced power of the Downing Street press office. Campbell had seen off his critics the year before, when the Cabinet Secretary rejected complaints from Conservative MPs that the Whitehall publicity machine had been politicised. Blair had inadvertently given the opposition the ammunition they were looking for when he acknowledged at Question Time that his press secretary was doing 'an effective job attacking the Conservative Party'. Armed with the Prime Minister's unexpected confirmation that his press secretary was acting improperly, Campbell was forced to defend himself at a hearing of the Public Administration Select Committee in June 1998. His return unscathed to No. 10 warranted a mention in *The Spin Doctor's Diary*. Price noted Campbell's response when he was congratulated by Blair: 'Alastair called him a "dickhead" and said the only problem had been Blair's comment that Alastair was very good at attacking the Tories, something he, and I, are not really supposed to do.'

The Cabinet Secretary's willingness to turn a blind eye to the political sharp practice taking place in No. 10 was perhaps understandable. Campbell and Blair's chief of staff, Jonathan Powell, who were the two most senior political advisers on the government's payroll, had both become extremely powerful civil servants, having been given executive authority to issue instructions on the Prime Minister's behalf. This unprecedented step, authorised by an order in council, had been approved by Wilson's predecessor, Sir Robin Butler, who had also asked Robin Mountfield, the permanent secretary to the Cabinet Office, to assist Campbell by chairing a working group which would recommend ways to strengthen the information service. When Mountfield's report was published in November 1997 it read like nothing less than a checklist of all Campbell's ideas for ensuring that the Whitehall publicity machine raised 'its game' and got to grips with the task of co-ordinating and delivering the government's message in an age when the news media were 'diversifying and multiplying as never before'. He had already told the heads of information the previous month that he wanted their departments to keep the Downing Street press office informed about their ideas for Sunday newspaper stories because the government should 'always be ahead of the game'.

This was a pivotal moment in the transplantation of the New Labour culture of spin, from opposition to government, and it was this shift which helped consolidate Campbell's control over the flow of news from the state to the media. He became an all-powerful information trader and regarded himself, in effect, as the editor in chief of an alternative news service, always trying to influence next day's headlines by setting the agenda for newspapers, television and radio. A newly revised manual entitled *Press Office Best Practice* told civil service information officers how to structure their briefings and write press releases to 'grab the agenda'. As the dates approached for the release of White Papers and reports, they should be poised to start a 'ring-round' of newsrooms so as to stimulate advance interest in the forthcoming publication of such documents. They should begin 'trailing the announcement during the previous weekend'. Departments were warned about the need to avoid breaching parliamentary protocol but there was no mistaking the path which civil service press officers were being urged to take: the information service would have to become proactive and go on the offensive, to undertake the aggressive selling of the government's policies and achievements. Having persuaded Mountfield to lend his name to the rewriting of the rule book, Campbell could henceforth ensure that civil servants reinforced the accuracy of the confidential information which he and his fellow spin doctors were already supplying to favoured news outlets on a selective and off-the-record basis.

Procedures for leaking had to all intents and purposes become institutionalised because for the first time government press officers were being instructed to back up what journalists had been told unattributably by the seventy or so Labour Party advisers who had the status of temporary civil servants and who worked alongside Cabinet ministers. Previously the standard response of government departments, when asked about the accuracy of Sunday newspaper 'exclusives', was to say they could not comment on speculative stories in advance of ministerial statements to Parliament. Post-Mountfield that changed: duty information officers answering calls from news agency reporters and broadcasters like myself started to open up; they would indicate which stories had some substance; sometimes they would volunteer more information or redirect the call to the relevant political adviser who they knew had given advance briefings to selected journalists. Campbell and his network of ministerial spin doctors already had the freedom to distribute confidential data; now their licence to leak had been given official approval and would be supported by the civil service. Sir Bernard Ingham shared my assessment: by establishing channels through which Whitehall departments could leak their policies 'by dictation to tame journalists', he considered the government had put political advantage before the authority of the House of Commons and MPs had only themselves to blame for allowing parliamentary accountability to be undermined.

In his book *The Wages of Spin*, Ingham acknowledged that the guidance given in *Press Office Best Practice*, that 'trailing helps set the context and news agenda', meant that the practice of trailing had been officially endorsed 'in black and white', despite the proviso that it 'must not offend parliamentary protocol'; to all intents and purposes the government had sanctioned 'leaking on its terms to pliable journalists'. However, he considered I had been rather unfair in one of my previous books, *Sultans of Spin*, in accusing Mountfield, who was knighted by Blair in the 1998 New Year's Honours, of having done 'Campbell's bidding' by accepting the rule change. I believed the new guidance required civil servants to verify politically inspired leaks and it meant they had 'become the spin doctors' accomplices'. Ingham sprang to the permanent secretary's defence: 'Mountfield, I am sure, did not write it. Nor, I am equally sure, did those who compose it mean ill. But they played right into the hands of Campbell's manifest contempt for anything, including Parliament, which gets in the way of his political mission.' Notwithstanding Ingham's belief that Mountfield should not have been criticised for 'running away' from his responsibility to protect the neutrality of civil servants, there was no doubting the willingness of Whitehall mandarins to go the extra mile in accommodating Campbell's determination to ensure that he and his staff in Downing Street would be able to control the advance planning of what was being said by each government department.

On taking office Blair had doubled the number of Labour Party advisers working for Cabinet ministers and to accommodate this greater political input Mountfield had also agreed, as part of his review, that a strategic communications unit should be established inside No. 10 to co-ordinate the presentation of policy announcements. In explaining why the unit was needed, Blair told MPs in January 1998 that it would prepare a diary of future events and 'show their coherence with the main themes of government strategy'. Downing Street's press release reinforced the point: the unit would make sure events were 'scheduled, launched and followed through to maintain impact and to convey the central story and themes of the government in all its communications'. At last Campbell had the kind of structure which he told lobby correspondents would fill 'a gap in the government's armoury' and help ministers 'get through unscathed' when they were 'getting a bad press'. Initially it had a staff of six, which included two pro-Labour former newspaper correspondents, Philip Bassett (*Times*) and David Bradshaw (*Daily Mirror*), who had both been hired as political advisers. They were required to give a hard journalistic edge to the task of devising a 'media plan' for 'big positive announcements' and one their first tasks was to write the stream of newspaper articles which began appearing under the by-line of the Prime Minister and other ministers such as the Chancellor of the Exchequer.

Each week the unit prepared, as Blair had promised, a list of future events set out in the form of a daily grid, which was marked 'restricted' and only meant for use within the government. The aim was to maximise the potential for publicity by ensuring that ministers' statements did not conflict with each other or clash with major news events or sporting fixtures. Philip Gould, Blair's long-standing political adviser, described in his book, *The Unfinished Revolution*, how he had helped draw up his first grid of events for the 1987 election campaign. Like Blair and Campbell, he believed it was essential to prepare a forward diary; it was not just a timetable but also imposed an all-important discipline in political campaigning by identifying opportunities to reinforce the key strategic messages that were about to be delivered. Such was still the novelty of publishing an article signed by the Prime Minister that in March 1998 the *Sunday Times* gave Blair prime position in the centre spread to promote his week ahead. It read like an expanded version of the grid: 'On Tuesday, I will announce the first products chosen to be "millennium products" . . . on Wednesday, the Foreign Office will launch Panel 2000, which aims to modernise the way we project Britain . . . The Asia–Europe meeting in London on Thursday will showcase Powerhouse UK.' Wednesday lunchtime was set aside in Downing Street for the grid meeting and once the various timings had been agreed each department was required to devise a strategy to trail its announcements; Campbell and the No.10 press office had to be kept informed of what was being planned.

Political appointees in some Whitehall departments had no need to wait for the official guidance provided in the Mountfield report because they had already begun to 'grab the agenda'. Within a few weeks of Blair taking office, campaign strategies and tactics which had been fine tuned in Labour's media centre in Millbank Tower during the 1997 general election had been transferred lock, stock and barrel to the Department of Health under the guidance of Joe McCrea, one of the party's sharpest communications technocrats, who had been appointed political adviser to Frank Dobson, the new Secretary of State for Health. McCrea's technological wizardry included the development of an information network which was designed to give ministers in his department '24-hour remote laptop access to lines to take, health line briefings and health rebuttals'. Another forte was his ability to identify potential stories and decide where best to place exclusives. A cascade of initiatives during Labour's first few months in office provided ample opportunity for the newly installed spin doctors to hone their skills in trailing announcements. In July 1997 the *Sunday Times* splashed on an exclusive by its political editor, Andrew Grice, reporting that the government was about to raise from sixteen to eighteen the age at which cigarettes could be purchased legally. I was told by the duty information officer that this was a possibility and was likely to be discussed at a meeting of health experts the following day. On being told the department could give me no further details, I contacted McCrea, who confirmed the story but insisted that I must not attribute this to an 'official spokesman' and should say instead that it had been confirmed by 'sources close to ministers'. Having experienced at first hand his expertise in grabbing the agenda, I began to track McCrea's success in trailing announcements and his output was so prodigious that the Department of Health became infamous for spin.

Reports about additional money for the NHS and falling hospital waiting lists became regular fare in the Sunday newspapers. After a rash of leaked stories in July 1998, Dobson appeared on *Breakfast with Frost* trailing his own announcements about a rise in health spending and progress on Labour's election pledge towards cutting waiting lists by 100,000. Finally the shadow health secretary, Ann Widdecombe, could take no more and in March 1999 she complained to the Speaker, Betty Boothroyd, about a catalogue of leaked news items in the preceding twelve months which she believed constituted a 'brazen contempt of Parliament'. In each of the cases she cited, she believed the Department of Health was the culprit: a nurses' pay award statement leaked two weeks before publication; an Ashworth Hospital statement leaked to the *Sunday Telegraph* the day before being made in the House of Commons; a mental health statement leaked to the *Sunday Times* two days before publication; a social services statement appearing in the *Independent* and the *Guardian* on the morning of publication, as did a statement on safeguards for children in the *Evening Standard;* a health spending statement appearing in the *Times* on the morning of its delivery. Dobson brushed Widdecombe's criticism aside and it was not until some years later, when a leading information officer in the Department of Health agreed to speak to me off the record, that I obtained an eyewitness account of the frenzied activity which was required to maintain what amounted to a production line of exclusive stories based on leaked data and documents.

I was told that each Thursday, once Downing Street had agreed its weekly grid of future announcements, McCrea set to work with Dobson and the minister of state for health, Alan Milburn.

> They were all obsessed with what stories would be appearing in the Sunday papers and they would spend real time deciding which exclusive should be leaked to which newspaper and then which minister should get the chance to do follow-up interviews on television and radio. As professional information officers we all thought this was terribly wasteful of ministerial effort. Milburn was always fretting about what the press team were doing and he'd get involved in the real minutiae of which journalist should get what. Milburn claimed he was close to George Pascoe-Watson on the *Sun* but when it came to a new initiative on nurses, Alastair Campbell overruled Milburn and said it had to be leaked to the *Daily Mail* because Downing Street was trying to win over the *Mail* group.

When Dobson resigned in October 1999 in order to mount his unsuccessful bid to become mayor of London, Milburn was promoted to Secretary of State for Health, after having spent ten months as chief secretary to the Treasury. With Dobson's departure, McCrea moved to Downing Street where he began to develop an electronic information and rebuttal system designed to give all ministers the kind of back-up which he had provided in the Department of Health. By sheer coincidence, two weeks after Milburn became the secretary of state, I obtained a copy of his confidential media plan for the week commencing Sunday 24 October 1999 and it revealed that the routines for trailing announcements, which McCrea had worked so hard to establish, were being followed to the letter. Dated Friday 22 October and marked 'restricted - policy', the plan listed the exclusives which had already been leaked to Sunday newspapers and, rather more ominously, I thought, it included a detailed résumé of what the department believed were the potentially hostile stories which it expected to appear that weekend. There had clearly been a considerable degree of collaboration because forty-eight hours before they had even been printed, the department seemed to have a good idea about the stories which most of the political and health correspondents were proposing to write. Under the section headed 'trails', it said Chris McLaughlin of the *Sunday Mirror* 'should run a news story' on the 'NICE announcement guidance on Taxol'; Michael Prescott of the *Sunday Times* has been 'briefed on the same Taxol story'; and on Monday 'the *Sun* will carry an article by Professor Michael Richards, the new cancer supremo' who was being 'lined up' to give an interview on the *Today* programme. The leaking of the statement which Milburn ultimately delivered on Monday 25 October, in which he announced that the anti-cancer drug Taxol would be made available to all patients, had clearly gone according to plan. 'We'll end the post code cancer lottery' was the headline over McLaughlin's 'exclusive', which said, 'Milburn has exclusively promised the *Sunday Mirror* that he will make Taxol universally available'; and in the *Sunday Times*, Prescott reported that the Secretary of State for Health would 'unveil reforms tomorrow' and order the 'expenditure of an extra £33 million' on anti-cancer drugs.

During their long years in opposition, Labour's press officers had always made a point of asking journalists and broadcasters to let them know what stories they were working on, especially at weekends, on the pretext that shadow ministers or party officials might be able to assist with background information or provide an informed comment. Some journalists resented these inquiries, believing they were nothing more than a blatant fishing trip. Bearing in mind my own reluctance to reveal exactly what I was pursuing in case of being thwarted by Labour's spin doctors, I had been taken aback on reading the media plan and discovering how much a Whitehall department purported to know, two days in advance, about likely story lines in the Sunday papers. The list ran to two pages of A4 and was signed off on Friday 22 October by the Department of Health's director of communications. It included the following: *Observer*, 'Anthony Browne planning story on body piercing regulations'; *Sunday Telegraph*, 'Jacqui Thornton writing story about pharmacists and anti-fraud forms' and another story about the 'drug

Propecia'; *Sunday Times*, 'Chris Dignan writing on general state of NHS readiness for winter' and 'Nick Rodrigues doing research into the import of Viagra'; *Independent on Sunday*, 'Jo Dillon writing about anticipated increase in millennium depression'; *Sunday Express*, 'Jonathan Oliver writing about NHS trust deficits' and perhaps 'running a story on beating the ban on tobacco advertising'. Having obtained an advance warning as to what was afoot, the department had drawn up lengthy guidance on the 'line to take' if ministers were challenged about any of the stories or if information officers were questioned by journalists.

The department's intelligence gathering had obviously been as effective as its leaking because most of the stories appeared as billed: Chris Dignan's story on page two of the *Sunday Times* had the headline 'NHS heads for worst cash crisis in 10 years'; 'NHS cash haemorrhage' was the headline for Jonathan Oliver's page lead in the *Sunday Express* and there was also a full page on the 'Battle to woo smokers before ad ban deadline'. The only minor slip-up was over the *Observer*: instead of examining body piercing, as had been predicted, the health editor, Anthony Browne, presented a news investigation on 'why we fail on cancer'.

Having established, with McCrea's help, a well-oiled regime which encouraged the release of confidential information, Dobson and Milburn found there were plenty of takers, even for what sometimes proved to be a blatant piece of kite flying. In the week preceding the release in June 1999 of the latest statistics on hospital waiting lists, the BBC's *Nine O'Clock News* swallowed the government's spin hook, line and sinker. As soon as Peter Sissons started reading the introduction, I suspected it was probably a planted story: 'The BBC has learned that the government has achieved its election promise to cut hospital waiting lists in England by a hundred thousand.' Unfortunately, when the official figures were published six days later the total had risen by 19,700 and the government was still 35,000 short of meeting its pledge. Judged by any yardstick the Department of Health had succeeded in raising 'its game' and the media plan showed that its information staff could hardly have been any more inventive in trying to comply with Alastair Campbell's diktat to 'grab the agenda'.

But the alacrity with which health ministers were willing to leak their own announcements to journalists for the sake of some easy headlines shocked and saddened leaders of the medical profession. At the annual meeting of the British Medical Association (BMA) in July 1999, its chairman, Dr Ian Bogle, accused Dobson and his colleagues of breeding an atmosphere of suspicion by putting media manipulation ahead of proper consultation with doctors' leaders: 'Floating policy initiatives by feeding stories to friendly journalists appears to have become the government's preferred method of communication. Authorised leaks and off-the-record briefings are commonplace even before doctors' leaders have had a chance to discuss the ideas.'

Bogle repeated his criticism the following year after the contents of a statement on the future of the health service were leaked three days in advance. No doubt after having probably started their Sunday seeing Milburn trailing the proposals on *Breakfast with Frost*, the heads of the medical colleges were invited to spend the afternoon reading copies of the government's blueprint 'Creating a 21st Century NHS', which the Prime Minister was to unveil the following Thursday. Despite having been sworn to secrecy, all the main proposals, including a plan to use private hospitals, appeared next morning on the front pages of the *Times*, the *Daily Telegraph* and the *Daily Mirror*. Interviewed later that day on *The World at One*, Bogle said he and his colleagues had no intention of breaking the undertakings on confidentiality which they had given to the Department of Health but they were utterly dismayed at the calculated way the government had leaked the contents of its own announcement: 'Health professionals have been working very hard on these proposals and I am certain they are not leaking this information. These are deliberate leaks by the government and they have devalued their own announcement.' Tight security had been in place that Sunday, when the heads of the medical colleges were given an opportunity to read the document. Nigel Duncan, the BMA's information officer, told me that although note taking was allowed so that those who were present could familiarise themselves with the contents, their notes could not be taken away. 'Government officials stood looking over their shoulders. We had to observe confidentiality but when it comes to leaking there is one rule for ministers and another for the medical profession.'

Bogle's attack on the government had followed hard on the heels of an investigation by *Panorama* into what its reporter John Ware suggested were tricks like triple counting to inflate the amount which Labour claimed to be spending on the NHS. Ware's accusation that it had been 'all spin and mirrors' was accepted by Romola Christopherson, who was head of communications at the Department of Health for the first eighteen months of the Labour government. She told *Panorama* that Blair and his Cabinet had remained in 'campaigning mode from day one' and she conceded that the health ministers had 'pushed the mirrors' further than before by reannouncing the same money. I described in *Sultans of Spin* how initially Christopherson had 'evidently accepted without rancour' Joe McCrea's hands-on approach in persuading journalists to run exclusive stories based on leaks about new investment. However, shortly after her retirement in December 1998 she revealed her true feelings in an article for the *Sunday Times*.

Christopherson declared that Campbell had become the 'monarch of all he surveys' and that his grip on the government's information service was absolute. Her assessment proved correct because despite all the accusations about triple counting and the 'fiddling' of hospital waiting lists, the Department of Health remained wedded to the Downing Street decree that in order to gain maximum exposure, announcements had to be leaked in advance. Again, by chance, I managed to obtain another of its confidential 'media handling plans', which in this case was marked for the attention among others of Milburn and his political adviser, Darren Murphy. It was dated Wednesday 8 August 2001 and outlined the strategy which was to be adopted when the junior health minister, Hazel Blears, announced that the government had purchased the privately owned London Heart Hospital for £27.5 million, a move that would double the cardiac capacity at University College London Hospitals. By any test this was a sizeable financial transaction, which, if not actually market sensitive, would certainly be of commercial interest to other private care companies. Instead of preparing to make a public announcement at a set time, so that all journalists and interested parties had simultaneous access, the media plan indicated how the information would be leaked in advance and it followed, almost point by point, the instructions issued four years earlier in *Press Office Best Practice*:

> We are trailing the story with David Charter at the *Times*. In addition we will brief the *Today* programme . . . Once the story breaks in the *Times* this evening, the duty press officer will ring round all broadcasters and picture desks to let them know of the morning photo call . . . A press notice will be issued at 9.30 a.m.

The *Times* did the story proud on Thursday 9 August. In addition to David Charter's report about the NHS spending £27.5 million on purchasing a 'state-of-the-art heart hospital' there was an accompanying feature describing it as a 'heartening example of NHS managers knowing a good thing when they see it' and calling for similar flexibility in the future. The media plan did not reveal any of the background as to why the *Times* had been selected for the task of 'trailing the story' but here in cold print was a classic illustration of the Campbell ethos: take advantage of the media's appetite for exclusives; ignore all civil service constraints on the dissemination of sensitive financial information; and do not inform other news organisations until the leaked story has been published or broadcast by the chosen outlet. If a civil servant had been caught 'trailing' news of such a transaction without authority there would no doubt have been grounds for instant dismissal and possibly a prosecution, not least for insider trading. Also at risk was civil service impartiality because the press release was couched in highly political terms: the first ever purchase of an 'entire private hospital' was described as being a 'huge boost' for the NHS which would cut waiting times. Yet the unpublished confidential briefing note prepared for Milburn and Murphy told another side to the story: it said the owners, Gleneagles Hospital UK, had decided to 'sell to cut financial losses' and unless its shareholders had agreed the London Heart Hospital would be 'forced into liquidation'. Because of opposition within the party and trade unions to the whole concept of the private finance initiative, the briefing note said the purchase of the hospital showed that Labour could have a 'modern relationship' with the private sector.

Having read all the accompanying notes and e-mails, I considered that no Labour Party spin doctor could have done anything other than applaud the press officer from the Department of Health's NHS media team who had prepared the media plan. It would be unfair of me to identify him, but the documents do support my assertion: under Campbell's instruction, and with the approval of Labour ministers, civil service press officers were ignoring well-established conventions designed to protect confidential data and they had become some of the most effective leakers in the land. Among the information officers of Whitehall, the Department of Health had become renowned for its strict adherence to a policy of trailing not just announcements but also a wide range of medical and scientific reports. One senior press officer who returned there after a break of some years spoke to me anonymously. He described his surprise on finding how rigid this rule had become:

> Even research papers have to be leaked to selected journalists prior to publication. Previously documents like that would have been sent out well in advance under a strict embargo to give correspondents time to digest what had been said. But now a new generation of information officers believe that it is only by leaking that their department stands any chance of securing favourable coverage.

Another indication of the long-lasting and pernicious effect of a culture which has required civil servants to trade information in order to 'grab the agenda' emerged in August 2005, when a league table was discovered on the Department of Health's website which graded the impact of newspaper articles written by medical and political correspondents as having been 'negative', 'neutral' or 'positive'. Among the journalists whose articles in December 2004 had the highest 'positive' scores were Lorraine Fisher from the *Daily Mirror* and three from the *Sun*, George Pascoe-Watson, Nic Cecil and Andrew Parker. The department said the gradings had been published as part of its wider commitment to freedom of information and the research was undertaken in order to help to 'prioritise resources' in its media centre. Despite the assurance that there was no intention to ostracise difficult or hostile reporters, *PR Week* feared the list could be used to 'black list journalists or withdraw press office co-operation'. What *PR Week* failed to spot was that the positive ratings in the league table might also have provided an extremely useful guide to those newspapers which would be most willing to accept leaks and trail announcements.

Notwithstanding the assurances given by the government, unhelpful journalists had been targeted in no uncertain terms during the two and a half years when Joe McCrea exercised control over which reporters would benefit from the Department of Health's largesse. His first recorded confrontation involved the *Evening Standard's* health correspondent Jo Revill, who switched on her telephone-answering machine in October 1997 and found herself being lambasted for having written the 'most negative possible write-up of extra health care cash for London'. If Revill was going to continue to 'kick shit out of us', McCrea deemed there would be no point him giving her 'an advanced briefing' in future. Here was a spin doctor laying down the terms of trade: exclusive information and advance briefings were available but only in return for positive coverage. Two years later the air was blue outside a Channel 4 News studio when McCrea took exception to a report by its social affairs correspondent, Victoria Macdonald. After being 'rather indelicately' described as a 'fucking lying bitch', Macdonald said she faced further abuse at the Labour Party's annual conference in Bournemouth. Her conclusion, in an article for the *Evening Standard*, was that Labour could get away with such behaviour because the party had done such a successful job in 'persuading journalists that they need the spin doctors more than the spin doctors need them' and it was time journalists realised that although spin doctors liked to think they were the only source of information, often they were not.

McCrea's spats with a couple of health correspondents paled into insignificance when compared with the well-chronicled exploits of Charlie Whelan, whose sharp news sense and expertise as a leaker were matched by a similar penchant for foul-mouthed tirades. Instead of lowering his profile in line with his newly acquired status as a temporary civil servant in the Treasury, Whelan went on taking liberties with confidential information on a scale that continued to infuriate even Labour's two most compulsive leakers, Alastair Campbell and Peter Mandelson. From the moment he let slip to the *Daily Telegraph* that Mandelson's codename during Tony Blair's leadership campaign had been Bobby until his forced resignation after being blamed for leaking details of Mandelson's controversial home loan, Whelan had journalists queuing up for exclusives. Once Labour were elected and he could brief on behalf of the Chancellor of the Exchequer, he showed the same cavalier disregard for authority that he had displayed in opposition. Of all the escapades which characterised the undemocratic and unaccountable way in which he traded information with carefully selected newspapers on Gordon Brown's behalf was his infamous alfresco briefing outside the Red Lion in Whitehall in October 1997. Within earshot of other Friday night drinkers he confirmed the significance and accuracy of the exclusive given to the *Times* and the *Sun*: Brown was ruling out British membership of the European single currency for the whole of Labour's first parliament.

This was one of the government's most momentous financial decisions, perhaps second only to giving the Bank of England power to set interest rates, yet it had been supplied exclusively to two of Rupert Murdoch's most influential newspapers, both of which were highly sceptical of Britain joining the euro. Although the Chancellor was saved by the long parliamentary recess from the humiliation of having to make an immediate statement to the House of Commons, there was no escape from the ignominy which he faced the following Monday morning when he visited the London Stock Exchange, switched on a new trading system and had to endure an excruciating photo-opportunity. A massive screen behind him went red, indicating that billions of pounds were being wiped off share values because of concern over Labour's sudden change of tack. After barely six months as Chancellor he had learned two essential lessons: when the ground was being prepared for an important announcement, leaks and briefings had to be properly co-ordinated; if not, there was a real danger that news of an unexpected decision could damage confidence in the City of London. In the years that followed, Brown demonstrated repeatedly during the build-up to successive Budgets that he and his team of political advisers had mastered the process of massaging media speculation; most of his major tax changes were trailed so successfully in advance that there were rarely any surprises left when he finally appeared at the despatch box.

Unlike Campbell, who had grown to detest most journalists, Whelan enjoyed their company and remained a free spirit, regularly poking fun at what he considered were some of the more ridiculous examples of the control freakery of New Labour. Inside the Downing Street press office there was a much tighter regime. Campbell demanded total loyalty from the political advisers who were under his control. They had to realise they were at war with the news media; that meant engaging in nothing short of hand-to-hand combat with the enemy, and most journalists fitted that category. The duties performed by Campbell's first deputy, Tim Allan, epitomised the job require-ments of a young, up-and-coming New Labour spin doctor. Allan started working in Blair's office in October 1992, after leaving Cambridge University, and when the shadow Home Secretary was elected Labour leader two years later, and Allan was still in his early twenties, he was appointed deputy press officer. He became Campbell's willing helper, eager to do all he could to assist in promoting the party as it prepared for the 1997 general election.

As I was already being treated by Campbell and his fellow spin doctors as the lowest form of pond life, I was hardly surprised to find Allan trying to ape his boss's bombastic approach whenever I needed to speak to him. I was instructed never to identify him by name; any information he gave to me should always be attributed to 'a senior Labour source'. Allan had obviously embraced Campbell's emerging vendetta against the BBC because despite his inexperience he regarded himself as an authority on the editorial standards of broadcasters and the conduct of lobby journalists. While I was probably the last person to whom he would have offered an exclusive story, there were occasions, as in late November 1996, when Allan had no other alternative but to deal with the political correspondent on duty on that day. In the haughty tone which he tended to adopt, Allan demanded to know why I had not responded sooner to the offer by Blair's office to supply the BBC with a copy of a leaked memo from the Deputy Prime Minister, Michael Heseltine, which revealed that controversial changes were about to be made in the civil service. Being pressurised in this way to report a story which might damage the Conservatives was nothing out of the ordinary. Labour's proficiency in disseminating leaked documents was second to none and Allan's hard sell was only to be expected from a party which believed it might soon be in government. But once the tables had been turned and Labour were in power, Allan's freedom to exploit leaks to attack the Conservatives should have been curtailed. On joining the Downing Street press office as Campbell's deputy, he had become a special adviser to the Prime Minister and one of the conditions of his newly acquired status as a temporary civil servant was that as a government employee he should not engage in promoting attacks on Blair's political opponents. Campbell, as the Prime Minister subsequently observed, had done 'an effective job attacking the Conservative Party', notwithstanding his status as a civil servant, and his deputy did his very best to keep up. Within a few months of William Hague being elected the new Conservative leader, Allan drew my attention to the fact that that as a result of Cabinet pay increases agreed by the Labour government the salary of the leader of the opposition had risen to £98,700, almost twice as much as Blair had earned.

Occasionally Allan stood in for Campbell at the daily lobby briefings and this was another opportunity, when political journalists were gathered together, to peddle titbits which might embarrass the Tories. I heard from fellow correspondents that after a briefing in January 1998, Allan stayed behind when the lead civil service press officer, Allan Percival, left the room. He suggested to the reporters who remained in the room that they might like to check out the accuracy of what subsequently transpired to have been a Downing Street-inspired leak to the effect that the taxpayer had ended up paying the air fare for Ffion Hague when she attended the Hong Kong hand-over celebrations. The use of a lobby briefing to pose questions about Mrs Hague, which the Press Association attributed to 'a Labour source', was the last straw for Conservative Central Office: as only the cost of her husband's air fare was met by the state and the party had paid for her flight, the Conservatives demanded an immediate apology from the Prime Minister for what it claimed was Downing Street's 'scandalous attempt to smear' the leader of the opposition and his wife.

A month later, after Allan had been blamed for another inappropriate briefing, he demanded that I should be 'chucked out of the lobby'. At issue was my interpretation on *The World at One* of the guidance he had given about the lack of Cabinet support for the Lord Chancellor, Lord Irvine, after he suggested the introduction of a judicial safeguard of prior restraint to curb invasions of privacy by the press. I had quoted a Downing Street spokesman as saying that not a single minister backed Irvine, which Allan considered misrepresented what he had said. What caused him even greater irritation was his suspicion, which was quite correct as it happened, that I was probably the journalist whom Roy Hattersley had relied upon to confirm that it was Allan who had given the briefing; Hattersley wanted confirmation for a newspaper article he was writing.

In my election diary *Campaign 1997* I had identified Allan on several occasions as having been the source of controversial off-the-record briefings, so I was expecting to be rebuked. I was not disappointed: 'On what basis is this conversation taking place? . . . You should be chucked out of the lobby for writing about conversations on lobby terms.' Allan's complaint about my broadcast was part of the Labour Party's ongoing assault on the news judgement of Kevin Marsh, editor of *The World at One.* As Peter Oborne and Simon Walters revealed in their biography of Campbell, Allan overreached himself in the run-up to the 1997 general election and had to plead for mercy. Marsh suspected that Labour had been caught red handed leaking a report by the House of Commons Committee on Standards and Privileges into allegations against the Conservative MP Neil Hamilton. Despite three or four calls asking *The World at One* to drop the story, Marsh stood his ground. 'An agitated Allan rang him again and said: "If you run this story, I'm finished" . . . Marsh knew the story was risky . . . and decided to play safe and drop it.' However, the accusation that Labour had leaked the committee's report was broadcast later in the day on the *PM* programme.

After completing a year as Campbell's deputy in Downing Street, Allan, at the age of twenty-eight, was appointed director of corporate communications for Rupert Murdoch's satellite television channel BSkyB, on a reported annual salary of £85,000. On my wishing him well in his new job, he seemed to relish the chance to warn me that he would continue to exploit every opportunity 'to go on baiting the BBC'. According to the *Observer's* report of the farewell party which the Prime Minister hosted for him at No. 10 in May 1998, he was 'lavish in his praise for Campbell, saying "he taught me everything I know" '. Allan was true to his word and regularly used the authority of his position with BSkyB as a platform to support Campbell's repeated complaints about the 'lack of accountability' in BBC journalism. After establishing his own public relations agency, Portland, whose first client was BSkyB, he kept up his criticism of the BBC's editorial standards and in an article for the *Spectator* in February 2002 widened his attack by arguing against further expansion of the corporation, claiming that it had become 'a world-class rip-off'. Allan continued to deploy another of the skills which he had learned at the feet of Campbell, his ability to identify a juicy leak and to use it to feed the media's perpetual demand for exclusives. After hearing in September 2005 that in a speech to public relations executives, the *Today* presenter John Humphrys had apparently launched an attack on the truthfulness of Labour ministers, he leaked the contents to the *Times*, which ran the story under the headline 'Radio's king of rude launches another salvo at Labour "liars"'. Humphrys said the report, by Andrew Pierce and Tom Baldwin, was 'a stitch-up' and in the ensuing row about the degree of impartiality which should be expected from one of the BBC's leading broadcasters, the organisers, Richmond Events, said the only videotape and transcript of the speech had been given to Allan in his capacity as managing director of Portland PR and he had reneged on a commitment to use it 'exclusively and confidentially'.

After the BBC's director general, Mark Thompson, rebuked Humphrys for 'inappropriate and misguided remarks', Allan justified leaking the video on the grounds that he did 'nothing other than any journalist could have done' in asking for a copy of a speech delivered at a public event. 'I was glad that I was able to bring Humphrys' inappropriate and misguided comments to the attention of the BBC.' Richmond Events consulted its lawyers but the company's chief executive, Mark Rayner, abandoned plans to take legal action against Allan after being advised there was little chance of gaining redress. Despite a flurry of newspaper reports suggesting that some of Portland's clients were not at all impressed by the underhand behaviour of its managing director, his own evident satisfaction at having forced the BBC to rebuke Humphrys reflected the sense of empowerment which I had detected before among compulsive leakers. His continued dabbling in the darker arts of media manipulation seven years after leaving Downing Street reinforced my contention that the practice of leaking, which had become so entrenched under Campbell's regime, was highly addictive, a conclusion which I felt was more than justified by a surprisingly frank insider's account in *The Spin Doctor's Diary*, written by Allan's successor in the No. 10 press office, Lance Price. While much of the news coverage about the book concentrated on revelations about indiscretions and infighting among ministers during his three years as a Labour spin doctor, I was struck by the author's repeated, almost throwaway references to the constant flow of leaks and tip-offs emanating from Downing Street and other Whitehall departments.

Price acknowledged in his introduction that in agreeing to become Campbell's deputy in June 1998 he had to be 'a one hundred per cent Blair loyalist'. Instead of 'balancing all opinions', as he had been required to do in his previous job as one of the BBC's political correspondents, he would be 'pushing just one line and selling it as hard as I could'. While he admitted that Downing Street's 'strenuous efforts to shape the news agenda' did allow Campbell's staff to take advantage of journalists who were asking for 'exclusives to keep them one step ahead of their rivals', he made no mention of having sacrificed in the process another tenet of public service broad-casting, a belief in the principle of free and fair access for all journalists. I felt Price had been rather more candid about his stint as an information trader in an article for the *Independent on Sunday* in August 2003 when he described how he manipulated the pack of newspaper journalists which queued up for juicy stories. It was, he said, 'spin-doctor heaven' and his diary provided yet another illustration of the way a Labour-appointed special adviser could cock a snook at the rules requiring temporary civil servants to desist from exploiting their position for party advantage. Price was in his element trading information with favoured contacts, only too happy to compliment himself, as revealed by his entry for the day of Tony Blair's speech at the 1998 Labour conference: 'It's been a triumph for spin all week, really. Lots of good stories on the morning of TB's speech, all selectively leaked by me. In fact, an almost universally good press yesterday and today. Trebles all round.'

Price approached with gusto his role as Campbell's accomplice: another entry for September 1998 explained how he forced two rival Sunday newspapers to bid for an exclusive leak about zero tolerance on crime.

> AC said give it to the *Mail on Sunday* but only if they splashed with it. They wouldn't guarantee to do that so I gave it to the *Express* who would. The *Mail on Sunday* has a new editor and we got a bit worried that they'd do a spin doctors' story, so I ended up giving it to them and asking them to attribute it to the Home Office to cover my tracks. Nothing too wicked in that, I suppose.

Having noted in my own diaries the times and dates of all the various contacts I had with Price, and having observed the way he immediately took Campbell's side in attacking the editorial standards of the BBC, I was intrigued to see how far he would go in *The Spin Doctor's Diary* towards accepting that he might have failed to honour the terms of his civil service contract not to take part in 'political controversy' and to 'avoid personal attacks'. He made no mention, for example, of the day in June 1998, three weeks after joining the Downing Street press office, when he tipped off the BBC that William Hague had been admitted to hospital in Darlington for a sinus operation. Price rang the Westminster newsroom at 10.30 a.m., a full hour before a statement was issued by Conservative Central Office. His action met a chorus of approval because none of the editorial staff on duty at BBC Westminster could ever remember him delivering an exclusive during the many years he worked for the BBC. Nonetheless his own diary indicated there was a possible ulterior motive in promoting a story about the leader of the opposition being admitted to hospital: an earlier entry referred to Price's very first private conversation with the Prime Minister, during which he informed him that many Tory MPs 'were very unhappy with Hague who is off sick at the moment and would like to replace him as party leader'.

Price was surprisingly upfront in hinting that he had possibly breached the rules for his part in mounting a covert attempt to thwart Ken Livingstone's bid for the Labour nomination for mayor of London. This story gave me my first diary mention, for 5 February 1999: I had a note of Price asking *Westminster Live* if the programme wanted the No. 10 press office to help find a Labour MP to 'bash Ken'. In Price's entries for 14 and 18 February, while giving no hint as to precisely what he had been up to in the preceding few days, he did mention that he had 'tried to co-ordinate a bit of opposition to Ken' but faced the 'perennial problem that neither Number Ten nor the party can really get involved, or at least be seen to'. Another omission was any reference to his action in January 2000 in trying to persuade the BBC to follow up a magazine interview in the *Face* in which Livingstone had praised anti-capitalism rioters in Seattle and London. I took the call and he said Downing Street wanted to alert the BBC because Blair considered that the remarks indicated that Livingstone would return to 'gesture politics'. 'We've just been tipped off about it by the *Daily Telegraph* and they're going to run it.' By acting in such a calculated way to stir up opposition to Livingstone's candidature, Price had underlined Campbell's utter contempt for the undertaking which he had personally given to the House of Commons Public Administration Select Committee that he and his staff would always refer internal party issues to Labour headquarters.

Price considered he was equally proficient in leaking information about changes in government policy. In December 1999, after Downing Street commissioned a report on the implications of the north–south divide, he remarked that the 'stuff we trailed in advance was very good'. After Blair failed at Prime Minister's Questions in March 2000 to mention all the initiatives being taken by the Home Office to stem the flow of professional beggars from Romania seeking asylum in Britain, Price said he thought the rest of the measures would be suitable for leaking to the Sunday papers. On some occasions Downing Street would also act as a clearing house for leaks: for example, in October 1998, when the BBC's director general, John Birt, was intent on stopping BBC Scotland broadcasting its own *Six O'Clock News*, he asked for the help of the No. 10 press office in 'leaking an internal BBC survey that shows most Scots don't want it'. Price's diary was equally revealing about the sense of annoyance felt by ministers who had either been accused of leaking or who were the victims of hostile briefings. An entry for July 1998 gave a flavour of this anxiety: Harriet Harman, Secretary of State for Social Security, called Price to complain that she had been 'wrongly accused of leaking'.

While the sense of persecution being experienced by some ministers began to mirror the paranoia that pervaded Downing Street in Harold Wilson's day, trading exclusive stories had increasingly come to be regarded by the Prime Minister and his wife, as well as by most of their senior aides, as one of the few ways in which they could hope to exercise influence over the editors of tabloid newspapers. Price gave his account of two of the most celebrated leaks of Blair's first parliamentary term: the news in November 1999 that Cherie Blair, at the age of forty-five, was pregnant with her fourth child; and her husband's decision to postpone by a month the date of the 2001 general election. Some questions still remain to be answered about the precise route through which these disclosures reached the press but the accounts given so far have illustrated the lengths to which the Prime Minister and his entourage went to secure the most sympathetic coverage they could obtain for the exclusive information they had on offer. According to the publicist Max Clifford the original tip-off about Mrs Blair's pregnancy came from a 'senior Labour politician' who was repaying him for advice he had given on thwarting a woman intent on selling a story about an extra-marital affair. In his autobiography, Clifford said he gave the news of Mrs Blair's condition to Piers Morgan, editor of the *Daily Mirror*, who then rang Campbell to check if it was true. 'Alastair said it was true and then tipped off the *Sun*, so both papers ran with the "exclusive" . . . Piers was furious. If he hadn't called Alastair he'd have had the story for himself.' In his diaries, titled *The Insider*, the former *Mirror* editor said Clifford demanded a fee 'not massively far from £50,000' for 'a dynamite, but not nasty, one-fact story on Cherie'. After Morgan had informed Campbell that his paper would be leading with the news that Mrs Blair was pregnant, the Prime Minister was told at 5.30 p.m. and was said to be 'pretty relaxed' about the *Mirror* having the story as an exclusive. Then at 8 p.m., after eleven pages had been written on 'every conceivable nuance of this one-fact story', Campbell rang Morgan to say that Rebekah Wade, deputy editor of the *Sun* had 'got wind of it too'. Campbell's explanation was that Wade had somehow got word that the Prime Minister's wife was seriously ill, had phoned her at the Downing Street flat and it was then that Mrs Blair felt compelled to tell the truth. Morgan said he 'didn't believe a word of it' and accused Campbell of having lied to him. Shortly after 9 p.m., when the *Sun*'s first edition appeared with 'World Exclusive' emblazoned all over it, the Prime Minister rang Morgan to assure him that it had indeed been the case that the *Sun* had phoned No. 10 and that Wade had spoken to his wife. 'I don't want you thinking we have been playing politics with our baby, because I would never do that or allow anyone to do that.' Ten days later, still convinced that he had been lied to by both Tony Blair and his press secretary, Morgan telephoned Campbell's partner, Fiona Millar, who was Cherie Blair's personal press officer. She told him that Mrs Blair felt she had no choice but to tell the *Sun* because she 'didn't want her pregnancy used as some commercial tool, so she gave the story to Rebekah as well'. According to Price's diary, it was not Mrs Blair but Millar who 'told her friend Rebekah Wade' that the Prime Minister's wife was pregnant. 'Cherie had been spotted at the hospital and the *Sun* were asking if she was ill.'

Despite the conflicting accounts over precisely who said what to whom, the saga of Mrs Blair's pregnancy illustrated the unseemly manoeuvring which the Prime Minister was prepared to tolerate in a desperate attempt to retain the support of both the *Sun* and the *Daily Mirror*. Rather than spike the guns of tabloid editors by issuing an immediate public statement through the Press Association, Tony Blair knew all about the value of exclusive information and did not want to squander the chance of trading it for political advantage.

Price left Downing Street in June 2000 on being appointed the Labour Party's director of communications and it was in that job that he had a ring-side seat when the *Sun*'s political editor, Trevor Kavanagh, was tipped off that Blair had decided to postpone the expected date of the 2001 general election for a month because of the severity of the foot-and-mouth outbreak. Rarely had there been a deliberate leak of such constitutional importance: instead of observing the formalities of first informing the Queen, the Cabinet and Parliament, the Prime Minister felt it was more important to retain the support of Rupert Murdoch's biggest-selling daily paper. There was considerable confusion on the morning of the *Sun*'s front-page splash announcing its 'massive political exclusive' under the banner headline 'Election off'. Ministers spent the morning scurrying to catch up. In an interview for *Today*, the Secretary of State for Culture, Chris Smith, denied that a decision had already been taken; he had failed to accept, as did most political journalists, that the *Sun* had come to be regarded as the official notice board for Downing Street.

Kavanagh revelled in his exclusive, which the paper attributed to 'a senior minister', although when pressed on *The World at One* as to whether it was Campbell, he admitted it had come from 'a usually reliable source' who had helped him in the past, which political correspondents took as confirmation that it was the Downing Street press secretary. Price acknowledged in his diary that the *Daily Mirror* had been 'pissed off' by the leak because Kavanagh had 'splashed on it authoritatively', but the Labour Party could not risk losing the *Sun*'s support. Four months after Blair's return to Downing Street, Price told an election seminar that Labour believed the *Daily Mirror*'s support 'could be taken for granted' but that the party could not be so sure about the *Sun*: 'We had a considerable task on our hands to mollify the *Mirror* . . . but having the *Sun* on board was a sufficiently important prize to take that risk.' Juggling the party's interest against the competing pressures of the news media was a task which Price clearly took in his stride when leaking information. He helped orchestrate the defection to Labour of the gay businessman Ivan Massow, who had previously sought the Conservative nomination for mayor of London. Price offered the story to the *Independent*, which agreed to make it the splash on condition that it was an exclusive. When Massow heard the night before that *Channel 4 News* intended to break the story, he rang the station's controller, Michael Jackson, and told him the programme's staff were breaking a promise to keep it confidential. 'Eventually Jim Gray, editor of *Channel 4 News*, agreed and backed off. Andrew Grice, political editor of the *Independent*, was paranoid about losing his scoop but we managed to preserve it.' Price did not tell the whole story: according to an entry in my diary he rang the BBC's newsroom late in the afternoon and alerted the duty political correspondent, June Kelly, to the news that Massow was defecting. Initially Price insisted on an 11 p.m. embargo, so as not to jeopardise the *Independent*'s exclusive, but then brought it forward to 10.30 so that it could be reported by *Newsnight*.

During his twelve months at Labour headquarters, no longer troubled by the pretence of having to steer clear of party political work, Price had a more or less free hand in deciding how best to dispense the leaks and tip-offs at his disposal. He also had the freedom to work out how best to neutralise hostile leaks, a trick which Campbell had frequently pulled off with considerable aplomb. In September 2000, after the Conservatives obtained an illicit copy of Labour's political broadcast for Scotland, Price turned a potentially damaging leak to the party's advantage, accusing the Tories of 'a massive own goal' for giving it so much publicity. Another potential disaster was averted three weeks before the general election in June 2001 after a briefing note listing Labour's manifesto stories had accidentally been e-mailed to the *Daily Express* by Jim Godfrey, the party's senior press officer. Price feared the *Express* could 'easily have done us over with a big "Millbank leak" story but Jim managed to negotiate us out of it brilliantly'. In return for not 'embarrassing us' Price arranged for a couple of good stories to be leaked to the *Express*, which, to the delight of the party, subsequently recommended its readers to vote Labour for the first time in the paper's history.

What I had found so instructive about Price's account of his frenetic relationship with those journalists with whom he traded exclusive information was that during the two years he spent in Downing Street he treated the whole business of leaking in such a matter-of-fact way. Campbell's insistence in November 1997 that the government's information service had to learn how to 'grab the agenda' had obviously been taken to heart within a matter of weeks, because by the time Price joined the No. 10 press office in June 1998 the practice of trailing announcements was such a well-established routine that it was barely given a second thought, as his diary confirmed. Nevertheless there had been a transformation in the way news was being disseminated by the government: the media market place was there to be exploited, and confidential information was increasingly being treated as a form of currency which could be traded with selected journalists in return for the most favourable coverage.

As I know only too well, few political journalists have ever had any wish to enter into a discussion about the basis on which they have obtained exclusive stories and this reluctance to discuss their terms of trade has presented a rather insurmountable barrier whenever outside observers have tried to penetrate the murky world of media manipulation. Notwithstanding the obvious difficulties presented by a refusal to reveal sources, a group of political correspondents, information officers and party spin doctors did agree to assist a Cardiff University School of Journalism student, Mary Ellen Armstrong, who was studying the role of leaking in government news management. She published her dissertation in September 2004 and her research convinced her that selective briefing and leaking had become 'common practice' within Whitehall.

She concluded that both sides benefited from the arrangement: as long as government communicators continued to see advantage in this method of news management, the practice was unlikely to change because 'a journalist is able to claim an "exclusive" and score points in the highly competitive UK media environment'. Armstrong thought it was important to distinguish between the comparatively rare genuine leak, typically delivered in a brown envelope, and the much more common authorised leak, which usually took place in the context of a selective briefing, a process which many journalists and information officers considered was entirely legitimate. Again what stood out so clearly from the survey Armstrong conducted was the fact that trailing government announcements had become standard practice; political advisers and government communicators did not consider advance briefing for tactical advantage to constitute a leak, because they were trading confidential information in the knowledge that they had the authorisation of their ministers. Although told repeatedly she had to differentiate between authorised and unauthorised leaks, Armstrong doubted whether the journalists always knew whether their exclusive briefings had been sanctioned internally, as often it 'all looks the same to them'.

One of the most revealing responses she obtained was from the deputy head of news in a major Whitehall department who wished to remain anonymous. He concurred that the use of 'planned trails' was 'completely entrenched' as a communication tool within the government; ministers determined which information was ready to enter the public domain. 'It's all organised now . . . and we then make decisions about how the information is going to be released, when, and to whom.' Leaking by civil service press officers tended to fluctuate in content and frequency because it depended on the outlook of the minister in charge. 'Some showed great enthusiasm for the practice, while others would not dream of it.' Further evidence of the key pump-priming role played by ministerial aides was contained in the responses of Conor Ryan, who was David Blunkett's political adviser during the four years he was Secretary of State for Education. Ryan told Armstrong that he believed it was 'entirely proper' to give exclusive briefings ahead of significant announcements; 'most Fridays' he supplied the Sunday news-papers with stories which were usually 'relatively small scale' but which were 'picked up more often than not'. After spending a total of eight years as an adviser, in both opposition and government, Ryan reflected on his experiences in an article for the *Sunday Times* in December 2004 and, in answering the charge that Labour had been guilty of 'spin over substance', he said Blunkett 'certainly recognises the reach of popular papers such as the *Daily Mail* and the *Sun*'. David Hughes, the *Daily Mail*'s political editor, provided corroboration: when Labour were trying to get elected in the mid-1990s his paper was a favoured recipient of exclusive information.

> I frequently received leaks from the party leadership who were desperate to woo the middle England voters who make up our readership . . . Leaks are just about the most useful tool at the disposal of government to try to influence the news agenda . . . A well-placed and carefully timed leak can ensure that a policy issue dominates the news cycle, and they are frequently deployed in an attempt to squeeze out less favourable items.'

Ryan's justification for Labour's tactic of leaking information to the *Daily Mail*'s political editor could hardly have been bettered by either Peter Mandelson or Campbell. He believed that once elected, Labour had no alternative but to recognise that the party had to share the task of communicating the business of government: 'You can either play a role in helping to set the agenda, or you can leave it entirely to the press to set that agenda for you.' The danger for the government and the civil service was that Campbell and the network of political advisers under his control were prepared to take ever greater risks in their desperation to 'set the agenda' and therein lay what I considered was the malign influence of the changes which had taken place. Nothing, it seemed, was off limits when it came to trading confidential information with those editors and journalists who were favoured by Tony Blair's kitchen Cabinet and the No. 10 press office. By loosening the civil service rules on confidentiality, and by failing to encourage procedures which ensured that all news outlets were informed of developments simultaneously, Campbell had dragged the government machine ever deeper into the murky world of media manipulation.

Ministerial offices across Whitehall were undoubtedly responding faster and more effectively to the pressures being imposed by newspapers, television and radio and Campbell could take considerable personal credit for the increased professionalism being shown by the government's information service. Nonetheless, by the end of Blair's first four years in office, Campbell had succeeded in establishing himself as the most powerful information trader in modern British politics. He had, in effect, become the editor of an alternative news service, able to deliver scoops, exclusive interviews and unprecedented access to a string of favoured journalists, action which had acquired the official blessing of the Whitehall machine.

Chapter 7

Alastair Campbell's promotion after Labour won the 2001 general election reflected the importance of his expanded role in Downing Street. His appointment, to the newly created post of Prime Minister's director of communications and strategy, relieved him of the daily responsibility of briefing lobby correspondents. He assumed overall control of the government's media strategy and as a result hoped to spend more time considering how ministers' objectives could best be communicated to the public. Although two senior civil service press officers, Godric Smith and Tom Kelly, took on the shared task of briefing journalists in the name of the Prime Minister's official spokesman, the lobby was told that Campbell would still 'talk to the press from time to time'. The message was clear: trading confidential information with trusted media outlets would remain one of the unseen and unwritten responsibilities of the director of communications, a role that would assume even greater significance during the build-up to the war against Iraq in March 2003 and the bitter recriminations which followed the US-led attack. In view of his own furtive behaviour during the controversy over the contents of the government's dossier on Iraq's weapons of mass destruction and the crisis which developed in the relationship between Downing Street and the BBC, it was perhaps entirely fitting that Campbell's own ignominious resignation in August 2003 should have been hastened by an unauthorised, off-the-record briefing given three months earlier by an equally adept and anonymous information trader, Dr David Kelly.

The circumstances which surrounded the death in July of that year of Britain's leading authority on biological warfare and one of its most experienced weapons inspectors were examined at length by the Hutton inquiry, which, coincidentally, did more than any other recent investigation to expose the covert exchange of information between the state and the news media. In their own individual way, but self-evidently for entirely different reasons, Campbell and Kelly had both become addicted to taking selected journalists into their confidence. Campbell never faltered in the justification he gave for his actions: his duty was to support Blair, the government and the Labour Party. Kelly's motives must remain a matter of conjecture but, however misguided his conduct might have appeared to ministers and the civil service hierarchy, he seemed to be acting in what he believed was the public interest, supplying the news media with information which he thought might help generate an informed debate about the need to stop the proliferation of chemical and biological weapons.

Campbell remained wedded to his addiction until the very last moment. Of all the revelations at the Hutton inquiry, perhaps the insight which got closest to unmasking his compulsion to trade information was the account of how he intended to outflank the BBC at the height of the row over Andrew Gilligan's allegation that Downing Street had 'sexed up' the British government's dossier on Iraq's weapons of mass destruction. Realising that he was getting nowhere with his complaint about the inaccuracy of the BBC's reporting, Campbell was desperate to keep up the pressure and in July 2003 he was overheard suggesting that one of the newspapers should be told that the Ministry of Defence believed it had discovered the source of Gilligan's story. Here we saw an information trader at work: a potential deal with an unidentified journalist was in the offing and in all likelihood the eventual currency for this transaction would have been the name 'Kelly'. Campbell was explicit in entries in his own personal diary about the likely impact once this news got out: 'GH [Geoff Hoon] and I agreed it would fuck Gilligan if that was his source.' Lord Hutton, who spent six months taking evidence and preparing his report into Kelly's death, failed to ascertain the identity of the likely recipient of this potential hot tip from Downing Street. Under cross-examination by James Dingemans QC, counsel for the inquiry, Campbell insisted that his plan to give this information to one newspaper was simply 'a thought that was born and died within minutes'. Nonetheless the Hutton inquiry, which set a new benchmark for openness and access to transcripts and official documents, laid bare the rotten, corruptive nature of Campbell's regime. Admittedly, in his own evidence, he did acknowledge that it had in the event been a mistake to allow the Ministry of Defence to confirm Kelly's name to five newspapers 'in an uncontrolled way', but his whole approach showed that his repeated calls for a 'more open and honest' dialogue between government and the media were nothing more than a sham.

Throughout his confrontation with the BBC, and what he said turned into 'a media firestorm' for the government, Campbell displayed scant regard to the moral obligation on Downing Street and the Ministry of Defence to act responsibly when briefing the media and to have some thought for Kelly's welfare. Whenever there was a discussion about how best to disseminate information, he seemed to develop tunnel vision and, whatever the eventual cost to the Prime Minister and his colleagues, Campbell's only concern was to put the BBC at a disadvantage. Although he tried to justify his reasons for wanting it 'put into the public domain' that Gilligan's 'source had broken cover' and that 'the biggest thing needed was the source out', his diary entries made no mention at any point of him ever having considered releasing this news to all media outlets at the same time and in a controlled manner, through one or other of the official channels available to Downing Street, such as a lobby briefing, the No. 10 website or a statement to the Press Association. Campbell could not let go; he appeared unable to control his compulsion to deal with journalists on a selective and partial basis, despite having told all and sundry as early as June 2000 that he intended to concentrate on future strategy and spend less time briefing political correspondents. Even after his promotion and the appointment of two official spokesmen to conduct the twice-daily lobby briefings, Campbell was still hard at it, talking on an off-the-record basis to his chosen elite of 'editors and senior journalists', never letting them forget that he was intent on controlling the market place in confidential government information.

Publicly Campbell lost no opportunity to berate reporters for their 'relentless negativity'; he complained regularly about the general decline in editorial standards, but privately his approach when dealing with political correspondents at Westminster remained one of divide and rule. As long as he retained the confidence of a number of journalists in key positions on what he thought were the most influential newspapers, he believed the majority of political reporters would have little alternative but to follow in the wake of the exclusives which he was releasing. The chain of events which ended with Kelly taking his own life illustrated the degree to which the importance of trying to influence the daily news cycle dictated the decision-making process in the No. 10 press office. Throughout the offensive against Iraq, Campbell had been critical of what he claimed was an anti-war agenda in much of the BBC's coverage. Therefore once Kelly agreed to an unauthorised meeting with *Today*'s defence correspondent in the Charing Cross Hotel, and once a weapons inspector of his authority started opening up on issues which were of concern to the intelligence services, such as the accuracy of the Iraq dossier, the BBC's subsequent coverage was bound to cause further annoyance. Andrew Gilligan did not pull his punches: he alleged the government 'probably knew' that the claim that Iraq was capable of deploying weapons of mass destruction 'within forty-five minutes of an order to use them' was wrong, even before Downing Street decided to put it in the dossier.

Effectively Gilligan was suggesting, on the basis of what he had been told by 'one of the senior officials in charge of drawing up the dossier', that Blair had taken Britain to war on a lie, which was certainly how *Today*'s broadcast was interpreted by Campbell. So great was his determination to force the BBC to apologise that he could barely restrain himself once he was informed on Friday 4 July 2003 that a Ministry of Defence employee had volunteered the fact that he was possibly the source of Gilligan's allegation that Downing Street had 'sexed up' its dossier on Saddam Hussein's weapons of mass destruction. Campbell noted in his diary that Gilligan's contact was 'an expert rather than a spy or full-time MoD official' and that was why he and Geoff Hoon, the Secretary of State for Defence, agreed that 'it would fuck Gilligan if that was his source'. Next day an exclusive story in the *Times* by its political correspondent Tom Baldwin revealed far more about the 'military expert' who was believed to be the source than Gilligan had disclosed in his own evidence when questioned by the House of Commons Foreign Affairs Committee. Hoon was so concerned that he asked Campbell about the story that Saturday morning. It was the following Monday, 7 July, after he had been informed that the MoD believed Gilligan's contact was in fact Dr David Kelly, that Campbell was overheard trying, as he recorded in his diary, to 'get it out through the papers' that the source 'was not in the intelligence community, not involved in drawing up the dossier'. At six that evening Godric Smith, one of the two official spokesmen, was in Campbell's office in Downing Street when Campbell, who was talking to Hoon, switched the conversation to a speaker phone.

Smith told the inquiry what happened next: 'Alastair floated the idea that the news that an individual had come forward, who could be the possible source, be given that evening to one paper.' A little later, after discussing what he had heard with his colleague Tom Kelly, Smith telephoned

Campbell to tell him that they both considered this was 'a bad idea'. They thought it was in the public interest that the government should make any announcement itself and that it 'seemed somewhat complex to have the story appear in one newspaper and then be subsequently confirmed that evening by the Ministry of Defence'. In giving his evidence to Lord Hutton, it was obvious Smith had chosen his words with great care and it was plain that both he and Tom Kelly had no wish to play any part in the kind of underhand trade-off which Campbell had in mind. As senior information officers in the civil service, the two official spokesmen would have realised the danger they might have faced if it was ever discovered that either of them had given their support or participated in the leaking of such a sensitive news item to a journalist. During his cross-examination at the inquiry, Hoon gave his account of the conversation. He said that Campbell suggested they 'might brief a journalist' that someone had come forward 'as a means of putting further pressure' on the BBC. Hoon recalled how definite he had been: 'I resisted . . . I was pretty doubtful about that . . . I was not thinking of briefing a newspaper and indeed I did not agree to that approach.' When Campbell was questioned about his motives, he told Hutton that on the morning of the day he made his suggestion to Hoon he was aware that David Kelly was 'judged by the Ministry of Defence to be in all likelihood Gilligan's source'.

What he was suggesting was that 'the fact of somebody coming forward should be put into the public domain' before the Prime Minister faced MPs' questions the following morning at a meeting of the House of Commons Liaison Committee.

> I hesitate even to call it a proposal, it was a thought which was very quickly rejected by the Defence Secretary. Godric Smith and Tom Kelly both thought it a bad idea. But more importantly I raised it with the Prime Minister, he thought it was a bad idea and nothing came of it . . . This was a thought that was born and died within minutes.

After Campbell had been pressed further and had assured Hutton that he was not envisaging that the name itself should be conveyed 'in anything other than an open way, making clear that this was information that would come from the government', it was put to him that in his evidence Smith had said he and Tom Kelly had both thought the government should make the source public itself and not give it that evening to 'one paper . . . without, as it were, the government's fingerprints on it'. Campbell insisted again that he had not proposed conveying the name: 'Had the decision been taken that, yes, this should be done, there would then have been a proper discussion about how. But that is not a piece of information that the government could reasonably put into the public domain in an anonymous, unattributable way.' Despite his protestations of innocence before the inquiry and his attempts to cover his tracks, Campbell knew that he had, in effect, been caught red handed, preparing the way for one of the transactions which became the hallmark of his six and a half years in Downing Street.

The clear implication of his evidence was that if he had not been restrained by his colleagues, he might well have been tempted to leak David Kelly's name, two days before it was eventually confirmed by the director of news at the MoD, Pamela Teare, when it was put to her by the *Financial Times*; Kelly's name was later confirmed to the *Guardian*, the *Daily Mail*, the *Daily Telegraph* and the *Times*. In the opinion of many political journalists, the most likely recipient of the leak would have been Tom Baldwin of the *Times*, who had developed the uncanny knack of reproducing the very phrases that Campbell had recorded in his diary. For example, the day after his entry about his attempt to 'get it out' that Gilligan's contact was on the point of being identified, Baldwin used almost the same phraseology in a question-and-answer column in his paper: the source was not 'a member of the intelligence services and was not involved in drafting the report, but more likely is a weapons of mass destruction specialist'.

Having drawn back the veil on this hidden world, Hutton was intrigued about the precise meaning of Campbell's diary entry for the day that he had 'floated' what his colleagues thought was 'a bad idea'. It read: 'Several chats with MOD, Pam Teare, then Geoff H re the source. Felt we should get it out through the papers, then have line to respond and let TB take it on at Liaison Committee. TB felt we had to leave it to Omand/Tebbit judgement and they didn't want to do it'. What, asked Hutton, did the 'it' refer to?

Campbell said that the Prime Minister had told him he wanted any follow-up action relating to the identity of Gilligan's source to be sorted out by Sir David Omand, the security and intelligence co-ordinator in the Cabinet Office, and Sir Kevin Tebbit, permanent secretary at the Ministry of Defence. Leaving it to the 'Omand/Tebbit' judgement meant they did not want to do 'anything out of the ordinary, untoward, anything like this'.

James Dingemans QC was mystified as to who did what in the Downing Street press office. How would information about the source be given to one newspaper? Was Campbell continuing to talk to journalists when it was the responsibility of the Prime Minister's two official spokesmen to brief the media? Campbell: 'Well, yes is the answer'. Dingemans: 'You did brief journalists at the time about this story?' Campbell: 'Yes, I was talking to journalists certainly . . . I mean, I talked to journalists when . . . I mainly talk to editors and senior journalists. At this time I was emphasising that I did not believe that the BBC source was a senior intelligence official and I did not believe that their source was somebody centrally involved in the drawing up of the dossier.' Although Campbell denied having 'any knowledge of any information' given to Tom Baldwin about Kelly's status, he was not questioned any further about the identity of the select clientele of 'editors and senior journalists' with whom he was in contact. But Dingemans had made the point: Campbell ran his own private operation to brief those newspaper correspondents whom he trusted and it was quite separate from the official system of Downing Street lobby briefings which served not just the papers but also broadcasters, news agencies and a growing number of websites.

When asked to comment on procedure adopted by the MoD press office on Wednesday 9 July of identifying Kelly if the 'correct name is given' by journalists, Campbell reminded Hutton that by then he had been asked by the Prime Minister to 'take pretty much of a back seat on all of this' and was therefore 'under strict instructions' not to get involved. On reflection Campbell felt it would have 'been better if there had been greater clarity and control' in the naming of Kelly. 'I think it is always a mistake to cede control on these issues to the press.' Campbell's belief was that Kelly 'understood' that he was about to be named by the MoD and again he agreed it would have been better if Kelly had been brought in earlier as part of an agreed strategy:

> You cannot just let this sort of dribble out . . . far better it would have been for that to be announced properly, cleanly, straightforwardly and then you can actually put in place all the proper support that somebody who is not used to this kind of pressure can then maybe better deal with.

As the evidence unfolded during the course of the inquiry it emerged that Kelly had been as discreet as the Prime Minister's director of communications when briefing the select band of journalists whom he trusted and whom he was prepared to take into his confidence about his work as a weapons inspector. Having established himself as Britain's foremost authority on biological warfare, he was authorised – and encouraged – to brief journalists on technical matters relating to weapons of mass destruction and their use by states such as Iraq.

While Kelly's motives for going beyond the strict limits on what he could say, and for talking so freely to Gilligan, were not probed to any great degree during the course of the inquiry, he was said by his colleagues and family to place a great importance on his media work. On occasion he would break off conversations at social engagements simply in order to take a journalist's telephone call and, by all accounts, he took a close interest in any news reports which were subsequently published or broadcast. He was regarded as an invaluable contact by numerous well-established newspaper correspondents and broadcasters, both in Britain and around the world, and although we may never know why he was prepared to take the risks which he did in exceeding civil service guidelines, I concluded that in many ways his profile fitted those who leak information in the belief they are serving the public interest, which in his case appeared to be a desire to encourage an informed discussion about the action which he believed was needed to curb the proliferation of chemical and biological weapons. Kelly had been authorised and 'actively encouraged' to talk to the press since 1991; in 1995 his resource manager at Porton Down, Andrew Shuttleworth, made the task of briefing journalists, government bodies and learned societies one of his key personal targets. However, he was bound by the Official Secrets Act; there were strict limits on what he could say; and he was advised to avoid being quoted by name. Operational information, which might be of use to an enemy, could not be referred to; 'politically controversial issues' were another no-go area.

Richard Hatfield, personnel director for the MoD, told the inquiry that in meeting Gilligan on 22 May 2003, and by revealing details of disagreements within the government over the content and wording of the Iraq dossier, Kelly had broken the rules. Within days of Gilligan's broadcast on 29 May, Sir Kevin Tebbit wrote to the chief of defence intelligence, expressing a 'high level of concern' about leaks and unauthorised statements to journalists. Members of the intelligence staff were asked to report their suspicions about the identity of any leaker or individual known to be unhappy about the 'forty-five-minute readiness' to use weapons of mass destruction. By mid-June, Kelly's dealings with journalists had begun to raise suspicion. His line manager, Dr Bryan Wells, director of counter-proliferation and arms control, looked into a report in the *Observer* which quoted a 'UK source' who had inspected mobile facilities in Iraq and who believed they were for hydrogen production, not biological weapons; Wells recalled Kelly 'expressing that view to me', but when questioned he had denied being the

Observer's source. Once Patrick Lamb, deputy head of the counter-proliferation department, recalled that Kelly had referred 'very fleetingly' to having spoken to Gilligan several days before the *Today* broadcast, he informed the deputy chief of defence intelligence, Martin Howard, who concluded that Kelly should be interviewed.

By then events were closing in rapidly: after Gilligan was questioned by the House of Commons Foreign Affairs Committee on 19 June, a close colleague and former weapons inspector, Olivia Bosch, warned Kelly that Gilligan's evidence seemed to indicate he might be the source, because she recognised similarities in references to Iraq's chemical and biological capacity. Finally, on 30 June, Kelly decided to own up. He wrote to Wells informing him that he met Gilligan on 22 May; that he did discuss the issue of 45-minute deployment; that he told Gilligan it was included in the dossier 'probably for impact'; but that when Gilligan raised the issue of Alastair Campbell, he replied that he was not involved and was unable to comment. He accepted that he had fallen under suspicion because of his long association with Iraq, and although he deeply regretted talking to Gilligan, he was convinced he was not the *Today* correspondent's 'primary source of information . . . the single source referred to': 'I most certainly have never attempted to undermine government policy in any way especially since I was personally sympathetic to the war because I recognised from a decade's work the menace of Iraq's ability to further develop its non-conventional weapons programme'. Once Kelly admitted having had an unauthorised and unreported conversation with Gilligan, there was no going back: within a matter of days his identity had been revealed and he had to face the ordeal of a televised hearing before MPs on the Foreign Affairs Committee.

The line of questioning which most disturbed him related to another BBC report on 2 June by *Newsnight*'s science editor, Susan Watts. She quoted 'a senior official intimately involved' in the dossier who said that the government was 'obsessed with finding intelligence on immediate Iraqi threats' and that the 45-minute claim had 'got out of all proportion'. Kelly was said to have been 'totally thrown' when the quote used by Watts was put to him, and the full significance of her off-the-record conversations with him emerged only after his death: she had a shorthand note of one conversation and a tape recording of another; the transcripts confirmed that he had indeed said that the 45-minute warning had been seized on by Campbell and that the government was wrong to have included it in the dossier. Watts's note of her conversation with Kelly on 7 May was precise about the claim that chemical and biological weapons were deployable within forty-five minutes: 'Mistake to put it in . . . A. Campbell seeing something in there . . . single source . . . but not corroborated . . . sounded good.' Anxious to follow up the *Today* programme of the previous morning, she spoke to Kelly again on 30 May and told him she feared she had 'missed a trick' because her notes of their earlier conversation showed that he was 'actually quite specific' about the 45-minute deployment and had 'actually referred' to Campbell. Kelly agreed and added that he had also spoken the previous evening to another BBC correspondent, Gavin Hewitt. His report for the *Ten O'Clock News* quoted 'one of those who was consulted on the dossier' as having said that 'some spin from No. 10 did come into play'.

When Watts asked whether he had been getting much flak over what the BBC had been reporting, Kelly laughed and said he had been away in New York. 'I mean, they wouldn't think it was me, I don't think. Maybe they would, maybe they wouldn't. I don't know.' In another response, Kelly confirmed that he had expressed his unease about the section of the dossier dealing with the 45-minute warning: 'I reviewed the whole thing, I was involved in the whole process.' Here in Watts's transcripts was the confirmation which Kelly's superiors had been looking for: they had the proof they needed about the true extent of the information which he was imparting to journalists. Sir Richard Dearlove, head of the Secret Intelligence Service, MI6, told Lord Hutton that he had been 'shocked' to find that Kelly had spoken to Watts about unhappiness in the intelligence community over the 45-minute claim; 'it was a serious breach of discipline'. Richard Hatfield declared that contact with Gilligan had been 'a fundamental failing' and he would have been 'forced to suspend' Kelly had he known what he was disclosing to the media. The sense of shock among the defence and intelligence chiefs was palpable: they found it hard to believe that a senior government scientist had leaked highly restricted information and shown such a clear disregard for official secrecy. Although Hutton did inquire into Kelly's dissatisfaction with his salary and grading and his perceived frustration over the lack of recognition for his work, few witnesses offered an opinion as to other factors which might have motivated him.

Needless to say members of the Downing Street press office were decidedly more forthright. Tom Kelly, one of the Prime Minister's official spokesmen, apologised unreservedly to the Kelly family after telling Paul Waugh of the *Independent* that he believed David Kelly had been a 'Walter Mitty' character. Campbell had been equally succinct in his diary: 'Kevin said the

guy claimed he never mentioned me, he was a bit of a show off though.'
When asked whether this was correct, Sir Kevin Tebbit bridled momentarily
before deigning to respond to what he dubbed Campbell's 'very racy diary
style'. He was adamant that he had not used the expression 'show off', which
prompted Jeremy Gompertz QC, counsel for the Kelly family, to ask if that
supported the evidence of other witnesses who had described Kelly as 'a very
modest man'. Tebbit thought that was only part of the story: 'I think it is also
true that he enjoyed talking to journalists, that he enjoyed very wide relations
with journalists and was regarded very highly by them. And that contrasts a
little with the idea of the modesty.' In my opinion Tebbit had correctly
identified a common characteristic of anonymous information traders: the
satisfaction they can derive from helping journalists; the kinship they feel
with well-known media figures; and the sense of achievement which they can
experience from having had some influence over the content and direction of
news coverage in the press and on television and radio. What also emerged
during cross-examination at the inquiry was that prior to the controversy
over the Iraq dossier, Kelly had always been regarded as having been 'very
scrupulous . . . very helpful' about informing the Counter Proliferation
Department of his contacts with journalists.

Patrick Lamb said the system for providing the media with 'expert
background briefing' on an unattributable basis had worked well and led to
'no embarrassments' for the government in the two years up to 2002. 'There
is an element of self-discipline and judgement . . . Dr Kelly, I think, understood very clearly that he should not become involved on commenting on
current UK government policy.' When giving his evidence Lamb had
appeared not to recognise, as Tebbit subsequently did, that talking to
journalists can become addictive. Wing Commander John Clark, a long-
standing friend who accompanied Kelly to the House of Commons, told the
inquiry there was never any secret about his colleague's work with the media:
'He was quite proud that he had many press contacts, from diverse
backgrounds.' As I can attest from my own experience as a journalist,
relationships of this kind do strengthen over time. Most established reporters
know how to flatter their contacts and we do put a great deal of thought and
effort into developing our techniques for eliciting information. Olivia Bosch
said Kelly always appeared 'fairly relaxed' about it: 'He seemed to enjoy
talking with the press and giving them background information. He knew
they were seeking information to better understand what some of the
processes were that were going on in Iraq.'

During the two years Watts was in contact with Kelly she found that he often made 'gossipy remarks' during their telephone conversations. Referring to the transcripts, James Dingemans QC asked whether she thought Kelly sometimes used 'a chatty aside' to impart information. Watts replied that she felt able to discern the difference between 'a glib statement' and remarks based on 'his expert opinion or his considered opinion'. She had not broadcast the quote 'mistake to put it in . . . Alastair Campbell seeing something in there', because she considered it to be 'a gossipy aside', not 'particularly controversial' and, as Kelly appeared to be 'speculating in a way that he did not generally', it was not a comment she would have wanted to use 'with confidence' in a *Newsnight* report.

> I think both of us began to trust each other more and I feel that he trusted the way that I was using the information . . . I formed the view very definitely he had extraordinary access to government information across the board . . . I would say that he was passing information to me that was not sensitive in any way, not operational information . . . and not whistle blowing in any sense.

Susan Watts's name was the last which Kelly agreed should be highlighted in a list of journalists being compiled at the MoD on the day he died. In order to reply to questions tabled by MPs after his appearance before the Foreign Affairs Committee, Kelly had been asked to list all his one-to-one meetings with journalists during the previous two years. As Watts's reports on *Newsnight* had been mentioned during the committee hearing, departmental officials thought her name should be included in the list, which referred to his specific rather than general contacts. The two had met only once, on a Foreign Office open day in November 2002.

Clark obtained Kelly's approval to the change in the list shortly before 3 p.m. on Friday 17 July; when he rang again twenty minutes later to check about a meeting with Nick Rufford of the *Sunday Times*, he was told by Janice Kelly that her husband had left for a walk, during the course of which he committed suicide. Listening to an account of how David Kelly spent his final hours, having to remember the occasions and names of the journalists with whom he had been in contact, was an awkward moment for the reporters covering the inquiry. I found it particularly harrowing because in my career I had known people in public life who had gone the extra mile on my behalf, who had provided me with information which their superiors would have been most reluctant to have seen divulged. An indication of the reliance placed on Kelly as an authoritative source on biological weapons was the seemingly endless roll call of news organisations whose journalists he had assisted: the BBC, ITN, *Channel 4 News*, Reuters, the Canadian and Australian Broadcasting Corporations, the *Sunday Times*, the *Financial Times*, the *New York Times*, the *Washington Post*, the *Wall Street Journal* and so on. Uncomfortable though it was to hear of the painstaking way Kelly had been required to collate details of his various contacts with the media, my personal reflections had to take second place to the task of keeping up with the relentless pace of the inquiry, because next day, Thursday 28 August, the principal witness was to be Tony Blair.

This would create another momentous event in recent political history: the sight of the Prime Minister arriving at the Royal Courts of Justice after having been called to give evidence at a judicial inquiry. Most of the questions were focused on Blair's involvement with the preparation of the dossier, his role in the dispute with the BBC over the accuracy of Andrew Gilligan's broadcast and the steps which were taken once Kelly had identified himself. Blair told Lord Hutton he thought from the start that there was 'a fair possibility' the name would leak and, after being alerted by Alastair Campbell to the danger of the government being criticised for withholding it, he told his director of communications that it was his 'firm view' that the naming of Kelly had to proceed in a way that Sir Kevin Tebbit and Sir David Omand were 'entirely content with'. As to the central allegation, that he had allowed the 45-minute claim to be included in the dossier contrary to the wishes of the intelligence services, and 'probably knowing it was wrong', if that allegation were true, then 'it would have merited my resignation'. Blair's determination to stand his ground and take 'full responsibility' for the decisions which he and his colleagues had taken was rewarded with a one-word headline on the front page of the *Sun*: 'Defiant'. Other newspapers were equally complimentary: the *Guardian* concluded that the Prime Minister had handled himself in the witness box with 'his usual great skill'; the verdict of leader writers for both the *Independent* and the *Daily Express* was that it had been 'an assured performance'. Finding that the Prime Minister had emerged apparently unscathed from the Hutton inquiry was of far greater importance to Campbell than most journalists had probably realised because it gave him an opportunity he had waiting for, the chance to carry out his long-threatened resignation and make a clean break from Downing Street. By taking advantage of a day when press comment was far more supportive than the No. 10 press office might have dared hope, he was able to brush aside suggestions that his departure had been purposely timed to follow Blair's appearance the previous day. Instead he stuck firmly to the line that it had always been his intention to leave in the summer of 2003; he had informed the Prime Minister of his decision to quit the previous April.

Campbell refused point blank to discuss the evidence which had emerged during the first phase of the inquiry but his position had become increasingly untenable in the face of continuing revelations about his prominent role in preparing the dossier, his feud with the BBC over the accuracy of Gilligan's reporting, and the subsequent naming of Dr Kelly. Like other high-profile witnesses Campbell was recalled for further cross-examination in late September but then had to endure the long wait until Hutton published his conclusions in January 2004. Under a blanket of tight security, and in order to give the leading players and their lawyers time to prepare their responses, copies of the report were supplied to Downing Street, the BBC and the Kelly family twenty-four hours before Hutton was due to announce his findings at lunchtime the following day. All the recipients had to sign a legally binding agreement not divulge the contents, but within hours of the advance copies being handed over, there was news of another breathtaking leak: the *Sun* had obtained a full summary of Hutton's conclusions. Next morning, as he prepared for a televised hearing at the Royal Courts of Justice, Hutton found that he had been comprehensively upstaged.

Under the strap line 'World Exclusive', the *Sun*'s front page said it all: 'BBC "at fault" . . . Gilligan's story was "unfounded"; Blair cleared of using sneaky ploy to name Dr Kelly.' A photograph of the paper's political editor, Trevor Kavanagh, holding a telephone to his ear was the only clue to as to how he had obtained what was billed the 'scoop of the year': 'It was the call every journalist in Westminster was waiting for . . . the conclusions of Lord Hutton . . . Trevor noted them all down from a trusted source.' The leak was so comprehensive and appeared so authoritative that its authenticity was not questioned by the rest of the national press. Most papers led their front pages with what the *Daily Mail* said was the 'furore over Hutton leak' and the news that Blair and Campbell had both been exonerated and were 'off the hook'. An immediate investigation by the commissioner of the Metropolitan Police was demanded by the Conservatives, who blamed Downing Street and pointed out that the leak had gone to the *Sun*, the one newspaper which had consistently backed the Prime Minister over the war against Iraq. Not unnaturally the *Sun* trumpeted other scoops by its political editor, including his exclusive on the postponing of the 2001 general election; to ram home the point, the hero of the hour toured television and radio studios to insist that the inquiry's findings had been leaked to him by someone who had 'no axe to grind, and nothing to gain either financially or politically'. Even so, given No. 10's long track record of co-operating with the *Sun*, the finger of suspicion fell immediately on Campbell, who issued a prompt denial: 'This is totally untrue and deeply offensive.'

Downing Street was similarly forthright, insisting the Prime Minister was 'very angry'; later Blair told MPs that he supported the demand for an inquiry and would take whatever action was recommended. However distracting the leak might have been for Hutton, and he did announce he would consider whether legal action could be taken against the *Sun*, the flurry of pre-publicity had not reflected anything like the full force of the judge's criticism of the BBC and the devastating impact his conclusions would have on the corporation's journalists and management. Not only were Gilligan's allegations judged to have been 'unfounded', but the BBC's editorial system was 'defective' because editors had not seen Gilligan's script and had failed to prevent *Today* broadcasting 'false accusations of fact impugning the integrity of others', the BBC's management was at fault for 'failing to investigate properly' the government's complaints, and the BBC's governors were criticised for failing to make 'more detailed investigations' to establish whether Gilligan's report was properly supported by his notes and also for failing to acknowledge publicly that these 'very grave allegations in relation to a subject of great importance should not have been broadcast'. Hutton's exoneration of the Prime Minister and his colleagues was as sweeping as had been his censure of the BBC. He concluded: 'There was no dishonourable or underhand or duplicitous strategy by the government covertly to leak Dr Kelly's name to the media.'

Caught up in the midst of 'a major controversy' provoked by Gilligan's 'very grave allegations', the government's main concern, that it 'would be charged with a serious cover up' if it did not reveal that a civil servant had come forward, was 'well founded'; media interest was so intense that David Kelly's identity was bound to become known and it was not 'a practical possibility to keep his name secret'. As to the process by which he was identified, Hutton said that to begin with it appeared to him that a case of 'some strength' could be made for thinking that Kelly's identity was going to be 'deliberately leaked to the press without the government appearing to do so'. However, as the inquiry proceeded, the judge changed his mind: 'As I heard more evidence about the surrounding circumstances and the considerations which influenced those in government, I came to the conclusion that the reality was that there was no such underhand strategy.' The government had 'acted reasonably' in issuing a press statement to the effect that a civil servant had come forward: 'It is unrealistic to think that the name could have been kept secret indefinitely . . . it was better to be frank with the press and confirm the correct name if it was given.' Nevertheless the MoD had been at fault in not having set up a procedure 'whereby Dr Kelly would be informed immediately his name had been confirmed to the press'. His exposure to press attention and intrusion had been 'very stressful' but he was not an easy man to help or give advice to because of his 'intensely private nature'.

Hutton concluded that while it was 'not possible to be certain' of the factors which drove Kelly to commit suicide, he must have been concerned about his denial of having been the source of the quotes used by Susan Watts on *Newsnight* and it would also have appeared likely to him that his discussions with journalists were going to come under investigation, escalating the possibility of disciplinary measures and diminishing the prospect of an early resolution of his difficulties. One word, 'Whitewash?', underlined and in red capital letters, was the headline splashed across the front page of the *Independent*, which declared that Hutton's 'ferocious condemnation' of the BBC's journalism and its management, while giving the government the 'benefit of the doubt', was 'unfair . . . this one-sidedness seems perverse'. Most newspapers led with news of the turmoil within the BBC following the resignation of its chairman, Gavyn Davies, who the *Times* said had been forced to quit after the corporation had been 'plunged into the worst crisis of its eighty-two year history'. On inside pages there were reports of Alastair Campbell's call for further resignations on the grounds that the director general, Greg Dyke, was still maintaining that the BBC 'basically stand by their story . . . that they basically were happy with the way the BBC conducted itself'. The prediction of the headline writers, that Dyke's future was 'hanging in the balance', proved correct and before the day was out he too had resigned. He made an emotional farewell, clutching e-mails from staff urging him to stay, and he told reporters he hoped his own departure, as well as that of the chairman, meant 'a line can be drawn under this whole episode'.

To the surprise and unease of many of the corporation's journalists, the acting chairman, Lord Ryder, then announced on behalf of the BBC and its governors that he had 'no hesitation in apologising unreservedly for our errors and to the individuals whose reputations were affected by them'. Blair responded immediately, saying an apology and the withdrawal of 'a very serious . . . false accusation' were 'all I ever wanted'. He fully respected the independence of the BBC and had no doubt it would continue to 'probe and question the government in every proper way'. Hutton had ranged far and wide in delivering his strictures on the inadequacies of the BBC's editorial system; he even went so far as to suggest that newspapers as well as broadcasting companies should be required to ensure there were procedures in place for editors to give careful consideration to any report impugning the integrity of others: 'The right to communicate information . . . obtained by investigative reporters . . . is subject to the qualification . . . that false accusations of fact impugning the integrity of others, including politicians, should not be made by the media.' By widening his attack on the BBC's editorial standards to include the press, he invoked the fury of leader writers, who derided his attempt to curtail investigative reporting and restrict the freedom of editors.

While I agreed entirely about Hutton's naivety when it came to his pronouncements on the working practices of the media, I had nevertheless drawn an entirely different conclusion from the inquiry's clinical exposure of the inner workings of the BBC and the deficiencies of its editorial proce-dures. I had felt all along that the storm of protest over Andrew Gilligan's reporting had been an accident waiting to happen: it was the price which the BBC's management eventually had to pay for its lamentable failure to encourage a shared sense of purpose among the corporation's journalists and its inability to foster closer co-operation between the various news and cur-rent affairs programmes. While the need to encourage internal competition has always been regarded as an important BBC objective, and although rivalry between different teams of journalists does guard against the acceptance or even imposition of a uniform line on the events of the day, there are some stories which are so critical and so far reaching that the timing of their transmission cannot be dictated solely by an urge to be first with the news and the rush to claim an exclusive. Gilligan's allegation, that Campbell had 'sexed up' the dossier and included the 45-minute claim when the government 'probably knew' it was wrong, was so sensational that in my opinion the *Today* programme should at least have taken the precaution of consulting and alerting other senior journalists within the corporation. Admittedly Gilligan was hired specifically to uncover 'stories that cause the government discomfort' and he was allowed by his editors to report in 'primary colours', but with that freedom went a responsibility to guard the BBC's reputation. Look at it this way: here was *Today's* defence correspondent claiming on air that Blair had effectively taken the country to war on a lie yet Andrew Marr, then the BBC's political editor, told me subsequently that he had not been informed in advance about Gilligan's exclusive report; he was only aware of the story after it had been broadcast. I think I can say without fear of contradiction that no national newspaper would have dared allow a defence correspondent to lead its front page with such a startling allegation against the Prime Minister of the day without having first taken the advice of its political editor.

An even greater flaw in editorial supervision is the fact that three BBC correspondents had been speaking separately to David Kelly but without alerting each other to what they were doing; nor did they, either as individual reporters or through their programmes, co-operate in any way over what was being transmitted by the BBC, either before or immediately after Gilligan's broadcast. By any objective test of journalistic sources, Britain's foremost authority on biological warfare was a much-prized contact, well placed strategically and by far the most reliable and confidential informant the BBC could ever have hoped for when it came to the difficult task of trying to disentangle the mixture of claim and counter-claim surrounding Iraq's weapons of mass destruction. If ever there was a 'deep throat' who needed to be nurtured and protected it was Kelly and if the three BBC journalists had pooled their information it might have been possible, through their co-operation, to have done much more to safeguard his identity.

Inherent weaknesses in the way the BBC has structured its news and current affairs output were alluded to in a *Guardian* paperback, *The Hutton Inquiry and Its Impact*, which identified what the authors concluded was a problem unique to the BBC: 'exclusive stories run by one section of the organisation often have to be independently corroborated before another part of the empire is prepared to run them'. Therefore the *Ten O'Clock News*, which did not have access to *Today's* defence correspondent, assigned its own reporter, Gavin Hewitt, to follow up the story. Without knowing Gilligan's source or the identity of Susan Watts's contact, Hewitt approached Tom Mangold of *Panorama*, who gave him Kelly's telephone number. I could not help reflecting on the possibility, given the authoritative nature of the guidance being supplied to its three correspondents, that if the BBC had been far more methodical in researching and reporting the background to the doubts about the dossier, and if coverage of the story had been properly co-ordinated, then the outcome might well have been very different. While his family might be offended by the comparison, in some respects Kelly was potentially as significant as Mark Felt, the former deputy director of the FBI, who in June 2005 admitted he was the 'deep throat' who helped the *Washington Post* reporters Bob Woodward and Carl Bernstein in their relentless exposé of the scandal surrounding the infamous 1972 Watergate break-in, which led ultimately to the downfall of President Nixon. In his book, *The Secret Man: The Story of Watergate's Deep Throat*, Woodward described how, despite Felt's 'piecemeal approach to providing information', his assistance was invaluable as he and Bernstein attempted to understand the 'many-headed monster of Watergate'. He was convinced that Felt's objective was to protect the FBI by finding a way, 'clandestine as it was', to push some of the information from the bureau's interviews and files out to the public, to help build pressure to make Nixon answerable.

Because of his position in the FBI, Felt's words and guidance had, in Woodward's opinion, immense, even staggering authority.

> The weight, authenticity and his restraint were more important than his design . . . I am disappointed and a little angry at both myself and him for never digging out a more exacting explanation, a clearer statement of his reasoning and motivation. At the same time, there is a certain consistency, even a nobility and courage, in what Felt did.

Few now doubt the accuracy of the concerns which Kelly expressed in his various conversations with the three BBC correspondents: as the transcripts and notes indicate, he believed that the intelligence used in the Iraq dossier was flawed and that the war was being fought on a false prospectus. When asked in April 2006 to reflect on his experience and what he might have done differently, Gilligan told the *Journalist* that journalism needed to be 'readier to defend itself'. Because Kelly appeared to have been less than frank when he was questioned by the Foreign Affairs Committee, he too was 'not exempt' from blame. 'He probably should have come out and said, "Yes, I did say that" but he was worried that he would lose his job. Had he but known it, he couldn't possibly have been sacked, because he'd have been a national hero.' Gilligan supported the widely expressed view at the Hutton inquiry that Kelly was quite willing to give off-the-record briefings to journalists, not least because he felt his expertise was undervalued. 'I think he had genuine concerns about the dossier, and I think he was somebody who genuinely liked to share his information. He was naturally chatty and enjoyed talking to journalists and displaying his knowledge.' Despite Gilligan's assertion that his original report was 'a terribly limp little thing, it's awfully measured and equivocal', I maintain that if, in a systematic way, the BBC had been able to reveal over a period of some weeks or months just a small proportion of the evidence which subsequently emerged about the concerns of the security and intelligence services and the alarm over Alastair Campbell's influence in the preparation of the dossier, then the Prime Minister might easily have faced such a sustained challenge in Parliament that his position could well have become untenable. What cannot be gainsaid is that the BBC undoubtedly had access to an exceptional source of information, a contact whose insights and expertise were squandered in hastily delivered live broadcasts rather than the considered journalism which the story cried out for.

In the event, what transpired was a worrying indictment of the BBC's journalism. Three correspondents found themselves working in an editorial environment which was hardly conducive to the kind of solid, step-by-step investigative reporting which was deployed by Woodward and Bernstein and which so patently lacked the team spirit which had served the *Washington Post* so well. Ultimately the responsibility for this collective failure to exploit an opportunity which most respected national newspapers would have jumped at lay with the corporation's weak and inept editorial management. On this point Campbell was correct: editorial supervision within the BBC was not just haphazard but ineffective; if the degree of control which Downing Street's director of communications exercised over the No. 10 press office and the government's information service had been applied with anything like the same rigour to the task of managing the corporation's output of news and current affairs, then the outcry over the likely disclosures about his own role in the build-up to the war against Iraq would have been such that he might well have been forced to resign not long after the story broke, instead of lingering on until the end of August 2003. After the dramatic departure of the BBC's chairman and its director general, Gilligan's resignation from *Today* hardly came as a surprise. But despite all the savage repercussions from Lord Hutton's report and having personally done all he could to exact revenge on the corporation's management, Campbell continued in attack mode, using a series of speaking events around the country to justify his criticism of the BBC's journalism and also to give himself a clean bill of health.

When it came to facing up to his own past, Campbell remained in denial, unable to recognise the damage which his regime in the No. 10 press office had inflicted on the democratic process. In the six and a half years he spent in Downing Street, he had an unparalleled opportunity to help raise the standards of political journalism. He could have done his bit to drive up levels of accuracy and fairness by ensuring a level playing field for all political journalists at Westminster; he could have tried to counter the growth in unsourced and exaggerated stories by insisting that he, and the rest of the party spin doctors under his control, always spoke on the record whenever possible and went out of their way to ensure that their own quotes were properly attributed. Instead Campbell took advantage of the commercial pressures which have resulted in a relentless downward spiral in journalistic standards. He exploited the demand for exclusives by offering access and interviews in return for favourable coverage; he encouraged the trade in off-the-record tip-offs; and he undermined the authority of the Speaker of the House of Commons by blatantly trailing ministerial statements before they were announced in Parliament. Deliberate leaking of confidential information was a trick which the political parties and their spin doctors had always been trying to perfect in order to take advantage of the growing sophistication of the news media but it became an indispensable tool in Campbell's daily struggle to manipulate the headlines. Despite his repeated protestations about the 'sourness and cynicism' of political coverage, his communication techniques only added to the continuing deterioration in levels of public trust for politicians, journalists and the whole political process.

Chapter 8

As Margaret Thatcher and John Major discovered to their discomfort, a fairly accurate indicator of rising unpopularity can be the level of hostile leaking against the government of the day and the policies which it is pursuing. Both Conservative Prime Ministers found the longer they were in power the more they became the target for damaging disclosures. By the end of Thatcher's premiership leak inquiries were averaging about thirty-five a year, almost twice the rate when she was first elected. Major enjoyed a similar honeymoon but by the final two years of his administration leak investigations notified to the Cabinet Office were running again at the rate of thirty-five a year. Tony Blair has proved to be no exception to the rule: in the first two years of his government, leaks averaged thirty a year but by the start of Labour's third term the rate of unauthorised disclosures which warranted an inquiry had escalated considerably and so had the seriousness of the illicit data being made available to the news media. Blair's support for the American-led invasion of Iraq in March 2003 became the trigger for a succession of highly embarrassing leaks relating to the conduct of the war, the role of the intelligence services and the likelihood of terrorist attacks. As the months went by, each new revelation about the government's handling of defence and security issues only served to strengthen and prolong opposition to the continued deployment of British troops in Iraq.

The inquiries by Lord Hutton into the death of Dr David Kelly and a further review by a committee headed by Lord Butler into the accuracy of the intelligence on weapons of mass destruction left many unanswered questions about the legality of the war. Bomb explosions in London, on the Underground and a bus, in July 2005 only added to public disquiet about Blair's backing for American military action. Four months later, faced with a particularly disconcerting leak about a conversation between the Prime Minister and the US President, in which George Bush was alleged to have talked about bombing the headquarters of the Arabic television channel Aljazeera, the Labour administration, like its predecessors, came to the conclusion yet again that it had no alternative but to invoke the Official Secrets Act in an attempt to stop the wider dissemination of highly sensitive information and to bear down on the likely culprits. Public anger about the Iraq war and the death and destruction which followed in its wake was so persistent that it proved to be something of a catalyst for a wider sense of disenchantment and within months of Labour's third general election victory in May 2005, Blair's senior ministers were having to come to terms with the fact that, as in the Thatcher and Major years, there was little if anything they could do to stem the flow of unauthorised disclosures. A senior civil servant of thirty years' standing told me in the autumn of 2005 that the secretary of state in her department had revealed a growing sense of paranoia within the Cabinet:

> The minister admitted that Blair and his colleagues had become really obsessed about leaks and the harm they were causing. What is so ironic is that most of the top secretaries of state were all so conscious of the extensive use they made of unauthorised disclosures when they were in opposition. As up-and-coming frontbenchers they all benefited from the enormous flow of confidential documents which Labour received from the civil service during the final years of John Major's government. And it is this realisation that history might be repeating itself, but that this time it is Labour which is the target, which is making them all so jumpy about the rising number of leaks.

I thought at the time, after hearing of the mounting unease within the government, that perhaps the only consolation for Labour was that most of the leaked correspondence and documentation was still going direct to the news media rather than to either the Conservatives or the Liberal Democrats, which I took to be a reflection of the lack of strong and effective opposition in Parliament, a point which had obviously not been lost on would-be traders in confidential information. When I sought the opinion of one of the five anonymous leakers who had helped with my research, my hunch was confirmed:

> People who are prepared to leak and take the risk of challenging the authorities tend to be left wing. While a lot them are highly critical of what Blair is doing, especially in

supporting George Bush, there is no way they would do anything to benefit the Conservatives, so that's why most of the leaks are going direct to the press. It's the journalists who are seen as providing the most effective opposition to the government, not the Tories or the Liberal Democrats.

Opposition to the war with Iraq was without doubt the key factor in motivating the leaks which gave rise to the greatest political difficulties for Blair. Thatcher had been there before him: most of the illicit disclosures which caused her so much trouble in the 1980s related to what were also perceived to have been acts of aggression by the state, whether it was the delivery of Cruise missiles, the Falklands war or the programme of pit closures which precipitated the 1984–5 miners' strike. What seemed at the time to be the leak which could cause Blair the most political damage was fired with almost deadly precision in the closing stages of the 2005 general election campaign. Ten days before polling day, much to the annoyance of the Labour Party's campaign team, the *Mail on Sunday*'s front page exclusive succeeded in pushing Iraq to the top of the election news: 'The proof: Blair was told war could be ruled illegal'. For the previous two years the Prime Minister had steadfastly refused to publish the full advice given by the Attorney General, Lord Goldsmith, and the seemingly interminable argument about the legality of military intervention in Iraq was the last issue the government wanted to see reopened. Simon Walters, the *Mail on Sunday*'s political editor, said the thirteen-page document, which was marked 'secret' and had been 'sensationally leaked', showed that Blair had been 'completely untrue' in asserting that a summary published shortly before the invasion was identical to the Attorney General's advice.

Although Walters was only able to give an outline of Goldsmith's main points, by the following Wednesday the story was commanding blanket coverage after the text of the six key paragraphs was leaked to the BBC, *Channel 4 News* and the *Guardian*; the three copies were handwritten to stop the leaker being traced. *Channel Four News* and the Guardian Unlimited website were the first to carry the precise wording, timing their exclusives for 7 p.m. The failure of the BBC to break the story earlier in the day, although the newsroom was in possession of the text from late afternoon, was blamed by media commentators on the cautious approach being adopted by senior executives in the wake of Lord Hutton's criticism of the corporation's editorial standards. Next morning's newspapers had a field day, reproducing the six paragraphs in full, showing all the qualifications which had been omitted from the summary, together with Goldsmith's warning that an international court 'might well conclude' that a new United Nations resolution was needed. Political commentators were convinced the leak was the 'smoking gun' which could be used by anti-war campaigners and opposition MPs to substantiate their claim that the Prime Minister had misled the country over the case for military intervention. In a last-minute bid to take some of the heat out of the story, Downing Street opted for full disclosure and the thirteen-page document was posted on the No. 10 website once the Prime Minister had appeared at Labour's morning news conference. Blair told the assembled journalists that the Attorney General's key conclusion was that it was 'lawful to proceed, so the so-called smoking gun has turned out to be a damp squib'.

Nonetheless the damage had been done, the party's campaign themes were ignored and most newspapers agreed with the *Guardian's* assessment that it had been Blair's worst day of the election; all told, Labour had effectively lost five campaigning days. There was wild speculation about the likely source and Labour's strategy team was quoted by the *Independent* as having accused the Tories of orchestrating the leak over a period of days so as to inflict maximum damage, a claim which Conservative Central Office took delight in dismissing as nothing more than Labour Party paranoia. The Prime Minister's sudden U-turn was all the sweeter for Labour's political opponents because the previous weekend Alastair Campbell had given short shrift to the threat posed by continuing dissent over the war. Campbell, who had joined the campaign team at Blair's request, had leaked a copy of his own election strategy note to the *Sunday Times*. Instead of highlighting Blair's concern about a low turn-out, which had been the intention, the headline sounded far more complacent than the party intended: 'Campbell: We're home and dry'. Because of concern about the loss of marginal seats, the text was published immediately on the party's website. Campbell said he knew Charles Kennedy was 'going big on Iraq next week' but people could not take the Liberal Democrats seriously and the answer Labour candidates should give was that if Kennedy's 'view had prevailed, Saddam Hussein would still be in power'.

Secret information about the diplomatic manoeuvrings ahead of the Iraq war began to leak out in the lead-up to the invasion, long before Dr David Kelly gave his unauthorised briefings to the BBC expressing his doubts about the validity of the dossier on Saddam Hussein's weapons of mass destruction. Early in March 2003, three weeks before the invasion of Iraq, the *Observer* published a 'top secret' American memo which had been leaked from GCHQ in Cheltenham; another name was about to be added to the roll call of Britain's most celebrated post-war leakers. Here was another genuine Sunday newspaper exclusive: 'Revealed: US dirty tricks to win vote on Iraq war'. A second headline filled in the details: 'Secret document details American plan to bug phones and e-mails of Security Council members'. Almost twelve months elapsed before Katharine Gun, a translator at GCHQ, was able to give an account of the day she surprised herself by becoming a whistleblower and emerging as a transatlantic cause célèbre. When I was able to piece together the various twists and turns of a year which obviously became something of an emotional roller coaster for her, I was struck by many telling parallels with the experiences of the five anonymous leakers who had given me an insight into their illicit behaviour during the Thatcher and Major years.

Gun's superiors in Cheltenham must have thought there could hardly have been a more unlikely whistleblower. Then aged twenty-eight, she was a linguist, the daughter of a university lecturer, and she had spent two years at the GCHQ eavesdropping centre translating Mandarin Chinese intercepts into English. Along with her colleagues she received an e-mail on Friday 31 January 2003 in which the US National Security Agency sought the help of GCHQ in discovering the voting intentions of six states with swing votes on the UN Security Council. Intelligence staff were 'mounting a surge' in the monitoring of diplomats' telephones and computers ahead of the debate on the second resolution on Iraq in the hope of obtaining 'insights' that could 'give US policymakers an edge in obtaining results favourable to US goals'. Gun subsequently told the *Observer* that at first she could not believe what she was reading; she was so shocked she took off her headset and went to the ladies' lavatory. She was opposed to an invasion of Iraq and thought that if the public knew that the US was acting illegally there might be a chance of preventing the invasion. After spending the weekend wrestling with her conscience, she went back to work on Monday, convinced that if anything was going to stop the war, this might be it. She retrieved the e-mail from her classified in-box, copied and pasted it into a Word document, printed off a copy and walked out of GCHQ with it in her bag. She gave the e-mail to a friend who had previously worked at GCHQ and who she knew was in touch with journalists. In February Gun travelled to London to take part in the anti-war march but it was not until Sunday 2 March 2003 that her story finally broke. When interviewed a year later for the London *Evening*

Standard by the former BBC correspondent Andrew Gilligan, she described her reaction on buying the *Observer* at her local newsagent's shop in Cheltenham:

> I saw the headline and then it just hit. There was a very brief moment of excitement and then it was like panic, oh my God, now they're going to know it was me. I was walking round and round this shop, holding this paper, thinking, oh God, it's me and it's all over my face.

Gun's name was on the list of the e-mail's recipients but she denied being responsible when interviewed by her vetting officer the following Tuesday as part of a mole hunt at GCHQ. Next day she decided to own up. 'I did lie at first but it was horrible. I just couldn't do it. Until you confess, everything you do is fake. There was no pretending any more, you couldn't imagine you wouldn't get found out.' Gun's line manager, who was also a woman, let her cry on her shoulder. 'I was sobbing by then, so she comforted me; she said, thank you for coming out, don't worry, everything is going to be all right, which was rubbish, of course, but you cling to any straw.' Once her manager had informed the security division she was allowed to have lunch in the canteen and then driven in an unmarked car to Cheltenham police station where she was formally arrested and spent the night in custody. Gun, who was dismissed from GCHQ in June 2003, had to wait until mid-November before being formally charged under the Official Secrets Act with having disclosed classified security and intelligence information without official authority. Her plight during long months of uncertainty was highlighted by the *Observer*'s columnist Nick Cohen, who revealed in July of that year how his paper had published its story the previous March without having known that the leaked e-mail originated in Cheltenham. All that Cohen could say four months later was that the source was a woman employee aged twenty-eight who had been sacked by GCHQ the previous month and who was at home on police bail.

> We didn't know the identity of the mole at the time, and aren't better informed now. Neither the police nor the woman's lawyers will name her . . . If this newspaper had known the source, we wouldn't say a word about him or her in any circumstances for fear of breaking our promises and frightening off future informants.

Two weeks after being charged Gun appeared before Bow Street magistrates' court and was committed for trial. In a statement read to the court she did not dispute she was responsible for leaking the e-mail but said she would deny breaching the Official Secrets Act. Her disclosures had been justified because they exposed 'serious illegality and wrongdoing' on the part of the US government which had attempted to subvert British security services, and her action was 'necessary to prevent an illegal war in which thousands of Iraqi civilians and British soldiers would be killed or maimed'. She insisted her motives had been sincere: 'No one has suggested, nor could they, that any payment was sought or given for any alleged disclosures. I have only ever followed my conscience.'

In January 2004, when her trial at the Old Bailey seemed imminent, the *Observer* rallied support with a feature headed 'US stars hail Iraq war whistleblower'. A statement declaring that Gun should not become a scapegoat for an illegal war had been signed by the civil rights campaigner the Reverend Jesse Jackson and the Hollywood actor-director Sean Penn. Another signatory was the US whistleblower Daniel Ellsberg, author of *The Pentagon Papers*, who said Gun's leak had been more timely and potentially more important than his own disclosures in 1971 about US involvement in Vietnam. The statement, which honoured Gun for having 'bravely risked her career and her very liberty to inform the public about illegal spying', was described by the *Observer* as a 'glowing tribute to the publicity-shy GCHQ mole who has avoided all media attention since her arrest'. Legal experts were quoted as saying they believed her defence of 'necessity' had been strengthened by the resignation of the Foreign Secretary's deputy legal adviser, Elizabeth Wilmshurst, who disagreed with Lord Goldsmith's conclusion that military intervention could be justified on the basis of an earlier UN resolution. As the trial approached, Gun's lawyers indicated that they were convinced the case would hinge on the advice given to the Cabinet about the legality of the war, a tactic designed to play on ministers' fears that punishing an anonymous junior official could prove fatal to the government when it was withholding information from the public. Five days before the trial, the *Guardian* reported exclusively that the case against her was going to be dropped and in the event the hearing lasted for only eighteen minutes. Mark Ellison, counsel for the Crown, refused to expand on a brief statement he made to court: 'The prosecution offers no evidence against this individual. There is no longer sufficient evidence for a realistic prospect of conviction. It would not be appropriate for me to go into the reasons behind the decision beyond that.' The day before the hearing the defence had demanded to see all government papers relating to the legality of the war and most newspapers were convinced that it was serious doubts about the Attorney General's advice which forced the government to abandon the prosecution, a conclusion supported by Gun's lawyer, James Welch, a solicitor for the human and civil rights group Liberty, which would have argued her case for full disclosure. Walking free from the Old Bailey, she told waiting journalists she was delighted that her nightmare was over and that she no longer faced the prospect of a two-year prison sentence: 'I feel I've acted with decency and honesty throughout this whole affair and I've absolutely no regrets about what I've done. I would do it again.' Later, at a news conference, she said that although she was strongly anti-war, she had not been looking for information to leak but had been horrified on discovering that British intelligence services were being asked to undermine the whole democratic process of the UN.

> I'm not prone to leak secrets left, right and centre but this needed to get out. The public deserved to know what was going on at the time. When I originally leaked the e-mail I had no idea if anybody would be interested. Personally I felt very strongly about it and hoped the press would get their teeth into it.

She suggested others in the intelligence services might also find their consciences urged them to leak. 'I know it's very difficult and people don't want to jeopardise their careers or lives but if there are things out there that should really come out, hey, why not?' Appearing to incite her former colleagues to become whistleblowers and reveal 'vital military secrets' was a step too far for the *Daily Express*, which headlined its report 'Whingeing GCHQ girl betrayed Britain'. Except for this one critical headline and the juxtaposition in the *Daily Telegraph* of her photograph alongside that of a young soldier killed in Iraq under the headline 'Which would you trust your life with?', the national press was almost entirely supportive and not unnaturally the following Sunday's *Observer* hailed her as a heroine. In his column, Nick Cohen described Gun as a defence barrister's dream because she was well spoken, well dressed and manifestly well intentioned:

> Jurors might realise that her well-intentioned arguments were morally ambiguous . . . But whatever they thought about the war, they couldn't deny that she was a nice young woman that any parent would be proud to call their own. I doubt if the government could have found a jury in Britain which would have risked allowing the judge to lock her up.

The *Observer* revealed that the leaked e-mail had been obtained from Yvonne Ridley, a freelance journalist, who had been handed it by Gun's former workmate. Because the paper's editorial staff had no idea whether the memo was genuine or a forgery, it had taken three weeks to verify its contents, which explained why Gun had 'almost given up hope' of ever seeing it made public.

Ridley gave her side of the story in an article for the *Sunday Express* in which she described how in a Soho coffee shop 'an intense young woman' she had arranged to meet 'took an envelope out of her bag, removed a piece of paper and slid it across the table'. Ridley, who was on her way to address a meeting of the Stop the War Coalition, said they had met for the first time the previous year after she gave a speech in Bristol. Her contact, to whom she later gave the codename Isobel, disclosed that she worked at GCHQ and wanted to know, whether as a journalist against the war, she was 'interested in receiving any intelligence communications that would expose the British government's duplicity'. Ridley handed over her card and never expected to hear from her again. Three months later 'Isobel', who by then had left GCHQ, told her that she had been given a copy of an e-mail by a former colleague who had been 'repulsed and outraged' by its contents. When she read the document, Ridley said a shiver went down her spine. 'It was a mixture of shock, revulsion and that feeling you get when you land an exclusive story which can only be described as sensational.' Apart from a couple of text messages, Ridley did not hear from 'Isobel' again until nine days after the *Observer* published the e-mail, when she received another text message telling her that 'Katharine Gun had been arrested and that both their homes had been the subject of dawn raids'.

Three months later she was contacted by John Wadham, the head of Liberty, who revealed that he knew she was the third person in the GCHQ spy case. Ridley was informed that transcripts of her mobile phone conversations and text messages had 'emerged' when 'Isobel' and Gun had been interviewed by the authorities. 'Like Katharine Gun I have absolutely no regrets over my role. I salute her courage and fortitude and that of "Isobel" – a truly heroic woman who deserves much more credit for her part in exposing illicit spying activities.' Among the many anti-war campaigners who welcomed the collapse of the prosecution was the former Secretary of State for International Development, Clare Short, who had resigned from the government shortly after the invasion of Iraq and who was about to join Gun in revealing official secrets. She was quoted in the morning papers as saying the government's decision to stop the case was extremely significant and 'very fishy'. When interviewed on *Today* immediately after the 8 a.m. news bulletin, the presenter, John Humphrys, was taken aback when she claimed that British spies had been bugging the office of the UN Secretary General, Kofi Annan, and had been sending back reports to London. Short assured Humphrys she was fully aware of this when serving in the government:

> But these things are done and in the case of Kofi's office it was being done for some time . . . Well, I know, I've seen transcripts of Kofi Annan's conversations. In fact, I have had conversations with Kofi in the run-up to the war, thinking, 'Oh dear, there will be a transcript of this and people will see what he and I are saying.'

Later that morning, at his monthly news conference, Tony Blair said Short had been 'deeply irresponsible' and he accused her of threatening Britain's security by attacking the intelligence services.

Three days later Short appeared on the *Jonathan Dimbleby* programme, brandishing what she said was a 'threatening' letter from the Cabinet Secretary, Sir Andrew Turnbull, reminding her as a former minister of her obligation under the ministerial code to safeguard national security. She was warned that 'purporting to breach confidences given you by virtue of ministerial office' was in direct conflict with the oath she had taken on being appointed to the Privy Council. Turnbull hoped Short would take part in no further interviews on the issue and as Cabinet Secretary he reserved the right of the Crown to take 'further action as necessary'. The Gun–Short double act provoked considerable comment among leader writers and columnists, including a suggestion by Ann Treneman, writing in the *New Statesman*, that women made the best whistleblowers. Gun had shown 'not an ounce of regret' and Short did not seem 'to give a damn' that nobody at Westminster had a kind word to say when she revealed that 'Britain had been bugging the UN'. Treneman concluded that women had 'blown the whistle the loudest' over the war because they were probably able to think more independently by virtue of their outsider status in most work places, a view share by Guy Dehn, director of the whistleblowers' charity Public Concern at Work. In his experience women felt they had less to lose because most work places were male dominated and women saw themselves as outsiders. Treneman included in her list of women ready to 'do their duty' the Foreign Office senior legal adviser, Elizabeth Wilmshurst, who had quit because of her doubts about the legality of the war.

One characteristic which I thought had been overlooked was that female whistleblowers not only had dogged determination but sometimes displayed the most cunning when covering their tracks, especially if they were women in poorly paid positions and were managed by men who had no idea their lowly subordinates might be well informed and have strong political convictions. During my own interviews with anonymous leakers I had been struck by the fact that it was often the women who had leaked over the longest periods, taken the most risks and experienced the greatest sense of empowerment. One woman who also fitted the Identikit picture which I had built up in my mind was the Soviet spy Melita Norwood, who died in June 2005 at the age of ninety-three. She was a former clerk and secretary at the British Non-Ferrous Metals Research Association, which undertook metallurgy research and was involved in a top-secret project underpinning Britain's nuclear programme. After being recruited by the KGB in 1937, Norwood spent forty years, until her retirement, passing information to her Soviet handlers at drops in the suburbs of south-east London. She systematically photographed research data left on desks or stored in the office safe; sometimes she was able to take spare copies of classified documents because security was so minimal; and when she typed up minutes of meetings, she made a spare copy. Her secret life was not exposed until 1999 after research by the Cambridge historian Professor Christopher Andrew, who examined the files of the KGB archivist Vasily Mitrohkin and tracked down the true identity of the agent who operated under the codename Hola.

Andrew was struck by her extraordinary resilience and how at the age of eighty-seven, despite having woken up to find the British press assembled outside her front door at Bexleyheath in south-east London, she had calmly answered reporters' questions. With typical British understatement Norwood said she had never considered herself a spy or of having been unpatriotic: 'I did not want money. It was not that side I was interested in. I wanted Russia to be on equal footing with the west.' Her only regret was that she had finally been exposed, as she thought she had 'got away with it'. She was not prosecuted or even interviewed by the security services because the Home Secretary, Jack Straw, decided it would not be in the 'public interest' to press charges against an elderly grandmother. His Conservative shadow, Ann Widdecombe, demanded Norwood should be prosecuted for her forty years of 'sustained treachery' but Straw considered there was little prospect of obtaining admissible evidence and 'Hola' had only been of 'marginal' importance. Despite doubts about her true significance, Dame Stella

Rimington, the first woman director of MI5, did support the thesis about her having been a risk taker. Rimington claimed that female spies were psychologically tougher than their male counterparts and also more discreet. On reading in Norwood's obituaries that she had declined a pension of £20 per month offered by the KGB, I remembered a comment column in the *Independent* by Liberty's spokesman, Barry Hugill, in which he had reflected on the fact that as bids came in for exclusive interviews with Gun after the GCHQ leak, and the 'money offers go up and up', she refused to accept payment.

The *Mail on Sunday* was one newspaper which made a particular point of telling its readers that no fee had been paid for its interview with her.

Six months after the case was dropped Gun joined whistleblowers from several other countries in establishing the Truth-Telling Coalition, which aimed to stand by people who leaked sensitive information. The group dedicated itself to helping whistleblowers 'hold their lives together' and she promised to assist after discussing her experiences with Daniel Ellsberg, whose own trial was dismissed in 1973 after he leaked a 7,000-page study which exposed the conduct of the US in the lead-up to the outbreak of the Vietnam war. In an article for the *Observer* Gun described how, after her own arrest, she ended up in a 'confidence-sapping limbo', too frightened to open the door. She was not a natural activist and was sure most whistleblowers were not 'wannabe celebrities', craving a platform. 'I did not make my disclosure about the deceitful manipulation of the UN . . . in order to garner fame or fortune.' One immediate aim of the coalition was to start a campaign for a fundamental reform of the Official Secrets Act so that it distinguished between 'espionage breaches which genuinely endanger national security and public-spirited whistle-blowing'. Adding his voice to the call for a review of the secrecy laws was David Shayler, a former MI5 intelligence officer who was sentenced to six months' imprisonment in 2002 for passing classified information to the *Mail on Sunday*. Although it did not help in his own case, Shayler's appeal to the House of Lords did succeed in establishing the defence of necessity which Liberty had planned to use on Gun's behalf.

Previously the judges had always rejected the argument put by defence lawyers that civil servants and others had been acting in the public interest when they leaked classified information. In a change to what had otherwise been a blanket ban, the Law Lords ruled that if defendants could show they were acting out of necessity or under duress, the jury had the right to hear them out. Despite the judge's direction that there should be a conviction, a jury acquitted Clive Ponting in 1985 after he leaked documents about the sinking of the *General Belgrano* during the Falklands war and Liberty believed that the Law Lords' concession, which would have allowed Gun to put her case to a jury and plead the defence of necessity, would have been a trump card, especially at a time when public opinion was so divided about the Iraq war.

The day after the GCHQ case collapsed the Prime Minister's official spokesman announced a review of the Official Secrets Act. Tony Blair had been 'disappointed' by the outcome and he thought it was only 'a matter of common sense' that government departments should consider whether changes were needed. A month later the *Sunday Times* reported that the Home Secretary, David Blunkett, was conducting the review and was seeking ways to 'gag the blabbers'. Apparently his intention was to restrict the defence of necessity by requiring defendants to show they had used 'every possible avenue' to alert the authorities before they engaged in illegal conduct. News that the law might be tightened alarmed the National Union of Journalists, which repeated its long-standing demand for the introduction of a wide-ranging defence to allow whistleblowers to argue they had acted in the public interest.

Shayler suggested that one solution would be to allow intelligence officers and other civil servants the right to give evidence to parliamentary committees without the fear of prosecution. He said he was 'driven to speak out' and leak classified information in a series of articles for the *Mail on Sunday* after he discovered that in February 1996 'MI6 had paid affiliates of Al-Qaeda about £100,000 of taxpayers' money to assassinate Colonel Gadafi of Libya'. Malcolm Rifkind, who was Foreign Secretary at the time, denied there had been an attempted coup and his successor, Robin Cook, said Shayler's accusations were 'pure fantasy'. Nonetheless, in the face of the growing threat of terrorist attacks in Britain and other countries which had supported military intervention in Iraq, ministers were finding they had to focus their attention increasingly on the emergency measures which were being introduced to combat the 'war on terror', and nothing further was heard of Blunkett's promised tightening of the secrecy laws. Bomb explosions on three London Underground trains and a bus on Thursday 7 July 2005, which claimed a total of fifty-two lives, followed by similar but unsuccessful suicide attacks on Thursday 21 July, added further volatility to an already unstable political environment. Strengthening opposition to the continued deployment of British troops in Iraq and mounting concern about the surveillance and detention of terrorist suspects had coalesced to generate a heightened level of investigative reporting and a set of circumstances which provoked a bout of whistleblowing that proved highly damaging to the police and the government. Such was the degree of interest that leaked documents which challenged the official version of events were pounced upon by the media and instantly made headline news.

The death of an innocent Brazilian suspected of being a suicide bomber led to sustained allegations about a cover-up by the Metropolitan Police. Speculation about there having been a terrible mistake was suddenly given fresh impetus by a series of exclusive reports quoting documents leaked from the Independent Police Complaints Commission (IPCC). For several days during August 2005 the lead item in the bulletins of ITV News was scoop after scoop based on witness statements and the interim conclusions of the IPCC's inquiry into the fatal shooting of Jean Charles de Menezes, which had occurred the day after the failed suicide attacks. The leaks suggested that de Menezes was already being restrained by armed officers before he was shot seven times in the head and that he had not run away from the police by vaulting over a ticket barrier and entering Stockwell Underground station as originally stated; a leaked photograph showed a body on the floor of a tube train. Police sources were quoted as saying that the documents had not been produced on Scotland Yard's computers. Next day the IPCC revealed that a member of its administrative staff had been suspended after being identified as the likely source. According to the *Times*, a clerk with links to the ITV News staff was responsible; the *Sunday Times* went further, suggesting that an administrator had offered the documents to a friend who had applied for a job at ITV News, a claim which the company denied. David Mannion, editor in chief of ITV News, refused to give any clue as to the identity of its informant. He said the job of broadcasters was not to make judgements but to reveal issues of public interest: 'I think our source has made a very brave and public-spirited decision. Once we got the material, I think we covered it without any sense of bravado. We have more information and more photographs than we have published.' Newspapers followed up the leaks with gusto and the failure of the BBC's bulletins to credit the exclusive information being broadcast by ITV News produced a forthright rebuke from the corporation's former director general, Greg Dyke. Writing in the *Independent*, he claimed the story was a 'classic scoop' which came from 'good old-fashioned journalistic research'; the editorial team got the first hint of their exclusive two days before it was broadcast and

ITV News waited until the very last moment before notifying the police about what they had obtained because of fears that Scotland Yard or the Home Office 'might try to injunct them'. Misleading versions of what happened during the shooting had been left uncorrected for three weeks and Labour MPs who were demanding a full explanation regarded the illicit disclosures obtained by ITV News as proof that none of the suspicious behaviour attributed to de Menezes was true. Frank Dobson, a former Secretary of State for Health, said that rather than wait for the IPCC's report, the law officers and the police should thrash out a clear statement of the basic facts, otherwise there would be yet 'more weeks of damaging leaks'. Sir Ian Blair, commissioner of the Metropolitan Police, who faced repeated calls for his resignation, ordered an immediate inquiry by a force outside London. A month later, after officers searched several buildings in London, a woman aged forty three-was arrested in connection with the unauthorised disclosure of IPCC documents to ITV News; she was released on bail. A short report issued by the Press Association said no details had been given about the grounds for her arrest by Leicestershire Police, which was investigating the leak. News of two further arrests was revealed by the *Guardian* in January 2006, which reported that a television news producer had been arrested on suspicion of theft along with a woman aged thirty, who had been arrested on suspicion of conspiracy to steal. Both had been remanded on bail along with the 43-year old woman employee of the IPCC, who had subsequently resigned from the commission.

ITV News hailed its exclusive reports on the blunders that led to the mistaken shooting of de Menezes as one of the biggest scoops of the decade and entered them for a Royal Television Society (RTS) award. Although his channel failed to win the recognition which he had hoped for from the RTS, Mannion remained as forthright as he had been the previous August in defending the use of leaked witness statements and photographs to deliver 'a piece of masterful journalism'. He told the *Guardian* that ITV's informant was 'an incredibly principled and brave person motivated by public spiritedness to right a wrong'. But it took an 'awful lot of work' to make sure the story stood up and it had to be done in double-quick time. 'People didn't say that Watergate fell into Woodward and Bernstein's lap and neither did this fall into our lap. We worked for it, we got a lucky break, sure, and we did our job properly'.

Dobson's warning that allegations of a cover-up over the killing of the innocent Brazilian would inevitably trigger other unauthorised disclosures proved fully justified. Numerous speculative stories continued to appear about the evidence being collected by the IPCC and a separate inquiry was launched into Blair's conduct because of mounting criticism of the way he was said to have misled the public by stating on the afternoon of the Stockwell shooting that it was 'directly linked to terrorist operations', an assertion which only served to endorse the news stories suggesting that de Menezes was a terrorist bomber. Most of the illicit information which emerged related to the action taken by the armed policemen and there were yet more leaks in January 2006 when the IPCC's completed report was handed over to the Crown Prosecution Service and the Metropolitan Police. According to the *Guardian*, ten police officers had been questioned under criminal caution and although another leak obtained by the *Evening Standard* suggested none of them had been singled out individually for blame, they were all said to face the possibility of criminal charges. Within a matter of days the *News of the World* printed what appeared to be a far more authoritative leak and claimed that the IPCC's report disclosed that Special Branch officers had 'faked vital evidence to cover up blunders' that led to the shooting of an innocent man. Initially the surveillance team believed that the Brazilian was the terrorist suspect Hussein Osman, who was being hunted for a failed suicide bombing the previous day.

Much of the *News of the World*'s exclusive was based on information obtained from 'a Whitehall source' but the paper was quite specific when it came to the allegation that undercover detectives had tampered with the evidence:

> Once it was realised an innocent man had been killed, the special branch surveillance log was altered to show that no positive ID had been made. Incredibly, reveals the IPCC report, their log, which originally said 'it was Osman', was changed by the insertion of two words to make it read 'and it was not Osman'. The report, which has sent shock waves through Whitehall and Scotland Yard, suggests this was done at a debriefing meeting at eight o'clock that evening, about ten hours after the twenty-seven-year-old de Menezes was shot.

Running in tandem with leaks about blunders surrounding the tube shooting were numerous unauthorised disclosures aimed at exposing the dangers to Britain of the government's continuing support for military action in Iraq. In January 2006 the *New Statesman* published a confidential memo from the Foreign Office which suggested steps which the Prime Minister could take to divert attention from criticism of the US practice of transporting Al-Qaeda suspects to interrogation centres where they might be tortured. 'Rendition: the cover-up' was the headline over Martin Bright's exclusive report. Advice prepared for Downing Street by the private office of the Foreign Secretary, Jack Straw, suggested that Tony Blair should 'avoid getting drawn on detail' of the US policy known as extraordinary rendition.

The secret memo was seized on by Liberty and used to highlight its campaign to stop 'torture flights' going through the UK. Full page newspaper advertisements reproduced the key quote from the leaked Foreign Office document: 'We think we should now try to move the debate on and focus people instead on [US Secretary of State Condoleezza] Rice's clear assurance that US activities are consistent with their domestic and international obligations and never include the use of torture.' Within days of the revelations about how to counter criticism of 'extraordinary rendition', *Channel 4 News* disclosed the contents of another leaked memo which gave an account of a discussion between the Prime Minister and the US President on 31 January 2003, six weeks before Iraq was attacked. The memo, obtained by Philippe Sands QC, Professor of Law at University College London and included in his book *Lawless World,* stated that Blair had said 'he was solidly with the President and ready to do whatever it took to disarm Saddam' despite the absence of a second UN resolution. Much of the press coverage concentrated on what the memo said about the President's plan to lure Saddam Hussein into war without the need for further UN support: 'The US was thinking of flying U2 reconnaissance aircraft with fighter cover over Iraq, painted in UN colours. If Saddam fired on them, he would be in breach.' Most of the leaks were so authoritative that their authenticity was rarely questioned. When asked to comment, the No. 10 press office fell back on its stock answer that Downing Street did not comment on the Prime Minister's private conversations; the leaked memo from the Foreign Office was merely a 'progress report' and Straw assured MPs in a written parliamentary answer there was 'no evidence of detainees being rendered through the UK or overseas territories since September 2001'.

By far the most sensational leak of this period related to another of the Prime Minister's conversations with the US President, during which Bush was said to have suggested bombing the headquarters of the Arabic television channel Aljazeera. The first hint of the story that was about to break emerged on 17 November 2005, when the police revealed that a former civil servant and a political researcher had been charged with separate offences under the

Official Secrets Act concerning the 'unauthorised disclosure between April and May 2004 of a confidential document relating to international relations'. The two men, who both lived in Northampton, were remanded on bail and ordered to appear before Bow Street magistrates on 29 November. David Keogh, aged forty-nine, who had been a communications officer at the Cabinet Office, was accused of passing the document to Leo O'Connor, aged forty-two, who was at the time was political researcher for the Labour MP for Northampton South, Tony Clarke.

Initially there was some confusion as to what the leaked document referred to. On the day of the hearing BBC News said it was a secret Foreign Office memo on American policy in Iraq which criticised 'heavy-handed US tactics in Falluja and Najaf' and the 'scandal of the treatment of detainees at Abu Ghraib'. The leak was assumed to be one of a series which first appeared in consecutive issues of the *Sunday Times* in May 2004; another leaked document, from 'more than a hundred pages of confidential papers' seen by the *Sunday Times*, revealed a secret project aimed at tackling the growing threat of Muslim extremism.

However, reports in the national press on the day after the men's court appearance suggested that the unauthorised disclosure related to an entirely different matter. In its report the *Independent* said the leaked document was a transcript of a 'confidential and controversial conversation' between the Prime Minister and the US President. Four days later a front-page exclusive in the *Daily Mirror* claimed the transcript was in the form of a five-page memo, stamped 'top secret', in which Bush told Blair that he planned to bomb Aljazeera's headquarters. The leak was described as being 'explosive and hugely damaging' because it would have meant the United States bombing the television channel's base in Qatar, 'a friendly Arab nation', a move which Blair talked Bush out of on the grounds that it would 'spark horrific revenge'. 'Explosive' it certainly was because the leak provoked a hostile reaction around the world. Scott McClellan, the White House spokesman, did his best to play down the story, insisting the *Daily Mirror*'s claims were 'outlandish and inconceivable'; an anonymous Downing Street official suggested Bush's remark was simply a joke. Aljazeera demanded an immediate explanation and its broadcasters held protest meetings to remind the President that a US missile destroyed its office in Kabul in November 2002 and that a journalist was killed after an air strike on the station's office in Baghdad in April 2003. Whatever was being said publicly, the government's law officers responded with alacrity. Next day, in another front-page story, the *Daily Mirror* declared that it had been gagged by the Attorney General, Lord Goldsmith, who warned that 'publication of any further details from the document' would be a breach of the Official Secrets Act. Unless the paper was prepared to confirm that it would publish nothing further, his office would issue an immediate High Court injunction. 'We have essentially agreed to comply,' said the *Daily Mirror*. Editors of other national newspapers were informed that they too would be liable to prosecution if they reproduced the contents of a document which had been 'unlawfully disclosed by a Crown servant'. Opposition MPs and media lawyers claimed it was unprecedented for the press to be threatened with the Official Secrets Act when data alleged to have been obtained illicitly had already been published; injunctions against newspapers had previously been obtained by the Blair government but it had never prosecuted them for publishing leaked documents. The *Guardian* concluded that the Attorney General had chosen to employ 'one of the most draconian pieces of legislation on the statute book' in order to put down a marker after so many previous leaks about the conduct of the war. In response to the suspicion that it was the Prime Minister who was trying to gag the news media simply in order to avoid embarrassing Bush and to protect Downing Street's intimate relationship with the White House, Goldsmith insisted he was acting on his own initiative, in his independent role to 'protect the administration of justice', and his intention was to remind newspapers they needed to take legal advice; the secrecy laws were not being used to 'save the embarrassment of a politician'.

The Aljazeera leak was unconventional in another important respect because the offending transcript had actually been returned to Downing Street eighteen months before the *Daily Mirror* published its exclusive story. In what appeared to be a throw-back to earlier levels of respect for the safekeeping of secret information, it emerged that the confidential document which the two men were charged with disclosing had been sent back to No. 10 by Clarke soon after it was discovered in a pigeon hole at his constituency office in Northampton. Clarke told the *Observer* that on being shown the document by O'Connor one Friday afternoon in June 2004, he realised immediately it was not a party political memo. Not only did it contain the transcript of a conversation that took place when Blair visited the White House and Bush talked 'openly' about bombing Aljazeera, but it also gave details of troop deployments. 'My researcher was worried about the content of the memo and did entirely the right thing. I realised it was highly sensitive and it was clear the lives of British troops would have been under threat if it had been made public.' Clarke considered he had 'no choice' but to inform Downing Street, telling the *Independent on Sunday*, 'After all, I was an MP and I am a special constable.' Next day he was interviewed at his home by officers from Special Branch and so was O'Connor, who lived not far from Keogh's Northampton home. The two men were arrested in September 2004; Keogh, who was on secondment to the Cabinet Office from the Foreign Office, was charged with sending the document, O'Connor with receiving it. When they appeared before Bow Street magistrates, O'Connor's lawyer, Neil Clark, said the defence had still not been allowed to see the document and unless it was disclosed he would be unable to defend his client. Rosemary Fernandes, for the prosecution, said that if information from the memo did emerge in open court she would seek the imposition of reporting restrictions in order to prevent publication.

One of the most prominent quotes in the *Daily Mirror*'s original exclusive was from the former Labour defence minister Peter Kilfoyle. He considered that the memo gave an 'insight into the mindset of those who were the architects of the war' and it needed to be put into the public domain. In an interview for the *Sunday Telegraph*, Kilfoyle gave a fuller account of why he was prepared to endorse the *Daily Mirror*'s story that Bush wanted to bomb Aljazeera; he was informed of the memo's contents soon after Tony Clarke was handed the document by his researcher. 'Clarke and I sat down and talked about the contents of it because he was seeking my advice on what to do with it.' Kilfoyle told the *Guardian* that in October 2004 they passed the transcript to the Democrats' national committee, hoping the contents might influence the 2004 US elections. Clarke was one of the Labour MPs who voted in 2003 to oppose military intervention in Iraq; he rebelled against the government on several occasions and lost his seat in the May 2005 general election. The *Observer* was certain the memo which turned up in Northampton was different to the one leaked the year before to the *Sunday Times*; they both revealed Foreign Office misgivings about 'heavy-handed US military tactics in Falluja' but it was the *Daily Mirror*'s memo which had 'metamorphosed into a major diplomatic incident' and attracted the attention of the Attorney General.

At a further court appearance by the two men on 10 January 2006 when they were committed for trial at the Old Bailey, the prosecution brought a second charge under the Official Secrets Act against Keogh of disclosing information which might damage the armed forces. Neil Clark told journalists after the court hearing that he had read the four-page secret document and he did not think it contained anything of embarrassment to the British government. Mark Stephens, representing Aljazeera, added his voice to those demanding publication of the Bush–Blair conversation on the grounds that if there was any suggestion that the station's journalists could have been killed, that would be legally indefensible and tantamount to 'counselling and procuring a war crime'; in such circumstances, the Official Secrets Act could not be used to stop publication. Aljazeera stepped up the pressure on the British government by demanding access to the transcript under the Freedom of Information Act. As a result Downing Street was forced to admit that it did have information 'relevant' to the request. However, the Prime Minister's official spokesman issued a categorical denial: the memo 'did not refer to bombing the Aljazeera television station in Qatar, despite various allegations to the contrary'. Although the No. 10 press office had been prepared to comment on the specific allegation, it insisted that the government was not obliged under the requirements of freedom of information to release details of 'private conversations between the Prime Minister and other world leaders'.

Nonetheless, having conceded that a transcript existed, Stephens was convinced the government would eventually have to publish it and in February 2006 he told a rally organised by the Campaign for Press and Broadcasting Freedom that he knew Aljazeera's request had caused consternation in Downing Street. An anonymous source within the Cabinet Office had told him that Bush had suggested using a missile. What was still not clear was whether the target would have been Aljazeera's studios in Qatar or one of its other bureaux in the Middle East. Stephens's fear was that Downing Street would continue to filibuster and 'drag this out until the end of the Bush Presidency' in the hope that journalists would lose interest. Because of the work he had done as a solicitor on Aljazeera's behalf, Stephens had come to the conclusion that the former civil servant and political researcher who had been charged under the Official Secrets Act with the 'unauthorised disclosure of a confidential document' would be well advised to follow the example of Katharine Gun and use the defence of necessity, especially as it seemed their trial might be held in secret.

> The only way to defend a case like this is to do what Katharine did and say this was a matter of conscience, that what was going on was a war crime; therefore take the moral high ground, just as Clive Ponting and others have done, and a jury will find for you.

Gun, who spoke at the rally in support of whistleblowers, said she too was concerned that the prosecution might seek to apply for restrictions on the reporting of the trial of the two men. She agreed with Stephens that the only way to stand up to the government was for a whistleblower to argue that a leak was justified. In her case, once the government refused to publish the Attorney General's advice on the Iraq war, the prosecution had no alternative but to concede there were 'evidential deficiencies' which made it impossible to disprove her defence of necessity. Gun was not at all surprised that her leak from GCHQ Cheltenham had been followed by a succession of unauthorised disclosures revealing other covert steps taken by Bush and Blair to try legitimise the war in Iraq.

> People like myself don't just stick our necks out for no good reason. No one wants to do this for fame, glory or money. We do it because we cannot stomach the lies any longer when the government has taken this country into a war against massive public opposition. Whistle blowing is our only guarantee against dictatorship; we should be celebrated not prosecuted.

Her determination to speak out in support of other government employees who might be prepared to put their careers at risk was applauded by Martin Bright, the journalist who broke the story in the *Observer* about Gun's leaked e-mail and the 'dirty tricks' which were being used in an attempt to persuade the six swing states to support a second UN resolution. Bright, who had subsequently become the *New Statesman*'s political editor, gave the rally an insight into how he had acquired a series of leaked documents from the Foreign Office, including the memo published by his magazine in January 2006 which revealed the steps being taken by the British government to distance itself from the US policy of extraordinary rendition.

> These leaks from the Foreign Office involve another extremely brave individual who stands to lose everything should anyone find out who it is . . . Publication of leaked documents is always justified. Journalists should not ask why. We know publication is always in the public interest. My only regret with Katharine Gun is that we didn't go with the story more quickly. Had the American press reacted more quickly it could have made a difference to what happened in Iraq.

On any reckoning 2005, like the preceding twelve months, had been another exceptional year for leaks and more often than not it was the *Sunday*

Times which led the way, leaving rival titles trailing in its wake. So confident was the paper in its ability to taunt the government that a front-page headline in August 2004 must have infuriated the ministers who had been most inconvenienced: 'No. 10 hunt for *Sunday Times* leaker is leaked'. Basking in its own notoriety, the paper revealed that at the request of the Prime Minister, the government's intelligence and security co-ordinator, Sir David Omand, had begun an unprecedented mole hunt within Whitehall to discover who was responsible for leaking a long list of confidential documents. A detective agency run by former MI5 officers was being employed by the Cabinet Office; civil servants in almost every department had been questioned; the estimated cost was close to £1 million. The investigation was revealed in a leaked letter from the Cabinet Secretary, Sir Andrew Turnbull, which advised permanent secretaries that he was putting 'more resources' into stemming the flow of unauthorised disclosures to the *Sunday Times* as this had become even 'worse' in recent months.

A leaked report of a presentation which Omand delivered to the Cabinet referred to twenty-six documents leaked to the paper's political editor, David Cracknell, over a period of fifteen months. Readers were reminded of the leaks which were thought to have caused the government the greatest embarrassment: a Cabinet split over plans by the Home Secretary, David Blunkett, to introduce identity cards; unease over 'heavy-handed' US military tactics in Iraq; a new strategy to placate the Muslim community; and the manipulation of the New Year honours to include an OBE for the tennis player Tim Henman in order to 'add interest' to the list. In a further swipe at the inability of ministers to protect their own correspondence, the paper quoted from fresh instructions issued by the Deputy Prime Minister, John Prescott, which were intended to safeguard any government paperwork containing references to 'serious ministerial disagreements'. In future he wanted such documentation to be 'double enveloped' and only a minister would be allowed to open the inner envelope; civil servants and political advisers would be permitted to see such documents but the paperwork 'must not leave the office of the minister unless it is in the minister's possession'. After indulging in an apparent orgy of self-congratulation the *Sunday Times* should perhaps have realised that it might be heading for a fall but the following month it published yet another 'leak from the heart of government', giving details of a possible pay rise for civil servants. Next day a temporary secretary at the Cabinet Office was arrested on suspicion of the theft of documents. She was aged twenty-three, a university graduate, and after a search of her home was released on bail pending further inquiries.

The national dailies, which had been waiting in the wings ready to exploit any sign of a slip-up by their weekend competitor, published prominent stories linking the arrest directly to the year-long series of leaks obtained by the *Sunday Times*. In a written parliamentary answer, the minister of state for the Cabinet Office, Ruth Kelly, said the secretary in question was from an agency which supplied temporary staff to government departments and 'following the incident, her assignment was terminated'.

After making further enquiries the *Guardian* identified the woman at the centre of the inquiry as Claire Newell, a 'would-be journalist', who had been temping in Whitehall after completing a postgraduate course in journalism and working briefly for the *Sunday Times* the previous summer. When approached by the *Guardian*, Newell refused to comment and the *Sunday Times*'s managing editor, Richard Caseby, said the paper 'would never discuss, let alone confirm or deny, the identity of any source'. Newell was also named by other newspapers and the *Observer* suggested she was one of two 'Whitehall moles who were feeding confidential documents' to the *Sunday Times*. After what the *Guardian* said appeared to have been 'slow-moving inquiries', the *Evening Standard* reported in August 2005 that Newell had been 'cleared of wrongdoing' by the Crown Prosecution Service following an eight-month investigation because of 'insufficient evidence' and the paper's Londoner's Diary noted with a slight hint of sarcasm that she had started a new job on the news desk of the *Sunday Times*.

I heard from other journalists that Newell wanted to become a foreign correspondent and, as she had not been charged, she hoped her arrest would not get in the way of her achieving her ambition. In standing firm behind the long-standing journalistic practice of going the extra mile to protect the identity of leakers and whistleblowers, the *Sunday Times* could, with some considerable justification, defend its record of breaking exclusive stories based on secret and confidential information. In the previous two years other journalists had been forced to look on with envy at a string of exclusives which did break new ground and often had far-reaching political conse-quences. Amid the seemingly unending flow of unauthorised disclosures about the lead-up to the Iraq war was a sequence of letters, memos and briefing papers obtained by the *Sunday Times*'s veteran defence corres-pondent, Michael Smith. His leaks were considered of such importance by American newspapers that his source was dubbed the 'British deep throat'. In a letter to the Prime Minister marked 'secret – strictly personal', Tony Blair's foreign policy adviser, Sir David Manning, who had returned from talks in Washington in March 2002, said he feared the US administration 'underestimated the difficulties' of going ahead with the invasion without stronger support from its allies and that President Bush had no answer to the question 'what happens on the morning after?' A Cabinet Office briefing paper revealed that Blair had promised Bush at a pre-war summit at the President's ranch in Crawford, Texas in April 2002 that Britain would 'back military action to bring about regime change'.

Despite Caseby's reluctance in the case of Claire Newell to even discuss the *Sunday Times*'s sources, Smith was allowed in June 2005 to reveal how he had obtained so many secret documents. One of the leakers was a friend and they arranged to meet in a quiet West End bar. 'The place was empty, but my friend chose the most secluded spot he could find. He was clearly nervous. He thrust two sheets of paper into my hand. It was a "Secret and Personal" letter from Jack Straw to the Prime Minister.' When Smith remarked with some understatement that he thought it would make 'a pretty good story', his friend said he had got 'five others just like it'. Eight months later another contact gave him a set of 'even more startling documents'. A series of exclusive stories published in March 2004 about the government's failure to conduct proper checks on visa applications by migrants from eastern Europe triggered yet more leaks, which, within less than a month, had forced the resignation of Beverley Hughes, the minister of state for immigration. Her hurried departure was due in large part to the effective way in which the shadow Home Secretary, David Davis, exploited a series of embarrassing revelations and used the very same tactics which Labour MPs had deployed so successfully against a Conservative government. After trying for three months without success to put a series of questions to Hughes, Steve Moxon, a caseworker at the Immigration and Nationality Directorate in Sheffield, approached the *Sunday Times*. He complained that his grievances had been 'repeatedly rebuffed' by his own department and also by the minister's private office.

'Lid blown on migrant cover-up' was the headline on the front-page story about the 'Home Office whistle-blower who has accused ministers of hiding the truth'. Once Moxon's revelations about the secret rubber-stamping of thousands of applications appeared in print, Davis raised the issue in the House of Commons; Hughes announced an internal inquiry; and Moxon was suspended the same day. His action in speaking out publicly prompted other disclosures including an e-mail sent anonymously to Davis by James Cameron, the British consul in Romania, which claimed that the concerns being expressed in Sheffield were just the 'tip of the iceberg'. Other leaked e-mails and documents were published in successive editions of the *Sunday Times*, including one memo from the Home Office which said Hughes had agreed that 'all applications over three months old should be granted'.

When Davis revealed that Cameron had been suspended for disclosing that visa applicants in Romania and Bulgaria were being allowed to by-pass checks at the embassies, the pressure increased and Hughes resigned. She had insisted all along that she had been unaware of the alleged abuses but in her resignation statement she admitted her parliamentary answers and television interviews were 'not in fact fully consistent' with a letter sent to her the year before by a former Home Office minister, Bob Ainsworth, who had drawn her attention to the unease of diplomats in Romania and Bulgaria about the abuse of immigration arrangements.

The day before she resigned Hughes accused the Conservatives of 'cynical news management' for having waited for three weeks before publishing the e-mail from the British consul but Davis said it was the job of MPs to protect civil servants who were prepared to reveal abuses and there should be a 'complete amnesty for them, no matter what they expose'. Davis confided to the *Sunday Telegraph* that he was buoyed up by his part in securing Hughes's scalp: 'The government is on the ropes because it doesn't know where the next whistleblower is coming from. But then, neither do I.' Four months later the *Sunday Times* had the front page headline 'Whistleblower sacked for upsetting ministers' over a report that Moxon had been dismissed by the Home Office for gross misconduct for 'disclosing official information without authority' and for failing to follow the rules obliging civil servants to 'exercise care in the use of information to avoid embarrassment to ministers'. Three weeks later the paper published an extract from Moxon's book, *The Great Immigration Scandal*, in which he described the grievances of caseworkers dealing with managed migration and how, having grown tired of the Home Office's stonewalling, he finally decided to ring the paper and blow the whistle. A three-page feature by David Leppard, the reporter who broke the story, gave an insight into the pressures Moxon had to endure when the government tried to rebut his allegations. 'First it accused the *Sunday Times* of making them up. When that did not work, it tried to smear Moxon. He was a maverick with a racist agenda, the spin implied . . . The whitewash failed. Other leaks – provided by ordinary citizens outraged by Moxon's treatment – flooded in.'

Hughes's colleagues were distraught about her resignation and furious that she had been forced out through a combination of leaks from civil servants, a press campaign against the government's immigration policy and some smart political footwork by the Conservatives. David Blunkett fought valiantly until the last moment to keep his minister of state. He was defiant at Question Time: 'The *Sunday Times*, the Tory party and anyone else can keep throwing mud, but my Right Honourable friend is not resigning.' When I discussed her downfall some weeks later with a group of Labour ministers, I could sense a real fear on their part about how vulnerable they had become to leaks from civil servants. John Healey, economic secretary to the Treasury, remarked ruefully on his concern that some government employees might be turning against Labour, just as they had lost faith with the Conservatives under John Major. Charlie Whelan, Gordon Brown's former spin doctor, was in no doubt as to who was to blame: leaks from civil servants were 'music to the ears of tabloid editors running campaigns against all foreigners'. In his weekly column in the *New Statesman*, he said 'tabloid hacks' had told him: 'We've got Beverley Hughes in our sights and we're out to get her.' Whelan was not surprised that a British consul had chosen the Tory party to leak his 'vile accusations' about immigration: 'My experience with FO staff abroad is that most of them are Tories. I hope this one gets sacked.' Whelan's fulminations were echoed across the Labour hierarchy, which in its fury seemed to have a collective memory lapse about the ruthless way ministers had exploited leaks when they were in opposition.

Blunkett, who had been so adroit in his use of unauthorised disclosures, told his biographer, Stephen Pollard, that he felt particularly exposed as Home Secretary. 'There's nobody been leaked against as much as I have: two White Papers, the ID stuff three times – including a letter that actually said "please do not distribute this letter", with the *Independent on Sunday* actually printing the words "please do not print this letter".' Andy McSmith, the *Independent on Sunday*'s political editor, took delight in complimenting Blunkett for remembering his paper's exclusive in July 2003, which was based on leaks about delays to the introduction of identity cards:

> As Blunkett rightly recalled, the report was based on a confidential document, on which he had included a plea that it should not be leaked. The exact words were: 'Only those in your office and the key official dealing with these matters should have sight of

this document, and I would be grateful if you would also keep a register of those who have seen this material.'

Blunkett's agitation about having become a target for leakers surfaced publicly for the first time when he was Secretary of State for Education and Employment. He was identified as being of one of the twelve ministers who had been strongly opposed to Tony Blair's decision to relaunch the Millennium Dome project within a month of Labour winning power in 1997. An apparently verbatim account of what Blunkett had said at the critical cabinet meeting was reproduced in the *Mail on Sunday* in November 2000. 'How the cabinet were steamrollered by Blair' was the headline over an exclusive report by its political editor, Simon Walters, giving an 'uncannily accurate' account of the comments made by each of the dissenting ministers. Several of those who had been quoted acknowledged that the views attributed to them about the Dome were broadly correct and Professor Peter Hennessy pronounced the account 'almost certainly genuine'; it was, he said, a 'Grade I listed leak'. After several days speculation about a 'high-level mole among officials or advisers at the heart of the government', the *Guardian* suggested the source was Mark Adams, a former Downing Street private secretary under Major who had continued working at No. 10 during the first three months of the Labour government. Adams was linked to the story because Walters had thanked him for help in writing his first novel, *Second Term*, billed as a story of 'spin, sabotage and seduction'. Instead of denying that he might have supplied the *Mail on Sunday* with a note of what each minister said, Adams admitted he was 'quite excited' to think he might be the 'prime suspect'. He thought it would be 'a shame to categorically deny it' because No. 10 had said that no such official document existed and there was no leak inquiry. Nonetheless Blunkett had felt so uncomfortable about the suspicions which had been aroused among members of the Cabinet that he had stopped taking notes himself. He told the BBC radio programme *In Touch* in January 2001 that he made a point at Cabinet meetings of switching off his Braille machine. 'I think we are all a bit wary of people who take notes.'

Over the years leaks became an increasing pre-occupation for Blunkett. The *Sunday Times* disclosed in January 2005 that his permanent secretary, Sir John Gieve, had done all he could to stem the flow of illicit disclosures from the Home Office; one whistleblower had been instantly sacked for leaking a report which indicated that ministers were seeking to cut up to

£25 million from the Criminal Injuries Compensation Scheme. Gieve told other government departments in a confidential memo, which had been seen by David Leppard, that the leaker had been identified and dealt with. 'His services were terminated on the spot and he was escorted from the building. The Home Office will be contacting the Cabinet Office to ensure that other departments are warned against employing him.' The previous year, at Blunkett's request, Gieve introduced a 'whistleblowers' hotline' in the Home Office to encourage officials who felt aggrieved about government policy to keep their concerns 'in house' but only eight enquiries had been received. At the height of the recriminations over Hughes's resignation Blunkett urged David Davis, as a fellow Privy Counsellor, to act responsibly and inform the authorities of possible abuses rather than undermine confidence in the immigration system by exploiting illicit disclosures. His request had echoes of the unsuccessful appeals which Margaret Thatcher made to Neil Kinnock in the mid-1980s when the Conservatives asked Labour MPs to have greater regard for the security of official secrets.

As Gieve did all he could to try to plug holes in the Home Office's defences, the Home Secretary suspected that the real villains were probably ministerial aides and advisers rather than civil servants. While he did not say so in as many words, like others in the party he seemed to be coming to the conclusion that Blair's government was slowly sinking in a sea of home-grown leaks which was entirely of Labour's own making. In Stephen Pollard's biography, *David Blunkett*, one of Blair's most trusted colleagues pulled back the veil on the way leaking was being used as a weapon in fighting turf wars within the Labour government: 'Somebody at adviser or minister level in other departments has got it in for me . . . None of it's been done with a helpful eye.' Increasingly bitter rivalry between committed Blairites such as Blunkett and the friends and allies of the Chancellor of the Exchequer was generating an apparently inexhaustible stream of unwelcome disclosures from Downing Street, the Cabinet Office and the Treasury. Endless speculation about the timing of Blair's departure and the likely date of a long-promised hand-over of power to Gordon Brown was a source of constant intrigue which fascinated political commentators and only added to the tension. As Lance Price confirmed in *The Spin Doctor's Diary* on his stint in the No. 10 press office, the feud between rival supporters and sympathisers of Blair and Brown was regularly fought out through leaking insider gossip and information to friendly journalists in the hope that unhelpful news coverage would annoy one side or another.

Blunkett, like Peter Mandelson before him, found that Downing Street's support afforded little protection once a media feeding frenzy had been unleashed and a Cabinet minister had become engulfed in a tidal wave of embarrassing and often unauthorised disclosures. Both men had the distinction of resigning twice from Blair's Cabinet and both were convinced that hostile leaking played a part in their downfall. Blunkett's first resignation in December 2004, after he intervened in the fast-tracking of the visa application of his former lover's nanny, was the culmination of a long-drawn-out saga which had been characterised by discreet tip-offs and off-the-record briefings by friends and colleagues of both the Home Secretary and his ex-lover, Kimberly Quinn, publisher of the *Spectator*. Disclosures in November 2005 about Blunkett's shareholdings in DNA Biosciences led to his second resignation, from the post of Secretary of State for Work and Pensions, after he admitted failing to consult the advisory committee on business appointments for former ministers.

During the early months of 2005 a similar tide of unwelcome leaks about the financial dealings of her husband David Mills dogged Tessa Jowell, Secretary of State for Culture, Media and Sport. After enduring weeks of damaging publicity, the couple announced 'a period of separation' while Mills continued to fight allegations that he had accepted a £350,000 bribe from the Italian Prime Minister, Silvio Berlusconi. While he was doing all he could to stand by Jowell, Blair found that his own position as Prime Minister had become endangered owing to leaks revealing that the House of Lords Appointments Commission had blocked four of his nominations for working peers because the individuals involved had donated money to the Labour Party. In the face of mounting pressure during March 2006, which was fuelled by a seemingly endless supply of unsourced information about donations and loans, the party finally published the names of the twelve millionaires who had secretly lent Labour £13.9 million to help finance the 2005 general election. One of the four whose peerage was blocked tried to discover where the leaks had originated. Dr Chai Patel, founder and chief executive of the Priory rehabilitation clinics, demanded an explanation. He told *The World at One* that his name must have been leaked either by the Lords Appointments Commission or Downing Street because only they knew that he had been nominated for a peerage.

Amid the claim and counter-claim of the 'loans for peerages' scandal, the *Guardian* disclosed that Blair had become so infuriated by the failure to stem unauthorised disclosures that the government intended to create a new post in the Cabinet Office to co-ordinate leak inquiries. David Hencke, the paper's Westminster correspondent, said he had been leaked a copy of the confidential job specification; it revealed that the new official, on a salary of £30,000, would be expected to co-ordinate investigations and draw up policy proposals to try to stop future disclosures. Extra money had been provided to 'beef up' internal security within the government and the new official, who would have the resources of the intelligence services at his or her disposal, would report to Sir Richard Mottram, who had been appointed Cabinet Office security and intelligence co-ordinator in September 2005. When the appointment of a leak inquiry co-ordinator was discussed on *Today* it was described 'as perhaps the most thankless job in the civil service' by Mike Granatt, a former head of the government's information service. In his experience leakers were rarely if ever identified, because most of the leaking was done directly from ministers' offices, either to fly a kite or scupper a colleague's idea, and no one had ever succeeded in bringing a minister to 'book for it'. Granatt thought the fear that ministers might be exposed by leaks was a good check on the executive. 'A completely leak-free government, with total control over information, would be less welcome than a government which feels vulnerable . . . Journalism is now more competitive and more expensive and there are fewer journalists who do proper investigations. We should treasure journalists who spend their time digging for the facts.'

Chapter 9

An increasing flow of unauthorised disclosures from within the government which were intended to disadvantage fellow ministers and party colleagues was more than matched in the first year of Labour's third term by the seemingly unending supply of deliberate leaks instigated by the Whitehall departments in order to trail ministerial announcements. Alastair Campbell's dogged persistence in encouraging civil service information officers to 'grab the agenda' had paid handsome dividends. Most weekends the Sunday papers offered a vast array of stories promoting policy initiatives and other developments. Rather than give any hint as to the likely origin or motivation for the disclosures which they featured so prominently, journalists tended to stress the importance of the confidential information which they were divulging and whenever possible they took pride in claiming that their reports were exclusive. With such a wide selection of stories on offer, the casual reader, viewer or listener could have been forgiven for finding it difficult sometimes to distinguish between a genuine leak, possibly the work of a whistleblower, and a planted story, which was often portrayed as a leak but which was more likely to have resulted from a planned and authorised disclosure designed to excite interest and manipulate the news headlines. The constant pre-empting of ministerial statements had become so entrenched within Whitehall by the start of Labour's third term that it came almost to be taken for granted by MPs and no longer seemed to trouble the Speaker, Michael Martin, as much as it had in his earlier years in the chair.

Martin's predecessor, Betty Boothroyd, had made a valiant effort during the first three years of the Blair government to stop his administration undermining the ability of Parliament to hold the executive to account. She issued six separate rulings against ministers she had caught disclosing detailed information to the news media before delivering statements to the House. When I made inquiries as part of my research for *The Control Freaks*, I discovered that in all six cases the trail of responsibility for leaking the contents of each announcement led back directly to the No. 10 press office and instructions issued by the Strategic Communications Unit. Yet in his 1998 appearance before the House of Commons Public Administration Select Committee, Campbell had given an explicit assurance that Downing Street did not 'pre-empt major announcements to Parliament' by trailing the contents of policy statements. Campbell's undertaking was never tested again by MPs during his six and a half years in Downing Street and the regularity with which secretaries of state sanctioned the leaking of their own statements by their political advisers and information officers so angered Boothroyd that she used her valedictory address in July 2000 to renew her plea to Tony Blair that his government should 'never overlook the primacy of Parliament', which was where in 'the first instance ministers must explain and justify their policies'.

Of the six cases I examined, one of the most blatant related to an announcement by the minister for sport, Kate Hoey, that £150 million was to be spent on improving school sports facilities. News of the extra money was revealed exclusively in the *Independent on Sunday*, followed up by a fuller story in the *Daily Mirror* and then trailed by Hoey herself in a *Today* interview on the morning of a news conference to announce the new sports strategy, yet no provision had been made for a parliamentary statement. Boothroyd was forthright in her ruling: there had been a 'clear breach of the convention' regarding such announcements and never again should there be a repeat of the position where 'the interest of Parliament is regarded as secondary to media presentation'. Shortly after Hoey apologised to the Speaker, I had to interview her and she inadvertently let slip that although she had been forced to take the blame, it was Downing Street which had whisked the sports strategy announcement out of her hands and leaked it to the press. After I disclosed this in *The Control Freaks*, I spoke to Hoey again some months later and she reinforced her criticism of the No. 10 press office for constantly changing her arrangements to fit the demands of the media. On succeeding Boothroyd, Martin issued several reminders to ministers that the House should be 'the first to hear of important developments in government policy'.

The stand taken by Speakers Boothroyd and Martin was supported by the Public Administration Select Committee, which asked Blair to reinforce a pledge he had given in December 2001 that the ministerial code would be strengthened to ensure that he and his colleagues made announcements 'in the first instance' to Parliament. Notwithstanding the build-up in parliamentary pressure, the No. 10 press office said the guidance could not be regarded as being 'hard and fast'. As the Prime Minister's official spokesman subsequently explained, ministers worked on the basis that they would make statements 'as soon as possible', which the *Times* concluded meant that Downing Street had 'no intention of sticking to the rules that prohibit ministers leaking policy announcements to the press'. The task of policing the ministerial code rested solely with the Prime Minister, and the government's continued refusal to authorise the preparation of a Civil Service Bill to update the regulations governing the relationship between ministers and civil servants was taken as an indication that Blair was content with the status quo. In the New Labour rule book for media management the importance of gaining the attention of journalists had a far higher priority than the conventions of the House. If ministers were reprimanded for trailing announcements, there was no way they could avoid apologising to MPs for their discourtesy but a rebuke by the Speaker would not been seen by Downing Street as having imposed any restriction on the freedom of ministers and their political advisers to talk to the news media; the rule about 'informing Parliament first' only applied where it was 'practical to do so'. Providing the No. 10 press office and Whitehall departments with the authority, if necessary, to by-pass the House of Commons in this way was one of the freedoms which Campbell had considered essential when civil service information officers were instructed in November 1997 to 'raise their game'. They were told they had to become more proactive and drive forward the news agenda by stimulating interest in government statements and White Papers; once a date had been fixed for publication, they should be poised to begin a 'ring-round' of newsrooms so as to trail parliamentary announcements. However, having pushed through the regime which Campbell had demanded, the committee, headed by Sir Robin Mountfield, failed to provide effective guidance on how civil servants should avoid a breach of parliamentary protocol once the No. 10 press office and the rest of the political advisers had whetted the appetite of journalists. In the light of numerous tortuous but ultimately futile attempts to hold ministers to account, I suggested in an article for *Political Quarterly* in July 2004 that the only remedy lay in the hands of MPs themselves. If they were serious in their wish to defend the 'primacy of Parliament' they should press for an immediate revision of the parliamentary rules to see if the disciplinary procedures of the House of Commons could be used to punish ministers who were implicated in leaking their own statements. What had struck me so forcibly was the absence of any penalty vested in either the Speaker or the House for the kind of wilful action which so self-evidently weakened the ability of MPs to challenge the executive.

According to Erskine May's *Treatise on the Law, Privileges, Proceedings and Usage of Parliament*, the ultimate authority on procedural matters at the House of Commons, the only existing parliamentary offence for divulging information relates to the premature disclosure of reports from select committees. Such was the level of unquestioning loyalty after Blair's landslide victory in 1997 that even this convention was flouted and a chain of events in the spring and summer of 1999 revealed a degree of complicity which shocked opposition parties and surprised even hardened journalists. Three Labour MPs were suspended for their involvement in supplying leaked copies of committee reports; a fourth resigned from a committee; a committee chairman had to apologise; and there was criticism of three of the most senior ministers in the Cabinet. An illicit copy of a committee report was considered to be of great value because it gave the responsible minister a head start in working out how to minimise the likely impact of any criticism. If a government department had been censured, once armed with a draft copy, the task of refuting a committee's findings could begin well before publication. The scale of Labour's duplicity surpassed all previous attempts to thwart the select committees, which had in fact struggled for three decades to stop leaks undermining the effectiveness of their work. In previous years, in the face of mounting frustration at their repeated failure to identify the source of leaks, the committees had tried without success to punish editors and journalists by recommending their exclusion from the House of Commons press gallery, but by majority votes on two occasions MPs refused to endorse punitive action. Throughout the 1970s the select committees grew in stature and importance. Their remit was strengthened further in 1979 at the instigation of the Leader of the House, Norman St John Stevas, and after they had been restructured to enable them monitor the work of each government department, their work assumed even greater political significance. Once leaks from draft copies of committee reports began appearing in the press, the Privileges Committee was asked for its advice and in 1978 it recommended that action should be taken where premature or unauthorised disclosure caused 'substantial interference' in a committee's work.

The leak which had attracted the greatest criticism and which precipitated the introduction of a formal procedure appeared in the *Economist* in 1975 after the magazine obtained a draft report from the Select Committee on a Wealth Tax. In a damning indictment, the Committee of Privileges declared that the editor had been 'reckless and blameworthy' and the journalist 'wholly irresponsible' for reporting an unauthorised disclosure but a recommendation that they should both be treated with the 'utmost severity' and be excluded from the precincts of the House for six months was rejected by MPs and no further action was taken. The inability of the select committees to stem the flow of leaks, despite repeated warnings that dishonourable conduct by committee members would be treated with 'appropriate severity', forced a re-examination of the rules in 1985. However, the Privileges Committee had no alternative but to admit that it was virtually powerless to take action because of the inability to 'unearth the sources of leaks', although the evidence it had amassed clearly showed that the majority of leaks came from within and were 'the deliberate work of members of committees acting for political or personal motives'. It concluded that as 'a leak supposes a leaker', all it could do was urge committee members to guard sensitive papers with the greatest possible care and remind them that a 'severe judgement' would be made against any MP found to have acted dishonourably.

Within months of its deliberations the committee discovered it remained as impotent as before, after the *Financial Times* published the conclusions of a draft report from the Environment Committee. A 'serious contempt' had been committed but an inquiry failed to trace the leaker and a recommendation that the paper's political correspondent Richard Evans should be suspended from the lobby and be excluded from the precincts of the House for six months was again rejected by MPs on the grounds that it would be wrong to 'punish a journalist merely for doing his job'. So great was the committee's irritation at its failure to identify the culprits that at one hearing the chairman, Sir Geoffrey Howe, voiced what he believed was their 'sense of collective abomination' at the failure of any of the 'leakees' to own up.

Despite the refusal of the House to heed previous recommendations and introduce a standing warning to journalists of automatic suspension for interfering with select committee work, another full-scale review had to be mounted in 1990 in the wake of an unauthorised disclosure which it was feared might jeopardise a right of access to official papers which had taken years to establish. In November 1989, in the first leak of its kind, the *Guardian* published classified data which had been supplied in confidence to the Public Accounts Committee. A report prepared by the Comptroller and Auditor General, John Bourn, disclosed that the government had paid £38 million in sweeteners to British Aerospace when it took over the Rover Group. The *Guardian*'s justification for publishing the story was that the revelation showed that MPs and the public had been misled about the real cost of the Rover sale. Such was the fury of the Privileges Committee that it demanded an explanation from the editor, Peter Preston, who, together with his two correspondents, David Hencke and Andrew Cornelius, was required to answer questions at a private hearing.

Preston explained in a prepared statement that they could 'offer no help as to the source of our story', a line which he stuck to resolutely when defending their action in printing facts which 'should clearly be in the public domain'. The *Guardian* did not believe that the 'expert and robust politicians' who served on the select committees were likely to be knocked off their course by a newspaper report and they should recognise that the 'leaking of facts is an inevitable part of the political process wherever power is disputed and that it is an umbilical role of the press'. When it was put to the editor and his journalists that publishing information classified as confidential was 'detrimental to the national interest', Preston disputed that either national security or commercial confidentiality were involved. Even if the Public Accounts Committee upped the classification of its data from 'confidential' to 'secret' the *Guardian* would do the same again because basing a report on a leaked document 'lent the story added credence'. Having failed in the past to persuade the House to discipline journalists, the committee decided against taking punitive action but it did not accept the argument that reporters were 'merely doing their job' and reserved the right to recommend punishment in the future. Because of fears that the 'sweeteners' leak might make it harder to obtain information from government departments, the committees were told they all might have to follow the example of the Public Accounts Committee and ensure that documents classified as 'secret' could only be inspected in a committee room or in the presence of a clerk.

Two leaks earlier that year from the Education Committee had so angered its chairman, the Conservative MP Timothy Raison, that he resigned in protest. Again an accusing finger was pointed at members of the committee but an inquiry failed to determine who might have supplied information to the *Guardian* about a report on teacher supply or the identity of the *Daily Telegraph*'s source for a story about museums and galleries. Being hauled before a parliamentary committee had come to be regarded as something of a badge of honour among lobby journalists and the appearance of the *Guardian*'s two reporters in front of the Privileges Committee had been preceded by the questioning of the *Independent*'s political correspondent John Pienaar by the Home Affairs Committee after a leak about a report on the work of the Crown Prosecution Service. So great was the determination of journalists at Westminster to protect the identity of their sources that they rarely gave any clue as to how they had obtained their information. Occasionally the temptation proved too strong and after an interval of eleven years Hencke disclosed in a media column in the *Guardian* how he acquired the leak on hidden government sweeteners for British Aerospace. He was sitting in his office in the press gallery when the telephone rang and he was invited to look at a piece of paper in the office of the caller. When he arrived he was handed four sheets of photocopied paper headed 'confidential'; it was the memorandum prepared by the Comptroller and Auditor General. The timing of the leak was 'impeccable' because it came the day after the publication of a National Audit Office report showing that Rover had been sold too cheaply. Hencke said his leaker had never been unmasked; to his knowledge had never leaked such damaging information again; and had been promoted to 'higher things in Whitehall and Westminster'.

I was intrigued by Hencke's assessment of the circumstances which precipitated the leak:

> The leaker told me he had looked at that morning's papers. 'I was going to give the document to the *Independent* but I saw the *Guardian* gave better coverage so I contacted you,' the person said. As a leaker, the person may not have been atypical but the motives were – nearly all really damaging leaks come because the person involved is angered by hypocrisy or by what they see as a serious "cover up". They are almost always looking for an outlet where the issue will be treated seriously – and only then are they prepared to take a risk that could wreck their career or public standing'.

Controversial inquiries into future spending on the National Health Service provided a regular flashpoint for the new Conservative Prime Minister, John Major, and an unprecedented hue and cry began in July 1991 after the Health Committee chairman, the Conservative MP Nicholas Winterton, discovered that a draft of one of his reports had been leaked to the Department of Health. Winterton believed that, assisted by the leak, the government persuaded the five other Conservative MPs on the committee to vote in favour of removing the seventeen most critical pages from the final report. Although he succeeded in stalling the committee's inquiries for three months, the Secretary of State for Health, William Waldegrave, finally acknowledged that a purported draft of the report had been sent 'unsolicited' to his department; after he discovered that it was not an official document he had ordered all copies of it to be destroyed.

After having been so frustrated for so many years, the select committees at last had a promising lead and in response to further questions Waldegrave revealed that the document had been passed to his department by Ian Taylor, his parliamentary private secretary. Taylor refused to elaborate on the 'channel through which' the report reached his hands but said rather ominously that he thought it was up to the committee member 'who may have been concerned' to clarify the matter. Armed with Taylor's tip-off, Winterton renewed his appeal for the leaker to own up and later the same day the Conservative MP Jerry Hayes admitted that without authority his American researcher had given the report to the Department of Health. 'I suspect that my researcher thought he was being helpful and know that he would have acted in total innocence of the consequences.' Hayes took full responsibility for the action of his research assistant, who had returned to the USA. After apologising, he said the only honourable course available to him was to resign. Waldegrave denied he had seen the leaked report but his political adviser, Richard Marsh, had discussed its contents with his civil servants, a disclosure which prompted Labour MPs to accuse the government of having 'nobbled' the Health Committee's inquiry. Not to be outdone, the Privileges Committee ordered Waldegrave to attend a private hearing but he refused to sack Taylor and rejected calls by Labour MPs that he should resign from the Cabinet. Winterton, who lost his position as committee chairman after Conservative whips withdrew their support, was disappointed when the committee failed to take decisive action despite having what he thought was conclusive evidence.

Allegations about government interference in the work of the Health Committee resurfaced in December 1992 after the Labour MP Alice Mahon obtained a leaked memo from the Department of Health revealing that the new secretary of state, Virginia Bottomley, and a team of eight civil servants had been told they would get 'confidential advance copies a few days before publication' of a report into NHS trusts. When the clerk to the committee explained there were procedures for reports to be released up to twenty-four hours in advance to ministers and lobby journalists, Mahon demanded that Labour's front bench should at least be afforded the same privilege.

A change of government in 1997 did nothing to lessen the temptation facing ministers and their advisers to use leaks as a way of rebutting critical reports from select committees. So strong was the tug of loyalty after Tony Blair won power that Labour MPs were prepared to take even greater risks than their Conservative counterparts. The full extent of Labour's double dealing was only revealed after it emerged in February 1999 that the Foreign Secretary, Robin Cook, had been given a draft copy of a report by the Foreign Affairs Committee into the delivery of British arms to Sierra Leone in contravention of a United Nations embargo. Ernie Ross, the Labour MP who admitted leaking the report, apologised for a breach of confidence. He was suspended from the House for ten days for what was said to have been a 'serious interference' in the committee's work. Cook denied that any use had been made of the report when briefing journalists, but he did not escape criticism, not least for his potential culpability in allowing senior civil servants to hold on to a leaked document for at least a month. Donald Anderson, the committee chairman, apologised for giving Foreign Office officials an advance briefing on the report's conclusions about the legality of the arms shipment.

Initially all eleven MPs on the Social Security Committee denied being the source of a leaked copy of a report on child benefit which was destined for the Chancellor, Gordon Brown, another minister renowned for his mastery of New Labour's repertoire of rebuttal. With an investigation having got nowhere and the Standards and Privileges Committee finally acknowledging that it could do no more than condemn whoever it was who had failed to tell the truth, the Labour MP Kali Mountford admitted she had tried to help the Chancellor by giving his parliamentary private secretary, Don Touhig, sight of her copy. Mountford, who apologised for her delay in being 'totally forthcoming', was suspended for five days; Touhig was suspended for three. Brown insisted that neither he nor any other Treasury minister had read the report.

The third leak was from the Scottish Affairs Committee; one of its members, the Labour MP David Stewart, resigned after he admitted having supplied extracts of a report to the Secretary of State for Scotland, Donald Dewar. In a concerted follow-up to deter potential leakers, the Speaker and the Standards and Privileges Committee joined forces to ask Blair to amend the ministerial code to require ministers and their parliamentary private secretaries to return leaked committee papers without delay. New guidance was issued not just to ministers but also to civil servants and diplomats. They were told that any future use of unpublished committee documents would be regarded as a contempt of parliament. The extent of the subterfuge uncovered during the investigation into the Sierra Leone leak was seen as a defining moment by the chairs of the thirty-three select committees and it triggered demands for a fundamental shake-up of the rules and procedures so as to strengthen their ability to hold the executive in check.

A procedure to protect committee reports from premature publication had been in force since 1837 and as the House of Commons had demonstrated so forthrightly that a cross-party consensus could be achieved in policing its own affairs, I suggested in *Political Quarterly* that if recalcitrant MPs could be held to account for leaking committee reports then there was no reason why ministers who had flouted parliamentary protocol could not be similarly punished. After all, the information being released by way of a ministerial announcement was in effect the property of Parliament and therefore it was the responsibility of the House of Commons to ensure that such a precious commodity was not traded in advance with the news media simply in the hope of benefiting the government of the day. I argued that a free and fair flow of news from the state to the public was a cornerstone of a democratic state and should go hand in hand with respect for Britain's parliamentary institutions. Needless to say, these lofty observations, together with my proposal that the advance leaking of a ministerial statement should become a parliamentary offence, failed to elicit any response in either Whitehall or Westminster. I was equally unsuccessful when I submitted evidence to an inquiry into the reasons for the lack of trust in the government's information service. I maintained, as I had many times before, that the constant, off-the-record trailing of ministerial announcements undermined the authority of the Speaker, damaged parliamentary accountability, and had hastened a decline in editorial standards because of the way the hand-over of data on a unattributable basis took advantage of competitive pressures within the media and fed the demand for 'exclusive' stories.

Although the review, chaired by Bob Phillis, chief executive of the Guardian Media Group, failed to address any of my concerns about the growth in the surreptitious trade in information, it concluded there had been a 'three-way breakdown in trust between government and politicians, the media and the general public'. In an interim recommendation, issued within days of Alastair Campbell's resignation in August 2003, the committee deemed that in future a senior civil servant rather than a political appointee should have strategic control over the government's publicity machine. Blair accepted the proposal with alacrity and No. 10's newly appointed director of communications, David Hill, formerly head of publicity for the Labour Party, was stripped of the unprecedented power to instruct civil servants which Campbell had exercised since May 1997. Admittedly it was rather late in the day, but Blair had finally conceded that the key media post in Downing Street should never again be held by a political propagandist like Campbell or Hill; instead he agreed that a permanent secretary should be appointed to take control of government communications and become head of profession for information officers. On taking up the new appointment in July 2004, Howell James was charged with the task of providing strategic leadership and building an authoritative communications service to be based on the 'reinforcement of the civil service's political neutrality, rather than a blurring of government and party communications'.

Well before James took up his appointment, one of the central proposals of the Phillis review had already been 'kicked into the long grass' after protests by the combined ranks of Westminster's political correspondents. At a meeting held in the press gallery they expressed their 'grave disquiet' about the recommendation that their twice-daily lobby briefings should be televised. Initially Downing Street had responded to the Phillis review by suggesting that a minister rather than the official spokesman should answer questions, but after hearing of the lobby's strong opposition to the prospect of their proceedings being held 'on the record, live on television and radio', the plan was quietly dropped. There was some justification for Downing Street's reluctance to pick a fight, because the lobby briefings had become far less combative since Campbell's departure and were being upstaged every month by the televised briefings which the Prime Minister was giving in No. 10. Blair introduced what he promised would become a regular question-and-answer session in June 2002 after allegations that he had tried to manipulate the preparations for the Queen Mother's funeral in order to enhance his own importance. By subjecting himself every month to questions from British and overseas journalists he hoped to demonstrate that his government was ready to be judged on substance rather than spin. While I applauded many of the other recommendations made by Phillis and his committee, especially those aimed at reining in the political advisers and preventing a repetition of Jo Moore's infamous instruction to information officers to 'bury' bad news, I felt that what had been billed as a 'radical review' had shied away from tackling the real mischief caused by partial and selective briefing.

I remained convinced that a root cause of the current malaise was the unregulated trade in confidential government information, one by-product of which was a daily line-up of confusing and often contradictory stories. If trust was to be restored, what better way to start than to introduce a new set of guidelines for those who briefed the media on behalf of the state? The closest the Phillis review got to addressing this challenge was advice on how information officers should respond when faced by a task which 'oversteps the mark' and might constitute a breach of the civil service code. If they found that requests made by ministers or political advisers were 'too onerous or problematic', they were advised to notify either their director of communications or their permanent secretary. Here was a chance for an authoritative group of senior civil servants and media professionals to have gone one step further; they could have reminded ministers of their collective responsibility to preserve the confidentiality of government information and their duty to uphold parliamentary conventions. Instead the Phillis review was a missed opportunity because it failed to turn the spotlight on to the government's own illicit behaviour.

In arguing the case for fresh guidelines on the way ministers and their political advisers traded information with journalists, I had frequently called in aid the action taken in the City of London to ensure the 'full, accurate and timely disclosure' of price-sensitive data. Rules introduced by the Stock Exchange to prevent insider dealing and stop the flow of leaks about bids and profit warnings were strengthened significantly and given the force of law under the Financial Services and Markets Act, which took effect in November 2001. The Financial Services Authority (FSA) was given the power to prosecute listed companies for abuses such as the 'Friday night drop', which involved holding back information until after the end of the week's trading on the Stock Exchange and then leaking it to a Sunday newspaper. As I had discovered during my research into the activities of public relations consultants who specialised in financial affairs, the practice of supplying journalists with tip-offs in the hope of influencing share prices was commonplace during the hostile takeovers of the 1980s and it was a technique which had been widely copied by Conservative and Labour spin doctors. Guidance issued by the FSA was explicit: a listed company was required to keep the market informed of price-sensitive information without delay; if there was a breach of confidence, the recipients must not deal in a company's securities before the relevant information had been made available to the public; and if there was no alternative but to issue the information over a weekend, when the stock market was closed, it must be supplied to no 'less than two national newspapers and two wire services'. If the FSA could establish and enforce a regime which held listed companies and their consultants to account, I failed to see why successive Cabinet Secretaries did not feel duty bound to devise a procedure which placed similar constraints on ministers and their political advisers. When companies were warned in 2001 that they would be fined if they were caught tipping off a reporter or failing to ensure the widest possible distribution for news of major corporate developments, the FSA chairman, Sir Howard Davies, said there was 'nothing more corrosive of market confidence' than the selective briefing of analysts and journalists.

Davies could hardly have put it any better if he had been describing the world of Whitehall and Westminster: ministerial leaks to favoured contacts have proved divisive among both politicians and political journalists and they have corroded the level of public trust in what the government of the day has been saying. If the City of London had been forced to clean up its act, there seemed to be no reason why the country's political establishment should not have been required to follow suit. I agree that without the political will there is no incentive for the head of the civil service to take any action but permanent secretaries should not be oblivious to the questionable activities which information officers have been required to undertake, especially when dealing with sensitive financial information. The first step in the Department of Health's media plan to announce the purchase in August 2001 of the privately owned London Heart Hospital was an instruction to leak the news exclusively to the *Times*, yet this was a transaction which involved £27.5 million of taxpayers' money and should have merited total transparency. The question I would pose is: how many other government information officers have been required to disseminate financial information in a manner which would not be in accordance with the spirit, let alone the small print, of the FSA's guidelines?

An earlier example of New Labour's casual approach towards the rules on the release of price-sensitive information was quoted by the authors Peter Oborne and Simon Walters in their biography of Alastair Campbell. They described a meeting in the No. 10 press office to discuss the arrangements for publicising British Airways' decision to purchase seventy-five planes from the European Airbus consortium at a cost of £3 billion. The announcement was made in August 1998 when Tony Blair interrupted his holiday in France and visited the Airbus base in Toulouse. Oborne and Walters claimed that BA officials were horrified when Campbell told them he intended to leak the story to one of the Sunday newspapers. They explained that such a tip-off would be 'highly irregular because of the market sensitivity of the deal' and it was only after BA managers warned him they 'could end up in jail' that Campbell 'got the message'.

If ever there is the political will in the future to ask the Cabinet Secretary to tighten the rules on the advance trailing of government statements, any review could hardly ignore the blatant leaking of Treasury announcements. In his nine years as Chancellor, Gordon Brown progressively disregarded virtually all the ballyhoo about pre-Budget purdah and the traditional secrecy surrounding the contents of the Budget box. During his long years in opposition Brown had become a regular conduit for publicising confidential documents leaked to him by civil servants and he was admired for the way he could put them to good use when attacking the government. In distributing his leaks and tip-offs among the political correspondents of Westminster, he had made some friends for life. Once Labour were in power, he demonstrated an equally deft touch when making use of the journalists whom he could trust; he realised that by choosing the correspondents to be briefed in advance he could exercise a degree of control over the presentation of his policies. The press build-up to the Budget and other financial statements was always carefully manipulated to prepare the ground for any changes which he intended to make in tax and spending. By the time of the 1999 Budget, his Conservative predecessor, Kenneth Clarke, could take no more and he accused Brown of engaging in the 'institutionalised leaking' of Treasury proposals. Clarke cited as an example a leak in March that year to the *Daily Express* which had reported exclusively that the Chancellor would give discounts on vehicle excise duty for the owners of small-engined cars. In disregarding the rule that Chancellors should not brief journalists in advance, Clarke said that Brown's leaks played into the hands of speculators. 'There are serious players in the City of London who analyse all this stuff and some people deal in it. They make bets on it, they make money, they lose money.' When it was put to him by the paper's chief political correspondent, Patrick O'Flynn, that the Treasury's response was that it could not be held responsible for speculative and often inaccurate stories, Clarke claimed Brown was equally adept at giving journalists misleading trails; it was time Labour realised there were good reasons why 'commercially confidential decisions' should remain confidential. Brown's decision to move gradually away from the idea that the Budget should remain a 'big bang', with all the significant changes kept secret until the Chancellor spoke at the despatch box, was welcomed by the Liberal Democrats' Treasury spokesman, Malcolm Bruce, because it helped opposition parties prepare their responses. 'All this Budget secrecy is a bit of a nonsense and I think if there is a general direction that the government is taking, step by step, then it is a good idea that the Budget should be trailed in advance.'

Two years later the *Daily Telegraph*'s chief political correspondent, Andy McSmith, listed all the leaks which had been published ahead of the 2001 Budget and argued that it was clear that the principle of keeping everything secret until the day itself had become 'one of the casualties of Brown's chancellorship'. Among the many tip-offs was one to the *Times* that the 10p tax band would be widened to help the low paid; the precise thresholds were then leaked over a period of days to other newspapers so they could flesh out the details. 'The story did two things for Brown. It killed speculation that he might cut the basic rate of income tax, preventing disappointment on the day, and it told the lower paid the Chancellor was thinking of them.'

By each succeeding Budget, financial and political commentators had been fed so much information in advance that there were rarely any surprises left on the day itself. Spooling forward rapidly to the pre-Budget report of December 2005 and then the Budget of March 2006, we see that Brown demonstrated his complete mastery of the art of trailing his own decisions; the demolition job on Budget secrecy was virtually complete. He had become so brazen in his disregard of parliamentary protocol that he was prepared to give a journalist the kind of exclusive briefing which had forced his eminent Labour predecessor Hugh Dalton to resign in 1947. On his way into the House of Commons chamber, Dalton outlined his Budget secrets to John Carvel, lobby correspondent for the London evening paper the *Star*, which printed the main tax changes in its stop press column. Almost sixty years later, the London *Evening Standard*'s political editor, Joe Murphy, pulled off the same trick: 'Speaking exclusively to the *Evening Standard* before delivering his annual pre-Budget report today, Gordon Brown said one of his priorities would be "making affordable housing available to young people and increasing support for hard working families".' Murphy explained how Brown's scheme would enable couples to buy a house even if they could only afford 75 per cent of the asking price; the remaining 25 per cent would be bought by their mortgage lender and the government. Among the other highlights which Murphy identified in the Chancellor's speech were a further freeze on petrol duty; a wider amnesty for families who had accidentally claimed tax credits; new tax breaks to boost the film industry; and the use of unclaimed assets in dormant bank accounts for youth and community projects.

The build-up to the Budget of March 2006 followed the usual pattern. Well-placed leaks were used to trail the main announcements and many of the tip-offs went to newspapers owned by Rupert Murdoch, whose support Brown was anxious to cultivate in view of heightened speculation about the timing of Tony Blair's departure and a likely handover of power. 'Sex tax cut' was the headline above the *Sun*'s exclusive report which revealed three weeks before the Budget that the Chancellor would reduce the rate of value added tax on condoms and other contraceptives from 17.5 to 5 per cent. Within days the *Times* declared: 'Budget could hold a shock for 4×4 drivers.' Its exclusive report revealed that Brown intended to impose a new top rate of vehicle excise duty on what had been dubbed the 'gas-guzzling Chelsea tractors'. The Sunday before the Budget the *News of the World* listed with great precision most of the announcements on taxation: fuel duty would 'remain frozen', there would be no increase in duty on spirits and 'a penny on the price of a pint'. By leaking his own decisions, Brown had shown once more his complete disregard for the traditional concept of pre-Budget purdah and, as in the previous December, Murphy was able to claim yet another scoop. His report illustrated the degree to which the Chancellor was prepared to co-operate with journalists: 'Speaking exclusively to the *Evening Standard* before briefing the cabinet this morning, Mr Brown revealed his confidence that the economy is on track, enjoying its longest period of uninterrupted economic growth.' Murphy's list of announcements to be made by the Chancellor included extra money for schools and funding for the 2012 Olympic Games in London.

Brown's trailing of his Budget proposals had become so thorough and so commonplace that this flurry of 'exclusive' leaks was accepted without question by MPs and although the *Evening Standard* made great play of Murphy's latest scoop, it failed even to notice the historic parallel with the fate of Dalton. I thought that far greater significance lay in the commercial sensitivity of much of the information being trailed in advance. For example, advance leaks about Brown's announcement in the 2005 pre-Budget report that he intended to help first-time buyers would, in my opinion, have been of assistance to Britain's biggest mortgage lenders and was to their financial advantage. As the *Guardian* commented next day, the only real surprise was Brown's decision to scrap his earlier proposal to widen the rules on personal pensions to include residential properties such as buy-to-let and holiday homes. Abolishing the property-related tax breaks associated with the planned self-invested personal pensions (SIPPs) four months before they had been due to take effect shocked leading providers such as Standard Life, which had attracted potential investments of more than £1 billion. If Brown had leaked this announcement in advance it might well have caused serious repercussions in the City of London because the Royal Institution of Chartered Surveyors estimated that 50,000 properties, worth around £24 billion, would be switched into the new pensions over the next few years. In the event Brown skated over the actual announcement, saying simply that his intention was to block 'misuse of SIPPs schemes to purchase second homes'; the details only emerged later in a briefing note from the Treasury. On completing his statement, one of the journalists the Chancellor telephoned personally to explain his U-turn was Alan Rusbridger, editor of the *Guardian*, which had highlighted the cost to the Treasury of potential abuses of the proposed tax break in order to fund property purchases abroad. Brown was anxious to secure as much favourable coverage as he could for his pre-Budget report because he was having to make a determined effort to recover from the damage inflicted the previous week during a bitter row over proposals for the reform of state pensions. After a two-year inquiry the Pensions Commission, headed by Lord Turner, was a week away from announcing its conclusions when a letter written by the Chancellor was leaked to the *Financial Times*, provoking a bruising round of political back stabbing over claims that the commission's main recommendations would be shelved by the Treasury. Turner was about to suffer the same indignity as Alan Pickering, whose report, *A Simple Way to Better Pensions*, was similarly sabotaged after it was leaked two days before publication in July 2002.

Turner's report had become yet another convenient flashpoint in the continued political infighting between rival supporters of the Chancellor and the Prime Minister. As had happened so often in the past, Brownites and Blairites ended up accusing each other of being responsible for an ugly bout of leaking, briefing and counter-briefing. According to the *Sunday Telegraph*'s political editor, Patrick Hennessy, the Chancellor had just finished giving a briefing about his forthcoming pre-Budget report to the *Financial Times*'s new editor, Lionel Barber, when Barber 'dropped his bombshell' that next day his paper would be publishing a leaked copy of Brown's letter to Turner. There was already an atmosphere of 'mild panic' in the Treasury because in mid-November 2005 the *Financial Times*'s public policy editor, Nicholas Timmins, had obtained a leaked summary of the commission's likely findings and its conclusion that the retirement age would have to rise if pensions were to increase in line with earnings. In the *Daily Telegraph*'s account of how the commission's report was 'sent spinning into the rough', its correspondent, Ian Cowie, said Turner was told by a Treasury spin doctor two and a half hours later, just after 8 p.m., that his report was about to be overtaken by a political storm because Brown's letter suggesting that the commission's solution was based on the wrong assumptions and would therefore be too costly had been leaked to the press. Cowie said the news was a 'heavy blow for the lord to receive at his home in Kensington' and friends said his language was 'uncharacteristic'.

Next morning the *Financial Times*'s exclusive on the leaked letter was taken a step further by the BBC's political editor, Nick Robinson, who told *Today* that he had been informed the Chancellor planned to 'shelve' Turner's key recommendation that the pension age should be increased in return for a restoration of the link with earnings rather than prices; the *Times* claimed the BBC's 'reliable source' was none other than the Labour MP Ed Balls, the Chancellor's former adviser. Amid denials all round, and fearing that his proposals were in danger of disappearing without trace, Turner urged all and sundry to calm down and wait until his report was published the following week, when the real facts could be debated. However, Brown appeared to be keeping up the pressure because he declared in a speech to the Institute of Directors the following day that pension reforms had to be 'sustainable, fair and affordable'. As the row intensified, Turner's appeal for calm got lost in a further flurry of claim and counter-claim. Brown's allies were quoted as blaming the original leak on the 'Teenage Taliban' of Downing Street, who were accused of seeking to portray the Chancellor as an obstacle to reform. The principal suspect was No. 10's policy director, Matthew Taylor, whom the *Daily Mail* described as the 'oddball Downing Street policy wonk' who usually 'staggered into work in tatty cycling shorts, dripping with sweat'. Desperate attempts were made by Downing Street and the Treasury to put a stop to the feuding. Tony Blair's official spokesman said Downing Street was not the source of the leak: 'I can categorically deny, as far as my knowledge goes and those I have spoken to in Number Ten, we were in no way responsible for it.'

Brown asked his permanent secretary, Nicholas Macpherson, to work with the Cabinet Secretary, Gus O'Donnell, to co-ordinate a leak inquiry across Whitehall. Copies of the Chancellor's letter had been seen only by officials in the Treasury, Downing Street, the Department of Work and Pensions and the Pensions Commission. Two days later Macpherson wrote to Taylor: 'I wish to put on record that the Treasury is not accusing you of leaking these letters, and I am discounting any press speculation about named individuals. As with any inquiry the Treasury will not prejudge the outcome.' Although the Treasury had no idea that Macpherson's letter was going to leaked by Downing Street, Taylor immediately welcomed it and issued his own statement to the *Evening Standard*: 'I hope it will correct and end the damaging and entirely unfounded speculation linking me with the leak of correspondence between the Chancellor and Lord Turner'. Not to be outdone, the *Financial Times* obtained a further leak, this time from the commission, suggesting Turner had calculated that his reforms would cost £12 billion a year, which the Treasury estimated would increase taxation by about 4p in the pound. When the report was finally published both the Conservatives and the Liberal Democrats welcomed the key recommendation that in return for more generous provision, the state pension age would have to increase to sixty-eight or perhaps sixty-nine. Both parties singled out the Chancellor as the main obstacle to reform. Alan Pickering, who believed his own report on pensions had been stifled ahead of its publication in 2002, told the *Independent* he saw close parallels with Lord Turner's experience:

> Two days before my report was published, it was selectively leaked and it was obvious the leak had come from government sources. By the time it was published, I was already busy defending the unpalatable bits that had been leaked. Lord Turner has been used to buy time for the politicians, in order to maintain the momentum of procrastination.

In the subsequent press analysis, many commentators blamed Brown and Balls for instigating a concerted attempt to discredit the Pensions Commission's report and then of trying to retaliate when the Chancellor's enemies in Downing Street portrayed him as an obstructive anti-reformer. In her column in the *Times*, Alice Miles ridiculed the Treasury and No. 10 for wasting their energy on 'playing that absurdly unconstructive Whitehall game: is your leak bigger than mine?' Despite repeated denials, she quoted unnamed No. 10 sources as suspecting that it was Brown's political adviser and chief spinner, Damian McBride, who had leaked the letter. What Brown could not deny, said a *Guardian* editorial, was that his letter 'strikes at the financing' of Turner's main proposal and it did undermine a rational debate on the future of pensions. In his column in the *Sunday Telegraph*, the Chancellor's biographer, Robert Peston, said Brown rarely wrote letters and when he did they were usually 'the underpinning of a campaign to do someone in'. Peston recalled that Brown had used the same tactic before: 'To be clear, the point of a Brown missive is not that he intends it to be leaked . . . It is simply that Brown likes to show his victims the manner of their impending doom.'

Peston was afforded considerable access when writing *Brown's Britain: How Gordon Runs the Show*, and one of his revelations about the soured relationship between the Treasury and Downing Street was that whenever a future handover of power was discussed, the Chancellor routinely said to Blair, 'There is nothing that you could ever say to me now that I could ever believe.' What had caught my eye was Peston's observation in the *Sunday Telegraph* that as a result of his insights he understood why writing a letter was such a special event for Brown:

> The Chancellor almost never puts anything down on paper, for fear of leaving an incriminating trail. It is a legacy of his career in the 1980s as a fearsome young opposition front-bencher, when he humbled the Conservative government of the day by obtaining a succession of damaging leaked official documents.

I felt I could have written a postscript of my own: my researches had demonstrated that not only did Brown become the Labour Party's most prolific and longest-serving trader in government secrets, but he remained its most experienced practitioner in the black art of using the news media to manipulate confidential information. Getting caught up in the saga of who leaked what during the row over the sabotaging of Turner's report was especially damaging for the Chancellor because he had been busy giving selected journalists guidance on how he hoped to rebuild voters' trust in the Labour government.

With his eye on Blair's eventual departure, Brown was anxious to set out his stall and I could not help feeling I was witnessing an action replay of the run-up to the 1997 general election, when he looked over his shoulder and realised that as Chancellor in waiting he had better begin showing some respect for the confidentiality of official documents. In a move which had echoes of his daring decision to give independence to the Bank of England, he gave a pledge at the 2005 conference of the Confederation of British

Industry to put the Office of National Statistics (ONS) at arm's length from ministers in the hope of lessening public suspicion about the accuracy of official statistics. As soon as legislation had been approved by Parliament, the ONS would be controlled by an independent board and would be answerable to the Treasury Select Committee rather than the government. Brown gave further hints in a series of unattributable briefings. Andrew Grice, the *Independent*'s political editor, outlined the far-reaching constitutional reforms being contemplated by a Prime Minister in waiting. One option would be to introduce 'a modern written constitution' giving MPs a guaranteed vote, for example, on whether the country should go to war; another might be the introduction of a Civil Service Act to safeguard the independence of civil servants and define the role of political advisers.

According to The *Times*'s political editor, Philip Webster, once Brown was installed in No. 10, he would 'return to a traditional style of running Downing Street . . . with all his senior officials being civil servants rather than political advisers'. He intended to dispense with the much-criticised order in council which Blair used after winning the 1997 general election to give unprecedented executive powers to his two key Labour Party appointees, the No. 10 chief of staff, Jonathan Powell, and the former director of communications, Alastair Campbell. While not saying so publicly, the Chancellor seemed to be signalling that a future Brown government would not permit the kind of behaviour which had led to the downfall of Campbell and other infamous spin doctors such as Jo Moore and his own former aide Charlie Whelan. In many ways Brown was pushing at an open door because his former permanent secretary at the Treasury, Sir Gus O'Donnell, who became Cabinet Secretary in September 2005, used his first few months as head of the civil service to flag up his determination to find ways of enhancing trust in government and public services. He told the *Independent* that he wanted to sharpen up Whitehall's act. 'I have a very straightforward view about trust. It is like the advert: we should do what it says on the tin.' In contrast to his immediate predecessor, Sir Andrew Turnbull, who had sided with Blair in failing to push ahead with a Civil Service Act, O'Donnell indicated that he was thinking on similar lines to the Chancellor and did see the need for a new statutory code to lay down clearer guidance on the differing roles of government officials and political advisers.

As a first step, O'Donnell promised to update the code of conduct for civil servants and he unveiled his plans in January 2006 publishing a draft of a revised code 'deliberately written in more everyday language' so that the 'core values of the 21st-century civil servant were clearer and more relevant'. Three months were set aside for consultation and comments were invited on the new code, which was explicit when it came to leaks and unauthorised disclosures: civil servants must not 'misuse information' acquired in the course of their official duties and they must not 'disclose official information without authority', a duty which 'continues to apply' after leaving the civil service. The new code was equally strict when it came to the outlawing of political interference: civil servants were told they must not let their own political views influence their work, nor use 'official resources for party political purposes'. In what appeared to be a strengthening of the safeguard designed to protect civil servants who might find themselves pressurised by ministers or political advisers, they were told they must not 'act in a way that is determined by party political considerations'. If civil servants believed they were being required to act in a way which conflicted with the code, or if they knew of action by others which was not in accordance with procedures, they were told to inform their line manager; if they believed they had not received a 'reasonable response' they would, for the first time, have the right to report the matter to the civil service commissioners. Freedom-of-information campaigners had argued long and hard for an independent channel through which concerns could be raised and there was an immediate welcome for the additional protection proposed by O'Donnell and his assurance that the commissioners would have the right to investigate complaints made to them directly.

In setting out his proposals for strengthening the core civil service values of 'honesty, objectivity, integrity and impartiality', O'Donnell made no mention of the repeated demands for stricter controls on the shadowy activities of ministerial aides. His room for manoeuvre had been somewhat curtailed by an order in council which was slipped through without advance warning two months before he became Cabinet Secretary and which was seen as having further entrenched the role of special advisers. While it did not go as far as the 1997 order in council which gave Powell and Campbell the power to instruct civil servants, the seventy-two political advisers on the government's payroll were told that in future they would have the authority not simply to 'advise' but also to 'assist' ministers in their work. To some extent the new wording was no more than a sensible piece of housekeeping because it acknowledged the reality of daily life in a ministerial office. Once they had been selected by the party in power, the political appointees immediately acquired the status of temporary civil servants. While some concentrated entirely on providing ministers with advice and support, most also had responsibility for a minister's party political work and, as seen during the years of the Blair government, many had increasingly turned their hands to the non-stop task of maintaining contact with the news media, which explained why they had come to be commonly regarded as spin doctors.

Trying to define the precise job description for an adviser was a task which had frustrated previous Cabinet Secretaries and proved equally troublesome for organisations such as the House of Commons Public Administration Select Committee and the Committee on Standards in Public Life. Numerous recommendations had been made over the years but successive heads of the civil service had taken the line of least resistance. O'Donnell's three immediate predecessors, Sir Andrew Turnbull, Sir Richard Wilson and Sir Robin Butler, had all shown considerable flexibility when in office and had quietly acquiesced as Blair extended the scope of the advisers' remit and blurred the boundaries of responsibility. Over the years, from the safety of retirement, the three mandarins have voiced a variety of concerns about the politicisation of Downing Street and the rest of the Whitehall machine and they have given the impression they think O'Donnell probably has a better chance than they ever had of establishing clear and enforceable guidelines to control the influx of a political cadre which they admit has had a greater impact than they anticipated. Sir Robin Mountfield, whose report encouraged government information officers to co-operate with ministerial aides in order the 'grab the agenda', has also acknowledged the need for restraint by the party in power. He feared that a further uncontrolled increase in the number of political advisers could lay the 'whole body politic' open to charges of 'patronage and jobbery'.

So far the strongest and most consistent advocate of change has been the Committee on Standards in Public Life, which, through its chairman, Sir Alistair Graham, and his predecessor, Sir Nigel Wicks, has called repeatedly for the introduction of a Civil Service Act to regulate the role of advisers and guarantee the political neutrality of civil servants. Its recommendations formed the basis of a draft Civil Service Bill drawn up by the Public Administration Select Committee. When the government responded in November 2004 by publishing its own version, there was no cap on the total number of advisers, nor was there any promise of the parliamentary time needed for legislation. Instead, in July 2005, the Cabinet Office finally conceded that as a result of the little-publicised order in council, the legal status of advisers had been changed to allow them to give assistance to ministers. Graham told the BBC he feared the consequences of a further strengthening of the powers exercised by political aides: 'Previously they could give ministers advice, now they may give assistance in aspects of departmental business and inevitably "assistance" covers a wider range of activities.' While he agreed that the Public Administration Select Committee had advised that a change was necessary, that had only been on condition that the various codes of conduct were put on a legal footing in a Civil Service Act and subjected to regular parliamentary scrutiny and approval. Instead the level of mistrust about the activities of the advisers had only increased, which in turn had further weakened confidence in the machinery of government.

On the Tory benches, the former Chancellor Kenneth Clarke has been another persistent critic of the extra powers given to ministerial aides and of the way he believed Blair has used them to help centralise power in Downing Street. After his election in December 2005, the new party leader, David Cameron, announced that Clarke would chair a democracy task force which would make recommendations on the steps a future Conservative government might take both to define the role of political advisers and to ensure the independence of the civil service. Cameron's predecessors, Michael Howard, Iain Duncan Smith and William Hague, had all added their names to a chorus of disapproval about the role of unelected advisers in Blair's 'kitchen Cabinet' and Conservative election manifestos had repeatedly given a pledge to restrict their activities and halve their number, taking the total back to the level of John Major's government. This long-term objective resurfaced in March 2006 in *Clean Politics*, a report prepared for Cameron by the Conservative MP Andrew Tyrie, who had been asked to devise proposals for the state funding of political parties. Tyrie calculated that halving the number of special advisers would provide an annual saving of nearly £3 million. Switching that money to help meet the cost of a general election fund for the parties could be justified on the grounds that paying the salaries of political aides for Cabinet ministers was already 'a form of state funding by the back door'.

I felt that however much support and encouragement O'Donnell was given for the introduction of a process to roll back the politicisation of the New Labour years and reinforce traditional civil service standards of integrity and impartiality, an incoming administration, whether it was led by Gordon Brown or eventually by Cameron, would in all probability face precisely the same pressures which made life so difficult for Blair. The twin task of delivering on election promises and controlling the message required a team effort and a steady supply of politically committed enthusiasts to do the work. My sense was that Brown or Cameron would become equally dependent on a network of trusted ministerial aides, not least when it came to managing the relationship between a new Prime Minister and the news media. O'Donnell's greatest challenge would be to find ways of attracting and sustaining an infusion of new blood into the administration of public services without endangering the values which civil servants hold dear, values which have been under attack from within as much as from without. By going ahead with the publication of his memoirs, *DC Confidential*, the former US ambassador, Sir Christopher Meyer, showed scant regard either for civil service propriety or for the confidentiality of conversations within the British embassy in Washington. Similarly Lance Price in his book, *The Spin Doctor's Diary*, revealed how, once installed in the No. 10 press office, it was possible to ignore almost every requirement of the special advisers' code of conduct. Judging by the way Price peppered his entries with references to the confidential data which he had managed to spread left, right and centre around the journalists of Westminster, he gave an unexpected insight into how highly Blair must have valued the ability of a Downing Street spin doctor to leak government secrets.

O'Donnell needed to look no further than Price's book if he required additional confirmation that the swift introduction of the guidelines enshrined in a Civil Service Act might provide at least some sort of mechanism to control the activities of a highly paid group of here-today, gone-tomorrow civil servants. Leaks, tip-offs and off-the-record briefings keep the traders in government information in business. Given the intense competition in the news media, journalists left to their own devices are unlikely to take the initiative and clean up their own act. Instant access for all journalists and the public can be provided via the internet and through the massive expansion in websites. There is no reason why Whitehall departments and state agencies could not provide a level playing field. I have never understood why the government does not see the value in treating journalists equally. Do ministers not realise it would make it so much harder for us to exaggerate or mislead if we all had simultaneous access to the same information? In that way, reporters inside the magic circle, as well as those outside it, really would be tested because the more official sources there are, releasing information to all comers on an on-the-record basis, and the fewer the leaks, the harder it would be to defend sloppy, cynical journalism. At least there would be a chance then to drive up editorial standards.

Index

Bowe, Colette 49–50
Boyds 44
Bradshaw, David 64, 160
Branson, Sir Richard 119–20, 141
Bright, Martin 219, 224
British Aerospace 59, 239–40
British Airways 141, 246–7
British Aluminium 128, 130
British Coal 44
British Journalism Review 54
British Leyland 41
British Medical Association 164–5
British Steel 40
Brittan, Sir Leon 49, 82
Broad Street Associates 124,
    130–4, 139
Bromley, Paul 144
Brown, Colin 21–2
Brown, Gordon 105, 149, 156,
    160, 229, 231
  and Tony Blair's future 231,
    249–54
  and Budget leaks 38, 83–5,
    88–89, 170, 247–50
  and Kenneth Clarke 79–84, 86,
    247
  denounces leakers 84–6, 90–1
  exploiting leaks 37–8, 67–8,
    79–85, 88–90, 104, 169–70
  and 'institutionalised leaking'
    247
  'king of leaks' 90
  and Piers Morgan 86–7
  and Pensions Commission leak
    250–3
  and political advisers 254, 257–8
  protecting leakers 60–1, 68–9
  and Rover Group 59–61

and select committee leak 242
*Brown's Britain: How Gordon Runs
    the Show* 253
Browne, Anthony 163–4
Bruce, Malcolm 248
Brunson, Michael
  and 'Bastardgate' 3, 6–8, 11,
    14–17, 19, 20
  and 'Dinnergate' 24, 25
BSkyB 172
BTR 132
Buckley, Sir Michael 109
Budget leaks
  (1947) 38, 87
  (1981) 34, 53, 87
  (1984) 87
  (1996) 83–8, 90–1, 104
  (1999) 247
  (2001) 248
  (2006) 248–9
  pre-Budget 248–50
Bush, President 204–5, 219–21,
    223, 227
Butler, Peter 82
Butler, Lord (Robin) 36, 61, 71,
    77, 105–6, 203, 256
Byers, Stephen 28, 116
Byrne, Colin 144, 147, 150, 154

Callaghan, James 40, 45, 47, 48
Cameron, David 257–8
Cameron, James 228
Campaign! 138
Campaign 1997 150, 172
Campaign for Press and
    Broadcasting Freedom 223
Campbell, Alastair 2, 68–9, 82,
    151